Presents for peace?

Nonetheless, the English pushed forward to the Indian villages, and a peace treaty was made between the British and the western Indians in 1764. Whites continued giving Indians presents for land, but most of the agreements were misunderstood by the Indians, who didn't believe individuals could own land.

The American Revolution began in 1775 and lasted until 1783, when the colonies became known as the United States of America. In the Northwest Territory that included Ohio, wars with Indian tribes lasted even longer, until about 1795.

Promised: Deeds

By 1786, a permanent settlement in the Miami Valley seemed possible. Like Christopher Gist and others before him, Benjamin Stites and John Cleves Symmes of New Jersey were delighted by what they saw at the confluence of the Miami, Stillwater and Mad rivers. In 1787, Symmes asked the government for a grant of land between the Miamis, and without delay — or approval from Congress — Symmes deeded 10,000 acres of land to Stites, who promised deeds to settlers for 83 cents an acre. Later, this hasty move caused much heartache among Dayton's earliest settlers, who were told their property rights were invalid.

In 1789, John Stites Gano and William Goforth negotiated with Symmes for land that included the area at the mouth of the Mad River. The new town, to be called Venice, was drawn, deeded and recorded, but the project was abandoned because of Indian conflicts and Symmes' problems with the government. If the deal had gone through, Dayton might have been known as Venice.

Bloody battles, peaceful settlement

Soon, Indian tribes began to bend beneath the blows of their American enemies. In 1794, Gen. Anthony Wayne was victorious over the Indians at the Battle of Fallen Timbers. On August 3, 1795, the Treaty of Greene Ville was signed, opening the Miami Valley to peaceful settlement by white pioneers.

On August 20, 1795, Gen. Arthur St. Clair (governor of the Northwest Territory), Jonathan Dayton, Col. Israel Ludlow and Gen. James Wilkinson paid Symmes his 83 cents an acre for the "Miami Lands" and agreed to establish a permanent settlement on 60,000 acres at the mouth of the Mad River. These four men were the town's first legal proprietors.

'It shall be called Dayton'

In September, Daniel C. Cooper, John Dunlap and their surveying parties arrived to break ground in the new town, where the Great Miami River joined the Mad, by cutting the first road and making a rough street layout. It is thanks to Cooper that we now have wide, straight, right-angled streets.

On November 4, Ludlow took it upon himself to lay out the new village. Ludlow named the town after his colleague Dayton, the lawyer, soldier and statesman who had a hand in the crafting of the U.S. Constitution. Streets Ludlow named after himself, St. Clair and Wilkinson. (Ludlow added the Jefferson Street to demonstrate the men's political loyalties.) Main Street was made 132 feet wide — enough to "turn a coach and four." Ironically, Jonathan Dayton is not known to have ever visited the town that bore his name.

Forty-six people expressed interest in coming to the new town. Each was to receive a platted piece of land, but only 19 made good on their pledge to move here. The first permanent settlers, from Cincinnati, finally arrived in Dayton on April 1, 1796.

And from that birth, our community began its rich and fascinating life.

ISBN 0-9616347-7-4 (hardback)
ISBN 0-9616347-8-2 (softcover)

Dear Reader:

In 1898 a young man named James M. Cox borrowed $26,000 and purchased two Dayton newspapers, the *Evening News* and *Morning Times*. He merged the two newspapers, renamed the new publication and, on August 15, 1898, 102 years after the settlement of Dayton Township, the first edition of the *Dayton Daily News* was published.

That small newspaper company has grown into something James Cox, who grew up on a farm near Middletown and was only 28 at the time he bought the newspapers, could not have imagined in his wildest dreams. In fact, the history of Cox and the company he founded could serve as a metaphor for much that was "made in Dayton" over these past 200 years.

James Cox went on to serve in Congress, be Ohio's first three-term governor and run unsuccessfully for president with a fellow named Franklin D. Roosevelt as his running mate. Today his company, started in 1898 with that $26,000, is one of the largest privately held communications companies in the world, with more than 37,000 employees and annual revenues of $3 billion.

As the Dayton region approached its 200th birthday it seemed appropriate that Governor Cox's newspaper publish a book of words and pictures creating an anecdotal narrative of the history of this community and its people. *For the Love of Dayton* is that book. It is not intended to be a definitive history of Dayton. Much like a daily newspaper, it is a collection of vignettes, some good, some bad, of our town and the people who have lived here for the last 200 years.

For the Love of Dayton was a labor of love by a very talented and determined group of people who are credited by name elsewhere in this publication. It is also a gift to the community on its Bicentennial from the Cox family and all of us who have followed in the footsteps of James M. Cox here in Dayton. All profits from this book go to support Celebration Dayton '96.

Happy Birthday, Dayton, from all of us at the *Dayton Daily News!*

Sincerely,

J. Bradford Tillson
Publisher

Before Dayton

Long, long ago...

Before there was a Dayton, there were glaciers and Indians and battles. Many battles.

The landscape and waterways we know today as the Miami Valley were carved by glaciers during the Pleistocene ice age 12,500 years ago. These massive rivers of ice retreated some 10,000 years ago, leaving behind rich fields, gently sloping valleys and flowing runoff that etched a new series of water channels.

By about 1000 B.C., the Adena Indians, the people known as the Mound Builders, settled in Ohio. This early woodland culture buried its dead in earthen mounds, alongside the things they had used in life: pottery, tools, ornaments and weapons. The largest in the area is the Miamisburg Mound; smaller earthworks can still be found above Huffman Prairie, on Wright Brothers Hill.

Later, in about the 12th century, the Fort Ancient people settled along the riverbanks in fortified agricultural villages. The tribe marked time by observing the sun and charting its course. Today, SunWatch Prehistoric Indian Village, in the south part of Dayton, shows how these people lived and used the fertile valley around them.

Land battles

By the late 1600s, the English and French were struggling to control lands in what was then considered the West — the Ohio Valley region inhabited by the Indians. Conflict between the great European powers, with the Indians caught in the middle, was inevitable.

In the 1740s, great bands of Shawnee hunted and fished in the Miami Valley. They were worried about the white settlers who were moving in and trying to "civilize" them. Other tribes in this part of Ohio were the Miamis, Pottawatomies, Wyandots, Delawares, Chippewas and Kickapoos. The Indians laid claim to the Valley as their own.

'It wants nothing but cultivation to make it a most delightful country'

But things were changing. In 1751, explorer Christopher Gist was attracted by the Miami Valley's "river-ribboned land," which he said was "very rich, level and well-timbered, some of the finest meadows that can be ... it wants nothing but cultivation to make it a most delightful country." He reported to the Ohio Land Company that "the country abounds with turkeys, bears, deer, elk and most sorts of game, particularly buffaloes, 30 or 40 of which are frequently seen feeding in one meadow."

The Treaty of Paris, signed in 1763 between France and England after the French and Indian War, gave Ohio and other lands east of the Mississippi to Britain.

Still, conflict lingered. Pontiac, the famed ruler of the Ottawas, Ojibwas and Pottawatomies, insisted that there was no such treaty and that England possessed no land. One chief even declared: "Englishmen! Although you have conquered the French, you have not yet conquered us! We are not your slaves! These lakes, these woods, these mountains, were left to us by our ancestors. They are our inheritance, and we will part with them to none."

FOR THE LOVE OF
Dayton

LIFE IN THE MIAMI VALLEY

1796–1996

1796

One by land, one by boat

Two groups of restless pioneers left Cincinnati on March 21, following the Great Miami River toward a new home on the land that soon would become Dayton.
Col. George Newcom's land party and Samuel Thompson's boat party followed John Hamer's overland group, already en route to the "river-ribboned" country some 60 miles to the north.

The land parties — kids in creels

Men, women and children alike followed the rough trail blazed by Daniel C. Cooper the previous fall. Cattle and pack horses carried hickory baskets called creels, laden with bedding, tools, seed corn, clothing and perhaps the luxury of a few chairs. The creels also bore the most precious cargo: the party's smallest children, who may have peeked over the basket edge as their weary parents walked alongside. Rafts were built to cross the largest creeks, and felled timbers provided makeshift footbridges over smaller waterways.
It was far from easy going.

Poling in pirogues

Men in the boat party poled long, narrow dugout canoes called pirogues. Evenings were spent ashore, where meals consisted of game (wild geese were plentiful that spring), fish, wild fowl eggs and cornbread.

April 1: Ahoy, Dayton!

After 10 days, Thompson's boat party, including famous first Daytonian Benjamin Van Cleve, arrived near the head of what we now call St. Clair Street.

First to set foot on the riverbank, according to one account: Catharine Van Cleve Thompson, great-great-grandmother of the Wright brothers.

Top: Dayton's first settlers arrived by boat, landing near what is now the intersection of St. Clair and Monument.

Left: Benjamin Van Cleve

Bottom: The first homes were built along the river, to take advantage of its plentiful resources.

Arrived...

The two land parties on April 5, after a two-week journey.

They found dense woods and silent wilderness ... rippling, sparkling streams ... hills and valleys of black, fertile soil ... birds and wild animals aplenty. They had timber, elbow room and, most importantly, the river — the rich and beautiful Great Miami, which provided not just food and fresh water, but sand and stone for mortar, gravel for roads and clay for bricks. The possibilities were endless, the resources seemingly inexhaustible.

Cleared and raised...

Ground, and then cabins. From sunup to sundown, the forest echoed with the steely ring of axes biting into wood.

■ Cabins sat on puncheon floors — split logs laid flat side up.

■ Furs covered the floors in winter. During warm weather, barefoot settlers got splinters.

■ Glass was precious; most windows were paper slicked with bear grease.

■ Nails were precious, too: Wooden pins held door and window frames in place.

Putting down roots

Settlers converted a clearing west of present-day Wilkinson Street into a cornfield. By midsummer, each family was allowed its share of the harvest — a fine crop, by all accounts. For 75 cents a week plus board, Col. George Newcom hired millwright and craftsman Robert Edgar to build the two-room Newcom Tavern — one of Dayton's first permanent dwellings — at the southwest corner of what's now Main Street and Monument Avenue. For timber, Edgar used ash, hickory, walnut, beech, elm, oak and sycamore; to make lime mortar, he burned stones from the river.

Newcom Tavern epitomized early Dayton. It was destined to be the town's first store, church, post office, courthouse and jail.

SLICE OF LIFE

Food, clothes and sickness

■ Cooking was back-breaking, endless work, as pioneer women stooped and slaved over open fires.

■ Most clothing was buckskin or homespun.

■ Malaria threatened, with chills, fever, weakness and deep, aching pain.

■ Despite the hardships, there was great natural beauty — the slow, lovely river, the fresh air, changing seasons and summer sunsets. But along with all that came thick mud, poison ivy, bitter cold, fever, mosquitoes and rattlesnakes.

Top: Newcom Tavern quickly became a gathering spot for the earliest Daytonians; it stands today at Carillon Historical Park.

Left: George Newcom

Bottom: The tavern's implement-cluttered fireplace provided warmth and a place to cook.

1797

The tax man cometh

June 10: James Brady became assessor of Dayton Township, which included all of Montgomery and western Greene counties. On August 25, Calvin Morrill was named collector. As Dayton's first constable, Cyrus Osborn was obliged to report "persons and property" to the assessor, who listed these accordingly and sent Morrill for collection. Brady got $5.20 for his services.

Summer bounty

After more than a year, basic provisions finally became more plentiful, as more pioneers arrived in the new community.

Squatters' rights

Newcomers arrived with big plans to build a new life along the river, but clear titles to land were hard to come by. Some moved on, unwilling to waste time clearing land they might not get to keep. Some "squatted" on land to which they had no legal rights.

Far left: John Cleves Symmes

Left: Daniel Cooper

1798

Above: According to legend, the first house in Dayton was built using wood from the first pirogue to reach the site.

How the garden grows

This summer saw a welcome variation in diet as the Wilkinson Street clearing yielded peas and beans, in addition to the corn that was the community's staple crop.

A hellish sermon

August 12: The Rev. John Kobler, a Methodist Episcopal presiding elder from Kentucky, preached Dayton's first sermon. Topic: "mainly hell," according to the record. (Hell, and how not to get there, was a popular theme.) Rev. Kobler organized the first Methodist Episcopal class of eight members. It later became Grace Church.

A stout, multipurpose structure

Col. George Newcom enlarged his tavern from two rooms to four during the winter of 1798-99. Newcom's became the gathering place.

Assessor, assess thyself

Tax assessor Daniel Cooper paid $6.25 in taxes, the highest amount in town. The average per Dayton taxpayer: $1.19. Total taxes: $29.74.

Worthless paper

Fear spread as settlers heard their land titles were invalid. The rumors proved true: John Cleves Symmes had been unable to secure a title from the government. The settlers did not own the acres they had cleared.

SLICE OF LIFE

Work, work, work

Dayton pioneers were a busy lot. They felled timber, dug out roots and stumps, plowed fields by hand and planted corn, turnips, potatoes and tobacco. They gathered and stored their crops, and stacked wild grass and fodder for their livestock. There were more cabins to be raised, roads to be opened and bridges to be built — and all the while, the settlement had to be guarded. Indians were a threat.

When the men had time to hunt, the woods provided deer, bear, wild turkey and pheasant.

Top: Rumors of Indian activity unsettled early settlers, though actual troubles around Dayton were few. This creek house was used by local Indians in the 1790s.

Right: One of Dayton's early maps.

Staples

Flour cost $9 a barrel. (Getting it from Cincinnati to Dayton, however, cost a whopping $5 more.)

Cabins

The whole of Dayton included nine of them (two on Main Street).

Sealing their fate

Two dollars an acre? Daytonians were astounded. That's the price Congress set on March 2 for untitled U.S. wilderness. Anyone who had made a land agreement with John Cleves Symmes before April 1, 1797, had to pay the price or forfeit their land — which all along had legally belonged to the government, not Symmes. Many had no choice but to leave Dayton.

Rumors: Indian troubles

Daytonians got word that Indians were banding together. They quickly built a log stockade at Monument and Main, large enough for all the villagers. Never needed for defense, the stockade was used instead for a church and for grain storage.

School days

The stockade also was used as a schoolhouse starting September 1. Lacking pencils, children used sharpened sticks to trace the alphabet in the sand. First schoolmaster: Benjamin Van Cleve.

Law and order

With civilization came squabbling: Daytonian Abram Richardson sued George Kirkendall for $8 on October 4. Court costs totaled 33 cents (including the summons, judgment and subpoena) as recorded in the docket of newly appointed Justice of the Peace Daniel Cooper. No idea, now, what they were fighting about....

First graveyard

John Davis, accidentally killed at Daniel Cooper's mill, was the village's first recorded death. Davis was likely buried at Dayton's first graveyard, at the northeast corner of Third and Main, on one of two lots Cooper gave to the Presbyterian Church. The town abandoned the cemetery after only a few years.

CITY OF DAYTON.

Only seventy years ago a few log cabins on the banks of the Miami River, shut in by forests and surrounded by red men, were all that marked the site of the now large and prosperous city of Dayton. The rapid growth of this city is one of the marvels of this progressive age, and a speaking tribute to the energy of the Anglo-Saxon race.

A history of the early settlement of Dayton has already been given, but a glance at the embryo city as it appeared in 1799 (three years after its settlement) will best show what its advance has been in the seventy-five years that have intervened. The outline of the following diagram represents the limits of the town plat as originally laid out, bounded on the north by Water Street, on the east by Main Street, on the south by Fifth Street, and on the west by Wilkinson Street. The plat was divided into two hundred and eighty lots, with reservations for markets, schools, churches, and burial-grounds.

Plan of Original Plat of Dayton, showing location and name of every resident in the settlement in 1799.

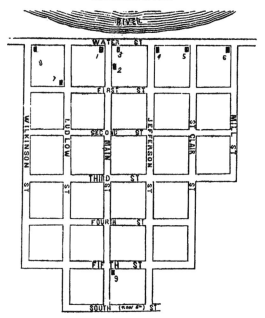

1. Colonel Newcom's tavern, built of logs, used as court-room after 1803. 2. George Westfall's log cabin. 3. Paul D. Butler's cabin. 4. Cabin where General Brown (who distinguished himself in the war of 1812) kept bachelor-hall, but unoccupied in April, 1799. 5. Samuel Thompson's cabin. 6. Cabin of Mrs. McClure, mother of James McClure. 7. John William's cabin, farmer. 8. Cabin of Thomas Arnett, shoemaker. 9. John Welsh's cabin.

1800

Century turns, commerce begins

Grain, pelts and 500 venison hams were among the items loaded onto the town's first flatboat, launched in the spring by Dayton businessman David Lowry. He reached New Orleans in two months, sold his boat and cargo and returned to Dayton on horseback.

Lowry had shown the way: Flatboats bound for long-distance trade soon became a regular sight on the Great Miami riverbank.

Initially, it was everyone for themselves; pioneer families raised and marketed their produce separately from their neighbors. No one thought about the advantages or efficiency of cooperation.

A year of firsts in Dayton

■ April 14: First child Jane Newcom was born to Mary and Col. George Newcom.

■ August 28: The village's first wedding saw Benjamin Van Cleve marry Mary Whitten. Van Cleve was one of the famous first Daytonians, serving as the town's first postmaster, schoolmaster and clerk of courts. (Folks came from miles around to wish the newlyweds well.)

■ First Presbyterian Church: a meeting house built of logs at the northeast corner of Main and Third streets.

■ First store: opened by George McDougal of Detroit on the second floor of Newcom Tavern. McDougal's suppliers included Indians and other trading posts up the Great Miami.

Tax rates

■ Horse: 40 cents.
■ Cow: 10 cents.
■ Bond servant: $1.
■ Single or young man: 50 cents to $2.
■ Houses, mills and other buildings: 40 cents on each $100 of valuation.

Skin currency

Real money? A rarity. Skins were dollars and cents to early Daytonians:

■ One buckskin bought a pair of cotton stockings (which cost as much as $1).

■ Two muskrat skins, 25 cents each, bought a yard of calico.

■ A bearskin bought a set of knives and forks, valued at $3 to $5.

■ A doeskin, worth about $1.50, bought a yard of shirting.

■ Only had a coonskin? You could still get a pair of moccasins, worth 37.5 cents.

Barter was common; in exchange for beeswax, lard, honey and squirrel pelts, pioneer women often got spools of cotton and papers of pins.

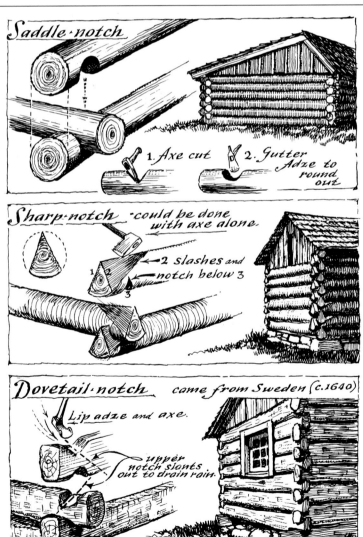

Top: Mary Newcom, wife of Col. George Newcom, gave birth to Dayton's first baby, Jane.

Left: Construction methods were basic but sturdy, and trees for lumber were plentiful.

Right: The original cabin built in 1804 by Col. Robert Patterson.

Below: Daniel Cooper's first plan of Dayton made the streets "four poles wide."

Bottom: An early Ohio map provides a key to Dayton's development.

Born...
Dayton's first male child, John Whitten Van Cleve, to Mary and Benjamin Van Cleve on June 27.

And that's why the streets are so wide, to this day
Daniel Cooper made Dayton's streets "four poles wide," in the measure of the day. A pole was about 16 feet 6 inches long, which made the town's original streets nearly 66 feet wide — a legacy still obvious if you drive downtown today.

The town plat, surrounded by dense woods, was divided into 280 lots, 100 feet by 200 feet each.

Would Dayton die out?
Since the title troubles with John Cleves Symmes were announced in 1798, many families had abandoned their land claims, left Dayton and moved to homes in the woods. By 1802, only five families remained in the 6-year-old settlement; four cabins stood vacant.

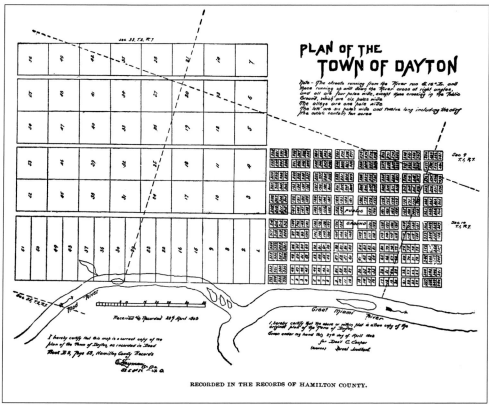

PLAN OF THE TOWN OF DAYTON

RECORDED IN THE RECORDS OF HAMILTON COUNTY.

Bad news, good news
■ Wild turkeys descended en masse on the settlement in 1801 and 1802 and threatened the corn crop, which was gathered early to save it from destruction.
■ The price of land wasn't the only thing out of reach — Daytonians couldn't afford wheat, either. A regional shortage pushed it to $7 a barrel in Cincinnati, nearly six times the U.S. wholesale price.
■ Dr. John Elliott became the first physician to live in Dayton. He followed the area's first physician, Dr. John Hole, who had moved to the Washington Township area northwest of Centerville in 1797. Silver Creek, along which Hole lived at the time, was later renamed in the good doctor's honor.

Map of the John Cleves Symmes Purchase. 1788

Dayton's savior
Daniel Cooper petitioned Congress, describing the town's land-title plight: Would it be right, he asked, to dispossess these settlers after they had worked so hard clearing land and raising cabins? The government named Cooper titular proprietor of the town. He paid the federal asking price of $2 an acre and bought 3,000 acres, including lots in Dayton.

Cooper executed the 1801 plat on April 26. He passed clear titles to the remaining settlers, who paid him "in accordance with their means." He even gave free lots for churches, markets, county buildings, graveyards and a park.

Admitted...

Ohio, as the 17th state of the Union, on March 1. The first state legislature meeting was held in Chillicothe.

Formed...

Montgomery County, on March 24. In April, Dayton became the county seat. Shortly afterward, four townships were established: Dayton, Washington, German and Elizabeth.

Gavel to gavel

The first session of Montgomery County Common Pleas Court was held July 27 at Newcom Tavern. Presiding: the Honorable Francis Dunlevy. The court adjourned at the end of the day. Business conducted: none.

Charged...

Peter Sunderland, with assault and battery against Benjamin Scott, on November 22. It was the new court's first case. Sunderland pleaded guilty and was fined $6 and court costs.

Convicts without money were fined in deer, skins, corn or pork. Justice could be harsh: Minor offenders might be sentenced to suffer up to 39 hard lashes on the bare back.

SLICE OF LIFE

Dayton's dark hole

Col. George Newcom became the first sheriff, serving until 1809. He took little pity on lawbreakers, lowering alleged offenders into his empty well, where they remained until trial.

Above: While Patterson Sawmill provided much-needed lumber for a growing town, domestic duties (below) were handled in much the same way they had always been — by the women.

Established...

Dayton's post office, in December. Benjamin Van Cleve, the town's ever-useful, all-purpose citizen, was appointed first postmaster.

First black resident

Daniel Cooper brought to town one of the first black residents, a young girl who became his servant at Rubicon farm. Her first child, whom she named Harry Cooper, was born shortly after her arrival. Young Harry was indentured to the elder Cooper, who agreed to teach the child tanning and milling (and possibly reading and writing).

Shaker town

On Beaver Creek south of Dayton, 14 Shaker families maintained a communal-style farm.

Right: Col. Robert Patterson, who would become a key player in Dayton, arrived from Lexington, Kentucky, where he'd also been a major figure. He bought land from Daniel Cooper, including his cabin, farm, sawmill, gristmill and distillery. Cooper built an elegant log mansion, lined with cherry wood, where he lived for the rest of his life.

Below: An example of the furnishings inside Newcom Tavern.

Held...

The first election for the Montgomery County commissioners, on April 2. Newcom Tavern was the site of the commission's first session, on June 11.

Jailhouse logs

While Col. George Newcom's dry well was an effective enough jail for a while, villagers realized something more was needed. On August 9, county commissioners released detailed specifications for a log jail. They wanted closely laid hewn logs, iron bars across the windows, heavy oak shutters with iron hinges and large locks in wooden cases. Low-bidder David Squier got the job at auction on September 28 for $299. Construction soon began on Third Street (across from today's Arcade).

A public square?

Daniel Cooper's larger, revised plat of September 9 proposed a town square at Third and Main, with the courthouse in the center.

Mail call

Benjamin Van Cleve opened Dayton's first post office in his cabin at First and St. Clair streets. The mail, which Postmaster Van Cleve sorted in his living room, was delivered biweekly as part of a route that ran from Cincinnati to Detroit. It often took weeks for important national news to become the talk of the town in Dayton.

Recipients, not senders, paid as much 25 cents for a letter. Van Cleve often let folks run up tabs for postage.

Street improvements

Villagers used logs to plug gullies in major streets; many existing streets were extended.

First house for business purposes:

Built at Main Street and Water Street (today Monument Avenue) by Henry Brown, who ran a store.

SLICE OF LIFE

Double duty

On weekdays, he was a physician; on Sundays, a preacher. Dr. James Welsh, pastor of First Presbyterian Church, was also one of several doctors who tended Dayton's sick, doling out such concoctions as "yellow bark, oil of vitriol, paregorick, Venue turpentine, and polypodium (a worm medicine)" to loyal parishioners. No word on how they fared under such treatment.

'Black Laws'

With 21 blacks in Montgomery County by 1804, whites began to fear job competition. "Black Laws" enacted by the state legislature starting in 1802 and running as late as 1878 spelled out rights, or lack thereof, for black Ohioans. Black laws in 1804 required each black person to hold a certificate of freedom, register with the county clerk and pay a registration fee. Even after all that, black children still could not attend state schools; a black man couldn't serve in the state militia or on juries, or give evidence against a white person on trial.

Social Library Society

Dayton was home to Ohio's first library association, formed February 1 by an act of the legislature. Benjamin Van Cleve was custodian of Dayton's first library, stocking two full bookcases in his log home/post office. Books were precious, and Van Cleve charged 2 cents for each drop of grease he found on a volume.

Incorporated...

Dayton, as a town, on February 12. "The Select Council of the Town of Dayton" included seven trustees, a collector, a supervisor and a town marshal and met in private homes for the next 10 years. The council president became mayor. Tardiness wasn't tolerated: Councilmen more than 30 minutes late to a meeting were fined 25 cents.

In a flood plain?

Rivers swelled after a week's rain in March. Pioneers raised earthen levees after much property was destroyed. Move Dayton to higher ground? The pioneers considered the idea, but decided that the rivers were too important to leave.

Recorded...

Cooper's larger plat (submitted in 1804) on November 20.

Accepted by Montgomery County...

The log jail, built by David Squier beginning in 1804, in December.

Dredged in flour

Ohio's — and Dayton's — surplus of flour, which brought only 25 cents a barrel in town, was worth 32 times that in New York City, or $8 a barrel. But how to get it there economically? There was simply no good way. (Twenty years later, construction began on the Miami and Erie Canal, which solved Ohio's commercial transportation problem — for the time being.)

They said no

Dayton's first-year municipal expenses totaled $72; townspeople turned down a proposition to raise the amount with taxes.

Jonathan Harshman, pictured here in later years with his family, bought 40 acres in Mad River Township and built a flour mill and distillery.
Other settlers included: Joseph H. Crane, one of Dayton's first lawyers; James Steele, who rallied for schools, libraries and churches; Joseph Peirce, who, along with Steele, opened a store at First and Main, selling clothes, farm utensils, dishes and food supplies; and H.G. Phillips, who opened a store at First and Jefferson in a two-story log cabin.

Opened...

The Fifth Street graveyard, bounded by Ludlow, Wilkinson, Fifth and Sixth streets, on land given by Daniel Cooper.

Around town

First and Main streets became the center of town, with two general stores: one operated by Daniel Cooper and the other by James Steele.

Friendly competition

McCullom's Tavern — built this year on East Second Street as the first brick structure and hotel in Dayton — edged out Newcom Tavern as a favorite gathering place.

Female mortality

Women, not men, often died first. A wife who managed to outlive her man — in spite of malaria, consumption (the term of the day for tuberculosis), hard work and child-bearing — typically had a tombstone revering her as a "beloved relic" of her husband. If she died first, however, she was called a "consort" of her husband, or merely "spouse."

The cost of ferries these days

Crossings on the Great Miami were made via two ferries — one at First Street, and the other at the foot of Fourth. Passage wasn't cheap:

- 75 cents for a loaded wagon and team.
- 50 cents for an empty wagon and team.
- 37.5 cents for a two-wheeled carriage.
- 12.5 cents for a man and his horse.
- 6.25 cents for a person on foot.

Above: With houses to build and land to clear, pioneers had little time to enjoy idyllic surroundings.

SLICE OF LIFE

Commerce by river

Imports and exports came and went regularly via flatboats. But over the next 10 years, a few short-sighted businessmen built mill dams and stretched fishing nets — making the river treacherous. (Some imports came by pack-trains, whose leaders complained about Dayton's muddy streets.)

Prospering professionals

Dayton was prospering, and boasted three doctors, one teacher, one minister, one lawyer and one editor.

Profitable drink

Their consciences told them not to, but selling whiskey brought a nice profit — so prudent businessmen often hid barrels of the stuff among the wheat, rye, tallow, corn, hides, furs and tobacco in their flatboat cargoes. Dayton businessman Thomas Morrison, who once added three casks of whiskey among the flour barrels for market, confessed to his diary: "And I hope the Lord will forgive me that sin."

Awarded...

A $4,766 contract to Benjamin Archer, on February 3, to build the first official courthouse, a two-story brick structure, at the northwest corner of Third and Main (the site of today's Old Court House) on land donated by Daniel Cooper.

Converts

Shaker missionaries arrived at the Shaker village on March 22. They soon converted nine people, establishing a permanent order of Shakers in the area.

Who were the Shakers? Plain, hard-working and deeply religious, they were skilled farmers and craftspeople. They were peace-loving, industrious — and celibate, which kept the order small. They worshipped at the Beulah Church near Beaver Creek in what is now Kettering.

'Cincinnati ... a little dusty hamlet'

Col. Robert Patterson, at long last, moved his family to the land he bought from Daniel Cooper in 1804. During the journey from Lexington, his children Robert and Elizabeth wrote: "The travelling was slow, but the novelty of it all, especially the night camps, was great fun.... We made but a short halt at Cincinnati, finding it to be but a little dusty hamlet of cabins strung along the river bank."

First newspaper (almost)

Chills and fever suffered by a Mr. Crane of Lebanon forced him to abandon publication of Dayton's first newspaper (name unknown) after only a few editions.

SLICE OF LIFE

Business boom, road wear

Daytonians who took a stroll down Main Street saw five stores, three taverns, one church and a dozen dwellings. And, depending on the weather, a lot of mud. Loaded wagons cut deep ruts.

Occupied...

Dayton's first official courthouse (used for both church and judicial purposes), in the winter. Furnishings were spartan — a single bench and a few three-legged stools.

1808

Incorporated...

Dayton's first school for boys, the Dayton Academy, on February 15. Daniel Cooper donated the bell that rang in the new two-story brick schoolhouse, built on the west side of St. Clair near Third Street. Public pledges paid for construction.

Villagers beat the winter doldrums by holding debates and spelling bees in the winter of 1807-08.

First regular newspaper

Townspeople paid $2 a year to get *The Dayton Repertory*, a four-page weekly first published September 18. Forerunner of the Dayton *Journal, The Repertory* continued until December 4, 1809.

B.Y.O.B....

For "Bring Your Own Bayonet," along with musket, knapsack, flints, balls and powder horn. The state militia enrolled all white men aged 18 to 45 who were "free and able" — but would-be soldiers had to furnish their own arms and supplies.

Loophole

David Reid got around paying the $10 license fee required to run his Main Street tavern by renaming it "Reid's Inn," a "house of private entertainment." Reid's became the place to meet.

Built...

Dayton's first brick residence, a Main Street two-story, by Henry Brown.

The bounty of the land

More cabins appeared as Dayton's rich farmlands drew a steady stream of settlers. Harvests were plentiful; farmers got 50 cents a bushel for wheat. (Whiskey sold for 37.5 cents a gallon.)

THE DAYTON REPERTORY.

DAYTON, OHIO, PRINTED BY WILLIAM ... PE & GEORGE SMITH, MAIN STREET.

No. 2. FRIDAY, SEPTEMBER 30, 1808. Vol. 1.

BOSTON, August 23.

FROM SPAIN

On Sunday arrived the brig Mercury, captain Bradford, from Alicant and Gibraltar. She sailed from the former place on the 29th of June—only 9 days subsequent to our accounts from Cadiz; and the cities are at a considerable distance from each other. She left Gibraltar on the 11th July, where she remained but a short time, fearing she might be detained, as she was without her regular papers, and the first vessel from a Spanish port that had put in there since the orders in council.

By captain Bradford's information it appears, that the hatred of the Spaniards for the French, has never been exceeded even among nations that were natural enemies. The French consul at Malaga, and several merchants, were said to have been put to death. At Alicant, every person born in France was imprisoned. Some who were confined, had resided 30 or 40 years in Spain. The patriots had heard that Napoleon had appointed them a king in his brother Joseph. ... all classes of Spaniards were enthusiastic in their determination to resist the French. The instances of suspicion that persons were in the public interest, were rare. At Valencia one per...

The account of the defeat of the French army under general Dupont, on its way from Madrid to Seville, is confirmed. It was said 5000 Frenchmen were killed.

It was said there was at Madrid, and in the neighborhood, about 50,000 French troops under the duke of Berg—several skirmishes had taken place. In Catalonia, there were said to be about 15,000. Desertions were frequent, and to prevent this at Barcelona, about 1000 selected troops had been stationed round that city. These the revolutionists contrived to surprise, and they were all cut to pieces.

A body of French troops (reported at 5000) had been dispatched from Madrid to take possession of the city of Valencia. They had been once attacked, succeeded in discomfiting the Spaniards, and continued their march. They had arrived within about 20 leagues of Valencia; but there was no despondency on that account—and about 30,000 regulars and volunteers had marched to give them battle, zealous in their country's cause, and confident of success.

We cannot learn that any fresh troops from France entered Spain in June.——American vessels which had been detained at Alicant and Malaga had been released by the Spaniards;—

Left: Early subscribers paid $2 per year for *The Dayton Repertory*.

Below: Reid's Inn, as it appeared years later.

SLICE OF LIFE

Divorce decree

Life on the frontier was not without drama. Folks in town may have seen this legal notice, posted by Elisha Spuryer: "Know ye that I do forewarn all persons from harboring, or trusting my wife Elizabeth Spuryer on my account, as she has left my bed and boarding, without any lawful reason, as I am determined to put the law in force against anybody that I find my property with." (Mrs. Spuryer had petitioned for separation, charging that Elisha had whipped her and betrayed the marriage vow.)

Medical care

They made house calls: Dayton's three doctors regularly saddled up and rode through the country to visit their patients. The most common diagnoses: rheumatism and fevers. Strong root and herb medicines were used as stimulants, tonics, astringents, emetics and laxatives.

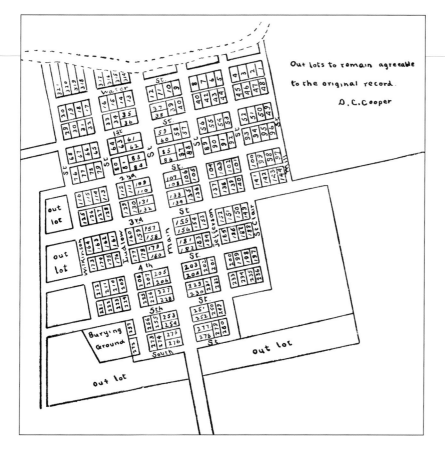

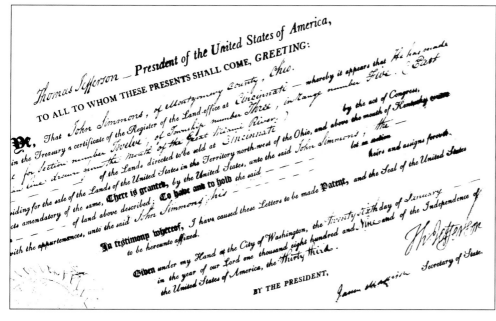

An old-fashioned Fourth

This was the year Daytonians hosted their town's first Independence Day celebration. Townspeople assembled on the riverbank, marched to the courthouse, sang together, heard an oration and artillery salutes, and then marched again, meeting at the home of Mr. Disbrow for dinner. (Tickets: 50 cents.) There were wrestling and shooting matches, foot and horse races. And then, folks danced the night away.

Held...

The county's first political convention, on September 6.

Opened...

The first drug store, by Dr. Wood in Reid's Inn.

Plat updates

Daniel Cooper again revised the town plat based on the most recent deeds and government land grants.

Connected...

Dayton — to Cincinnati, Franklin, Hamilton, Springfield, Urbana, Piqua and Xenia — thanks to improved roads. (After roads connected the Miami, Auglaize and Maumee rivers this year, Dayton had more-or-less direct access to Lake Erie. Still an extremely arduous trip, however.)

Elected...

Joseph H. Crane, one of Dayton's first lawyers, to the Ohio General Assembly.

Dayton's most wanted

Dayton's jail was considered first-rate when it was built in 1804, but it couldn't contain one determined inmate. Daniel Williams caught the escapee, a debtor, and earned a $9 reward.

SLICE OF LIFE

Retail buyers, colorful style

If the man of the house was a merchant, his family accompanied him back east to collect merchandise to sell in Dayton. Merchants depended on Conestoga wagons — covered with white canvas and drawn by a six-horse team — to freight goods over the mountains from Philadelphia, Baltimore or other cities.

In fashion this year: anything in deep blue. James Beck opened a dye house, coloring cotton for 75 cents a pound. Coloring linen and wool was cheaper (62.5 cents a pound).

Top: Daniel Cooper's revision of the Dayton town plat.

Bottom: The land grant to John Simmons of Montgomery County.

1810

Another $2-a-year weekly

After *The Dayton Repertory* ceased publication in December 1809, Daytonians had no newspaper until May 3, when *The Ohio Centinel* was founded. It continued until May 19, 1813. The subscription was payable in advance. No money? The publisher accepted produce at market prices. News coverage included official announcements and legal notices from Detroit to Chicago.

Fourth of July toasts

At this year's celebration, Daytonians made 17 toasts, including:

■ Toast No. 3: To "The Constitution of the United States — May its duration be as lasting as the solar system."

■ Toast No. 10: To "Agriculture — May our plowshares never rust, and may the hungry of nations be fed with our superabundance."

■ Toast No. 11: To "Manufacturers — May our exports exceed our imports."

Bogging down

Rain and snow still made road travel hazardous. Poles and logs, which covered holes and low places, floated in wet weather. A poor horse whose feet got caught was literally sunk. Men might struggle for hours to save their beasts from the muck.

They're back!

Indians, egged on by the British, camped north of Dayton at Greenville in the summer, harassing white settlers.

Infant industries

Besides smiths, carpenters, masons, tailors, weavers and dyers, a count of Dayton businesses and industries in August showed six licensed taverns, five stores, three saddlers, three hatters, three cabinet makers, two cut-nail factories and a tannery, brewery, printing office, gunsmith, jeweler, watchmaker, sicklemaker and wagonmaker.

Militiamen on parade

Businessmen closed their doors and country folks came from miles around to see the parade and drill of Dayton's Fifth Regiment, which assembled for training exercises September 18.

Walk this way

Flat stones, laid side by side, made up the first improved sidewalk along Water Street (now Monument Avenue). The Select Council improved sidewalks on principal streets as it could.

Cut...

The state road east and west through Dayton, and a 200-mile bridle path from here to Vincennes, Indiana, during the winter of 1810-11.

Growing

Dayton's population reached 383.

Above: Patterson Stone Mill, as it appeared in the mid-1800s.

SLICE OF LIFE

The mill

Cornmeal while-you-wait: Farmers picnicked with their families at Rubicon gristmill — built by Col. Robert Patterson on what's now Brown Street — while waiting for their corn to run through the stones.

Mobbed...

Shakers living in Dayton, on May 3. The attack wasn't a surprise. Through the newspaper, the mob had warned the sect to leave Dayton, or suffer the consequences. The Shakers refused — and resolutely stayed put afterward.

May 13-14

Flour, grain, salt pork, bacon, pelts and whiskey loaded on nine flatboats left Dayton for New Orleans. Eight made it; one wrecked just 12 miles downriver.

Foiled, but not forgotten

At the Battle of Tippecanoe in northeast Indiana on November 7, Gen. William Henry Harrison foiled famous Shawnee leader Tecumseh, who had planned to rid the region of whites. War between the United States and Great Britain, meanwhile, seemed inevitable — a war in which Tecumseh would side against the Americans who continuously encroached on Indian lands.

December 16: Earthquake!

Daytonians awoke at 2 a.m. in horror. The ground was shaking! Like people all over the Midwest, they felt the rumbling from the great New Madrid, Missouri, earthquake. People ran from their homes in fright and farm animals scattered, but Dayton escaped any real damage. (Aftershocks continued through February.)

SLICE OF LIFE

Wooden pavement

Laid: Walnut logs, at the southeast corner of Third and Main, by blacksmith Obadiah Conover. (Conover's version of customer service, the logs gave a smooth surface for shoeing horses.)

Left: Tecumseh

1812

January 10: Masons in Dayton

The town's first fraternal organization: St. John's Lodge of Free and Accepted Masons No. 13, chartered by the Ohio Grand Lodge.

Twister!

A tornado swept the area eight miles north of Dayton on June 27.

Born...

David Zeigler Cooper, to Sophia and Daniel Cooper.

MILESTONE
War rumblings

Travelers to Dayton brought the news: Near Lake Erie, the British continued to incite and arm the Indians.

Great Britain couldn't keep from messing around with its former colonies. The British were interfering with American shipping on the East Coast, and turning up the heat on the U.S. frontier, including the Miami Valley. When the second war of American independence came to Ohio, Dayton had its part to play.

April 27: Assembly

Off to fight the British, a company of U.S. rangers left Dayton for Ft. Loramie. Soon afterward, Ohio Gov. Return J. Meigs Jr. responded to President James Madison's request to call out the state militia. Place of assembly: Dayton.

May 25-26: Rendezvous

Under Gen. William Hull, troops assembled at Camp Meigs (established in Dayton on the west side of the Great Miami) and then marched on to Detroit. Quartermaster for the troops: Col. Robert Patterson. The quartermaster's headquarters: Newcom Tavern. (Where else?)

June 16: War!

After war was declared, Dayton became a busy and exciting military camp where plans were made and communication exchanged. Army roads were built to replace the pioneers' rough highways. New businesses and stores sprang up. Trade increased dramatically.

Top: Troops assembled at Camp Meigs for the long march to Detroit.

Bottom: The exploits of Gen. William Henry Harrison, hero of the 1811 battle at Tippecanoe, were later reflected in this 1840 campaign poster.

He flew the white flag

But in August, terror swept Daytonians when they heard the news: Gen. Hull had surrendered everything — 38 cannon, ammunition, provisions, cattle, horses and his 2,500-man army — without firing a shot. And the British were only half that number!

Southwest Ohio stood unprotected. Montgomery County responded with new militia companies, blockhouses, food, ammunition, arms and supplies. The new leader was Gen. William Henry Harrison. (Said one Dayton citizen: Our men are "no longer, thank God, commanded by an old Woman.")

Hero Harrison

Daytonians loved Harrison. At his request they hand-stitched 1,800 shirts in a single month for the soldiers. Harrison proved himself again as he had at Tippecanoe in 1811. On September 12, he led his men to Fort Wayne; soon afterward, the enemy disappeared. The Battle of Mississinewa in Indiana was another Harrison victory, but a costly one. In late November, 200 of his 700 troops trudged back to Dayton — limping, hurt, hungry and frostbitten. Wounded men were carted in wagons. Their blood froze into icicles.

First hospital

How to nurse the wounded? Daytonians quickly erected a tent hospital, directed by Dr. John Steele, on the courthouse lot; both men and women took care of the suffering soldiers. Over the next two years, Dayton remained an important point of communication during the war. ■

Right: William Huffman

Below: The Henderson & Elliott shop at the northwest corner of Fourth and Main streets.

SLICE OF LIFE

Working for a living

Working men and mechanics met at McCullom's Tavern on March 15 to organize the Dayton Mechanical Society, the town's first working-men's organization. The War of 1812 had been good to these men; money they made allowed them to buy land and build homes. Some townspeople enjoyed a prosperity they had not known before.

Died...

Dr. John Hole, who lived near Centerville and was the area's first doctor, on January 6.

Extra, extra!

The Ohio Centinel ceased publication May 19.

Completed...

The rubblestone jail, in December.

Shaker community dubbed 'Watervliet'

The Shaker community at Beaver Creek was now called Watervliet, named after a Shaker village in New York.

Built...

The first stone residence, at Third and Jefferson by William Huffman, who used the place as both a home and a store. It was later the site of Dayton's famous Beckel Hotel.

Continued...

The War of 1812. In spite of nearly constant rain that year — which flooded rivers and made roads practically impassable for military supply trains — Dayton remained a focal point for Gen. Harrison's army.

1814

Banker's hours — all three of them

Dayton's first bank, named (oddly enough) the Dayton Manufacturing Company, was incorporated on February 11, shortly after 16 Dayton businessmen gathered to discuss the need for a bank in town. Some statistics:

■ Cost of the bank's lot: $200.

■ Initial capital stock: $61,055.

■ Initial assets: $123,505.

■ First loan: $11,000 (to the federal government, for financing the War of 1812).

The bank board, organized on May 19, set the bank's hours of operation from 10 a.m. to 1 p.m. Doors opened in August.

In time, the Dayton Manufacturing Company (later renamed The Dayton Bank) became one of the strongest U.S. banking institutions.

Counterfeiters were at work before the end of the year, defacing $2 bills to be $20s and $1 bills to be $100s.

One potato, two potato

A Dayton citizen established *The Ohio Republican* on October 3, more than a year after the death of *The Ohio Centinel*. *The Republican* was doomed from the start. Two out of three subscribers never paid the $2 subscription, and the rest paid in potatoes rather than cash. Since a paper cannot live by potatoes alone, *The Republican* disappeared two years later, on October 9, 1816.

First regular ferry

Charles Tull launched it on the Great Miami at the head of Ludlow Street, in December.

Added...

A gristmill, at the Watervliet Shaker community.

1815

Ended...

The War of 1812, when the British gave up.

For your entertainment

Southern Ohio towns had grown large enough to make trips worthwhile for traveling shows and theater troupes. Dayton's first was a February 13 display of "wax work and figures."

Bogged in the basin

Dayton nearly lost some $100,000 in cargo that was packed and ready for export — but which was on boats that were stuck in the river mud near Wilkinson Street, thanks to a long drought. Once the rain came in March, the boats got going — much to the town's relief.

First school for girls

It opened on Main Street, south of Third.

Good deeds

Ladies who had replenished provisions, clothes and medical supplies during the War of 1812 formed the Dayton Female Charitable and Bible Society on April 12.

Established...

About 100 dwellings (mostly log cabins).

Fire

It happened in October, at the gristmill operated by Col. Robert Patterson, where NCR later grew.

A cordial invitation

At this year's Fourth of July celebration, Dayton women were finally welcome to join the festivities, which included a procession and dinner at a 100-seat banquet table.

Calling all single men

Dayton bachelors and gentlemen organized the Dayton Bachelors' Society, also called the "Society of Associated Bachelors," in July.

No immorality allowed

Meanwhile, the Moral Society met for the first time on July 22. Its objective: "the suppression of vice and immorality, Sabbath-breaking, swearing, and other immoral practices...."

Flood protection

Daniel Cooper, ever industrious, gave shovels to idle war recruits and sent them digging. The result: a new earthen levee following the turn of the Miami. The levee later became a winding parkway named Robert Boulevard.

To market, to market

Dayton's first market house opened July 4 in a long wooden building on Second Street between Main and Jefferson. For the next 40 years, that area was known as Market Street. It was the man of the house — not the woman — who rose long before dawn every Wednesday and Saturday to grab a basket and make the market's 4 a.m. opening. Market food was affordable:

■ A pair of venison hams or a turkey: 50 cents.

■ A pound of butter: 12.5 cents.

■ A dozen eggs: 8 cents.

■ A dozen chickens: 75 cents.

Above: The Patterson Homestead, a Federal-style farmhouse on eight acres of Col. Robert Patterson's 2,038-acre farm, at 1815 Brown Street. The farmhouse, a center of hospitality, was the birthplace of John H. and brother Frank Patterson, co-founders of the National Cash Register Company.

Bridging the gap

Unlike the Great Miami, the Mad River was tough to ferry. Townsfolk met on January 27 at Col. Grimes' tavern to discuss bridging the Mad at Taylor Street.

Formed...

Dayton's first medical society, on July 3. Secretary: Dr. John Steele.

New newspaper lasts four years

"Truth, Equality and Literary knowledge, are the three grand pillars of Republican liberty." So went the motto for *The Ohio Watchman*, a weekly newspaper first published on November 27. Subcriptions cost $2 a year. It stopped keeping watch on December 18, 1820.

Enjoy the show (and please, no smoking)

Patrons paid 50 cents to see local talent present the town's first play, an elegant comedy entitled *Matrimony*, on April 22.

SLICE OF LIFE

The mail

Daytonians paid dearly for long-distance letters:
- 0 to 30 miles: 6 cents.
- 30 to 80 miles: 10 cents.
- 80 to 150 miles: 12.5 cents.
- 150 to 400 miles: 18.75 cents.
- 400 miles: 25 cents.

SLICE OF LIFE

Elite transportation

Nearly all Daytonians still traveled on horseback. Only two enjoyed the pleasure of the carriage: Daniel Cooper and H.G. Phillips.

Military spirit

Men drummed up support for the military, forming three "hoss critter companies." Arms included war relics such as long sweeping sabers, flintlock horse pistols and muskets.

The sun also rises

Newcom Tavern was reopened as the Sun Inn in December by Blackall Stephens, whose storefront sign sported a rather large illustration of old Sol.

Busy congregation

At their meeting house, Presbyterians established a Sabbath-School Association in March. Later in the year, they erected a brick church building at Second and Ludlow.

Sold...

The contract for bridging the Mad River, on March 21 to William Farnum. Price: $1,400. The high, 160-foot-long bridge, painted red, was finished in December but opened for travel several months earlier.

Built and occupied...

A new two-story brick building, north of the courthouse, for housing county offices.

Changed...

The motto of *The Ohio Watchman*, to "A Free Press is the Palladium of Liberty."

1818

Coach was first-class in those days

It was slow going at first for the Cincinnati-Dayton passenger and mail coach service, which made its first run on June 4. The four-horse coaches, each carrying 11 passengers, left Cincinnati at 5 a.m. Tuesday; passengers stopped for the night in Hamilton, making Dayton by Wednesday night. Travelers paid 8 cents per mile and could carry 14 pounds of baggage (no more). The return coach left Dayton at 5 a.m. Friday, making Cincinnati by Saturday night.

"Travel light" was the advice from seasoned travelers. (After all, what if you had to walk or help push the coach from the mire?) It wasn't uncommon for a swollen stream to sweep a coach off the road ... for a robber to bunk in the tavern overnight ... or for scam artists to dig a quagmire deeper and offer to pull out the coach — for a fee, of course.

Overexertion, stress and strain

A burst blood vessel claimed the life of 45-year-old Dayton benefactor Daniel Cooper on July 13, six weeks after he was injured while wheelbarrowing a bell to the Presbyterian church. Cooper left a wife and a 6-year-old son.

Outdoor worship

Folks were used to seeing the Methodists conduct "camp meetings" in local groves. The first was held June 26 at the foot of Ludlow Street for 3,000 worshippers.

Rented...

The upper story of the courthouse office building, in August, to *The Ohio Watchman* for $50 a year. (A fringe benefit for the county: *The Watchman* agreed to print — for free — election notices and the treasurer's annual report.)

Organized...

The Methodist Sunday School Society, in August, for teaching kids and adults to read.

Begun...

Construction on the Bridge Street span, Dayton's first toll bridge over the Great Miami.

Above: Dayton was beginning to take on the appearance of the city it would become in this drawing by an unknown artist.

1819

Lion taming

The curious flocked to see the African lion brought to town and shown in the barnyard at Reid's Inn on Main Street, April 22-25. Adults viewed the caged beast for 25 cents, while children paid half that.

Bridge Street bridge completed

The red covered bridge let Daytonians cross the Great Miami at Bridge Street and Salem Avenue. On foot? The tollkeeper charged 2 cents before raising the pole. On horse? Then it cost 3 cents. Loaded wagons crossed for 12 cents, and empty wagons for 6. Revenues paid for road improvements — which usually meant extra layers of gravel.

Established...

St. Thomas Episcopal Church, in October, served by the Rev. Ethan Allen. It was Dayton's first Episcopal church, eventually leading to the formation of Christ Church.

Arrived...

A keelboat, from Cincinnati. More advanced than those square-ended, hard-to-steer old flatboats!

Another animal showing

Columbus the elephant was brought to Reid's Inn and shown in the log barn out back from April 11-14. Agog adults paid 37 $1/2$ cents for a look; children paid half-price.

First major fire

It was the worst fire the town had seen: More than 4,000 bushels of wheat, 2,000 bushels of wool, the gristmill, fulling mill and machinery were destroyed at Cooper's Mills on June 20. The town wasted no time afterward, organizing its first fire company the very next day. The Town Council bought ladders that were hung outside the Market House on Second Street, and each household was ordered to keep two black leather buckets handy in case of fire.

Oops! Too much partying?

The editor of *The Ohio Watchman* apologized in a July edition for having omitted several advertisements in the previous issue. He sheepishly admitted to having simply forgotten them, "owing to the celebration of the Fourth of July."
On Christmas Day, *The Ohio Watchman* changed its name to the *Dayton Watchman and Farmers' and Mechanics' Journal.*

SLICE OF LIFE

Mutual instruction

All were abuzz at the Dayton Academy, which had just launched the Lancasterian teaching method:
■ Student monitors guided their peers, who recited aloud from lesson cards on the walls.
■ Inappropriate behavior cost students "tickets of merit." (Playing ball on Sunday? An automatic 25-ticket deduction.)
■ The youngest scholars used sticks to copy the alphabet in a thin layer of silver sand spread across the teacher's desk.

Black businessmen

Black barber John Crowder teamed up with Jacob Musgrave to begin a regular stagecoach service between Cincinnati and Dayton.

Census reports

Dayton's population topped 1,100; of these, 114 were "free persons of color." Ohio's population jumped to 571,295, up from 45,365 only 20 years before.
By 1820, Ohio's population was the fifth largest in the nation.
Although Ohio was populous, its people were relatively poor; there was still no easy, efficient way to get the state's products to larger markets.

SLICE OF LIFE

Malaria

One in three Daytonians was stricken between August and October with a severe fever that was probably malaria. Nearly 400 people got sick; the dead were buried in the Fifth Street graveyard.

Top: Two black businessmen from Dayton teamed up to establish a Dayton-Cincinnati stagecoach line.

Above: An early drawing of the Dayton Academy.

Talk of the town

The place: Reid's Inn. The topic: raising funds for a survey of a canal route. Horatio Phillips, James Steele, George Smith, Alexander Grimes and Joseph Crane led the movement in Dayton for an Ohio canal. Quite obviously, something was needed. Stages and wagon trains couldn't handle the Miami Valley's imports and exports. River shipment, while affordable, was unsafe and seasonal. Costs for a canal were estimated at $2.5 million, but officials predicted it would pay for itself in just six years.

1822

Just like lemmings, but hungrier

It was a strange sight: The surface of the river was brown — with hordes of squirrels! On March 29, men and boys grabbed clubs to bludgeon the swarming critters, who were ready to feast on the town's crops. A full day of clubbing bagged 1,000 squirrels.

The cost of eating

Because crops were plentiful, people typically paid less for food in March than they had several years before:
- Flour: $2.50 a barrel.
- Whiskey: 12.5 cents a gallon.
- Beef: 1 to 3 cents a pound.
- Bacon hams: 2 to 3 cents a pound.
- Butter: 5 to 8 cents a pound.

THE RUBICON FACTORY,
Two miles below Dayton.

THE subscribers inform their friends and the public, that their Carding and Spinning machines are now in complete operation, having this season made considerable improvement in their Factory—they are prepared to Card and Spin wool in the best manner.

For Carding common wool 6 1-4 cts. per lb
" Spinning chain per doz. 18 3-4 cents,
do. filling per do 15 do.
" Carding, Spinning and Weaving Cloth in 500 } 31 1-4 do.
Reed,
do. all above 500 in proportion,
do Casinett, do.
do. Satinett, 37 1-2 cts.

Every attention shall be paid to work committed to them, that it shall be done in the best manner and to the satisfaction of those employing them.

Produce will be received, in part payment, at the market price.

R. PATTERSON,
H. HYATT.

May 12th, 1823. 73 tf

1823

Wool for produce

Col. Robert Patterson advertised on May 12 that his carding and spinning machines were now up and running at Rubicon. Patterson's pledge: "Every attention shall be paid (to the work) ... it shall be done in the best manner and to the satisfaction of those employing them.... Produce will be received, in part payment, at the market price."

Traveling zoo

Daytonians were delighted to see an African lion and leopard (both rather bedraggled), an elephant, Brazilian cougar, ichneumon (an Egyptian mongoose), Shetland pony and rider, and more on September 22-23. An extra treat: exotic music on such instruments as the ancient Jewish cymbal.

CHEAP SUMMER GOODS,
H. G. PHILLIPS

Is just receiving a large and general assortment, including

DRY GOODS,
HARDWARE,
BOOKS & STATIONARY,
BONNETS,
LOOKING GLASSES,
MILL & X CUT SAWS,
IRON & STEEL. &c. &c.
GROCERIES,
MEDICINES,
PAINTS & DYE STUFFS,
SHOES,
SADDLERY, AND
PLATED WARE,
CASTINGS,
COTTON, &c. &c.

The above were purchased on the best terms, and are offered WHOLE-SALE or RETAIL, at the most reduced prices for CASH, COUNTRY LINEN, BEES WAX, WHEAT, WHISKEY, &c.

Dayton, May 12th, 1823. 21 tf

Beyond tavern talk

Canal planning became more serious after a commission was appointed to survey possible routes and pin down cost estimates.

Departed...

Seven flatboats and one keelboat, bound for New Orleans.

Mysterious money

Reports listed the sheriff's salary at $50 a year, the clerk's at $50 per year and the auditor's at a comfortable $150. "Of course," one record noted, "there was a schedule of fees that the officers were entitled to, in addition to their salaries." Hmmm....

Top: Col. Robert Patterson's advertising promise, as it appeared.

Bottom: Needed supplies were arriving in town, and merchants wasted no time letting customers know.

Published...

The Miami Republican and Dayton Advertiser, for the first time on September 23, until September 7, 1826. Like other newspapers of its time, it was a $2-a-year weekly. Despite its name, *The Republican* was a Democratic Party paper (there was no Republican Party yet).

Music to their ears

Daytonians with the best voices gathered to sing under the direction of John Van Cleve, who organized the Pleyel Society. The talented Van Cleve, organist and choirmaster of Christ Church, held rehearsals in the courthouse's jury room.

Right: Where were the ladders? No one knew. In the meantime, two stores on Main Street burned to the ground. The loss: $1,000 — a huge sum for that time. After this disaster, Daytonians were fined $10 for removing fire ladders from their appointed places. Town Council members realized Dayton was long overdue for a fire engine.

Below: The Miami Canal opened up transportation between Dayton and Cincinnati.

Hold on to your hat

Stagecoach travel to Cincinnati had become cheaper ($2) and quicker (12 hours).

Budding industries

Flour mills and distilleries peppered the Miami Valley. Records estimated 50 flour mills and 100 distilleries on the Great Miami River.

Troubled bridge

They had an inkling it was unsafe, so workers installed a new floor and extra braces on the 1817 Mad River bridge. No matter: The old red span collapsed anyway by spring. (It was a year before a replacement was built.)

Invited...

Black residents, to leave Dayton for resettlement in Haiti, on October 21. Twenty-four of them accepted money from the Haitian government to make the move.

Appointed...

Issachar Bates, on October 24, to lead Dayton's Watervliet community of Shakers.

Organized...

The First Baptist Church. Place of worship: a new church on the west side of Main Street between Water Street (now Monument Avenue) and First Street.

Built...

Dayton's first cotton factory, by Thomas Clegg.

1825

MILESTONE

Transportation solution

It was a huge venture — an estimated $5.7 million, nearly 10 percent of the total valuation of all taxable property in Ohio. But money was no object to Ohioans, who wanted a statewide canal system at nearly any cost. The legislature agreed and authorized construction of the Miami Canal, from Dayton to Cincinnati (and eventually to Toledo), and the Ohio Canal, from Cleveland to Portsmouth.

1825

Trading poverty for prosperity

The task ahead was monumental, but Ohioans were undaunted. Their land was rich, but they were undeniably poor; it was simply too expensive and difficult to send enough of their goods to market. A canal would produce navigable, level waters year-round, and offer a direct route to eastern markets.

The dream couldn't come true soon enough — just this year, 30 riverboats were stranded by low water, a typical dry-weather problem. When the river was up, boatloads of cargo could be lost on rapids.

Ohio looked east to the success of the Erie Canal, which connected New York City and Buffalo. Completed in 1822, the Erie Canal brought development and prosperity; a ton of freight that once cost $100 to ship across the state now cost only $10.

Where to run the canal in Dayton? The Watchman suggested Main Street, but the canal landing ended up three blocks east, between Second and Third streets (along today's Patterson Boulevard).

Cutting the ribbon

Dayton's excitement grew after New York Gov. DeWitt Clinton came to town July 8 during his tour of Ohio to drum up support for the canal. Clinton and Ohio Gov. Jeremiah Morrow went on to Middletown, where they hosted groundbreaking ceremonies for the canal on July 25.

The turning of the spade marked a turning point for Ohio. The next step: hiring workers to build the canal. The force consisted of local contractors, small operators, farmers, farmers' sons and black, Irish and German laborers. For 30 cents a day and a jigger of whiskey (sometimes two or three), workers agreed to wield pick and shovel from sunup to sundown. The work week was easily six days, sometimes more, totaling 26 working days a month. For some foreign workers, a jigger of whiskey every two hours wasn't uncommon. Said one jigger boss: "You wouldn't expect them to work on the canal if they were sober, would you?"

In addition to back-breaking work, shack-dwelling canal crews risked malaria during the summer and freezing during the winter. Despite the obstacles, they pressed on. The canal's last section, the Miami Extension Canal from Dayton to the junction of the Auglaize and Maumee rivers near Defiance, was completed 20 years later.

Total cost of the canal: $8,062,680. ■

Dayton's first execution

The "other woman," Hetty Shoup, was there at the March 28 hanging of John McAfee, convicted in 1824 of murdering his wife. Shoup, who had wanted to continue her affair with McAfee, convinced him to do away with his spouse. The smitten McAfee tried and failed with poison, strangling his wife instead. The hanging, at 3 p.m. on the edge of the woods, attracted a huge crowd that apparently didn't mind trudging through heavy mud to get there. When it was over, the crowd quickly dispersed. And Shoup? She escaped without punishment.

The greatest show in Dayton

People came from miles around to see the first full circus to hit Dayton, July 19-21. The crowd enjoyed horse acts, bareback and fancy riding by men and women alike, running and vaulting, a clown and "ground and lofty tumbling." The circus pitched its tent in the barnyard of Reid's Inn.

Set up shop...

The first real estate agent in Dayton, George Houston, who announced himself in the newspapers.

Top and above: Once established, the canal had its peaceful moments.

The 'coffee mill' engine
Men and boys alike learned how to operate the long-handled pump of Dayton's first fire engine — a box with a pump and crank — which arrived from Philadelphia in the spring. (The cost: $226.) Bucket brigades filled the engine's 4-by-6-foot wooden tank from the public pump; another relay team worked the engine by pumping handles up and down to douse the fire.

Every male in Dayton was a volunteer firefighter. A night alarm meant leaving warm beds to work the engine, but no one dared miss a fire — for fear they'd be abandoned if their own property was ever ablaze.

Opportunity knocks
It was no coincidence that the town's first fire insurance agent, James Perrine, opened up shop in June, shortly after the fire engine's arrival.

Built...
The first county infirmary ("for a poor house"), on farmland bought from Dr. James B. Oliver in April. County commissioners paid the good doctor $10.50 an acre. The infirmary was completed in July.

Purchased...
The Miami Republican and Dayton Advertiser and the *Dayton Watchman and Farmers' and Mechanics' Journal*, by William Campbell in April. In November, he consolidated them into the *Ohio National Journal and Montgomery and Dayton Advertiser*, the Whig Party paper, which later became the Dayton *Journal*. The motto of this $2-a-year weekly: "Principles and not men, where principles demand the sacrifice."

Let them eat cake
Dayton celebrated the nation's first jubilee — the 50th anniversary of the signing of the Declaration of Independence — on July 4 with a procession, church services, a dinner at the former Newcom Tavern (by then Rollman's tavern) and a picnic near the site of today's University of Dayton. Featured speakers included John Van Cleve, who read the Declaration of Independence, and Peter P. Lowe, who delivered a distinguished oration.

A question of temperance
The gutters on Main Street swallowed gallons and gallons of whiskey dumped by businessman Obadiah Conover outside his prominent Dayton store. What made him do it? Conover's Presbyterian conscience had been eating at him. Whiskey meant profits, but whiskey was a bad thing — according to the Bible, anyway. Whiskey kegs filled his store cellar. For years, Conover's customers had been welcome to take a free nip or two from the jug on the back counter. Sigh. What to do? Before he could change his mind, Conover dumped it — every bit of it — down Main Street. Did his decision hurt business? No one will ever know.

Left...
Twelve boats, bound for New Orleans, in February. Only nine made it; two hit rocks and one sank immediately.

At last!
After nearly two years, canal work in Dayton began in April with surveys to run the Miami Canal from the Mad River to Middletown. The town was talking that spring. It seemed everyone wanted a piece of the canal pie; on May 17, canal commissioners opened some 600 construction bids. By June 1, contractors began work near Dayton. And with a cannon shot on September 3, Daytonians marked the start of construction at the canal basin between Second and Third streets.

Died...
Col. Robert Patterson, on August 5.

They quit
Afraid of malaria and hoping for better wages, some Irish and German canal laborers abandoned their jobs and left Dayton. They were replaced by black workers who lived in a settlement called "Africa" near Fifth and Wayne.

Connected by stage
Daily coaches between Dayton and Columbus began June 25.

Want to see Lake Erie? The Cincinnati, Dayton, Columbus and Portland coach traveled from Cincinnati to the lake in four days. (Fares: Cincinnati to Dayton, $3; Cincinnati to Columbus, $6; Cincinnati to Erie, $12.)

Improved...
The Dayton economy, after the long economic depression that followed the War of 1812. Since the end of the war in 1815, barter had largely replaced gold and silver on the frontier.

Organized...
The first official volunteer fire company (appropriately called the Dayton Fire Engine Company), on March 10. Eighty-eight leather fire buckets were purchased by Town Council for $112.50; 44 buckets were kept on the fire engine and 44 were distributed to homes.

1828

Changed...

The name of the *Ohio National Journal and Montgomery and Dayton Advertiser*, established in 1826, to the *Dayton Journal and Advertiser*, on January 1. John Van Cleve became owner of the Dayton *Journal*, contributing articles and editorials.

Flooded...

The Stillwater, Great Miami and Mad rivers, on January 7. The flood washed away a canal bridge and all the mill race bridges.

The best-laid plans

A few bugs in the canal system? Perhaps. That's what canal officials thought on September 26 after most of the first water let into the canal leaked out through the embankment in Mad River Township. They headed back to start tweaking the system.

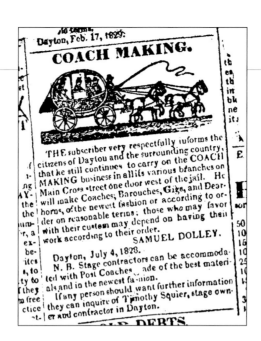

First UFO

War? Death in the family? That's what an elderly lady predicted when she saw something strange and frightening floating east over her farm on June 7. The object? A paper balloon, probably the first to be sent up in the area.

Test runs

The first canal boat built in Dayton, The Alpha, was launched August 16. Trouble was, the canal wasn't open yet. So they made several test runs by building a dam south of town and turning on the water near Second Street. By December 17, The Alpha carried folks to Hole's Creek near Centerville, and on December 22 more passengers went to Miamisburg and back, in time for Christmas Eve. The canal rides were the talk of the town that Christmas.

Established...

The first iron foundry, by McElwee and Clegg, later called Globe Iron Works. The proprietors made their first "heat" December 2.

Regular routes

Dayton was becoming a hot spot for travel. By 1828, 20 stagecoaches arrived in town every week.

1829

MILESTONE

A new era dawns

It was sighted at daybreak. The arrival of The Governor Brown — the first canal boat to reach Dayton — marked the formal opening of the Miami Canal in Dayton on January 25. Crowds cheered as the cannon boomed. Travel time from Cincinnati to Dayton: a mere 20 hours!

Marking the occasion

Later that day, three other boats reached Dayton: The Forrer, The General Marion and The General Pike. As always, Dayton celebrated with a grand banquet. Orators praised the great water highway that connected Dayton with the rest of the world.

Facts and figures

■ Dayton's section of canal began at the Mad River, wound through Miamisburg, Franklin and Hamilton and then followed the Mill Creek to Cincinnati. The Dayton-Cincinnati section was 67 miles long and cost $1 million.

■ A typical canal boat was 78 feet long, less than 15 feet wide and cost just over $2,000. Horses or mules drew the boats from a 10-foot-wide towpath.

Top: Early advertising highlighted transportation.

Above: The Miami Canal opened Dayton to the rest of the world. Shown here years later, the canal was a focal point for departures, arrivals and celebrations.

■ Big business was afloat. In April alone, 71 boats arrived in Dayton and 77 departed; more than $43,000 worth of goods were shipped out.

■ By the end of the first year, Dayton had exported 27,121 barrels of flour, 7,378 barrels of whiskey, 3,429 barrels of pork and 423 barrels of flaxseed oil.

Packet lines

Once freight service was established, passenger service began. Passenger boats, called packet lines, featured seats, awnings and reasonably

Land values

Real estate was at an all-time high. At Fifth and Brown streets, 27 building lots sold for a total of $220.

comfortable bunks. Black fiddlers often provided entertainment to passengers, who danced on deck. The mule-powered canal boats were slow — typically going 3 mph (the speed limit was 4 mph). The view from the top deck was pleasant, though, and provided a respite from the stuffy, mosquito-ridden cabins.

Growth follows

As predicted, prices rose, buildings went up and the economy boomed. Wrote John Van Cleve: "The streets are all busy, drays running, hammers and trowels sounding, canal horns blowing, stages flying, everybody doing something...." Still, there were critics. One pundit called the canal a "ruinous and useless expenditure," and a few dubbed it obsolete the day it was done. Why? Something about a contraption called an "iron horse." ■

What the town was made of

By January 1, Dayton boasted:
■ 125 brick buildings.
■ Six stone buildings.
■ 239 wooden buildings.
Residential buildings alone numbered 235.

Chief executive

The president of Town Council wore a new hat and title as mayor under a new town charter that took effect this year. Daytonians elected John Folkerth as the town's first mayor.

Constructed...

A dam, by James Steele, on the Great Miami River north of town, creating a water channel called a hydraulic race, which provided power for industry. Steele's dam was later called the Dayton View Hydraulic.

Right: With heavy canal-boat traffic, Dayton was a commercial success.

Below: An artist's conception of slaves seeking freedom.

Published...

The Dayton Republican — yet another $2-a-year weekly. It began on January 5 and continued until 1834.

Sowing the seeds for the Civil War

By giving food and shelter to runaway slaves, many people in and around Dayton broke the federal Fugitive Slave Law throughout the 1830s by refusing to turn in known fugitives — even to gain a $50 reward. One of many local stations on the Underground Railroad was the home of Dayton's Dr. Adam Jewett, who housed and fed escaped slaves in his cellar and barn.

Opened...

The National Hotel, on April 13, on Third Street. Edmund Browning kept the place for six years.

All aboard!

After calling a special meeting May 31, the Town Council granted a special license (for free) to an Englishman who promptly assembled a railroad track inside the Methodist meeting house and offered around-the-room excursions on a locomotive. At 25 cents a ride, it was Dayton's first taste of railroading.

By leaps and bounds

Dayton's population more than doubled in five years, to 2,954 in 1830.

Abandoned...

The Second Street Market. (Apparently, shoppers preferred the new market house built in 1829.)

1831

Shipping port

Canal freight became big business. In March and April alone, Dayton canal boats carried:

- 58,000 barrels of flour.
- 7,000 barrels of whiskey.
- 12,000 barrels of pork.
- 18,000 kegs of lard.
- 750 hogsheads of ham.
- 1.8 million pounds of bacon.

Organized...

Christ Church Parish.

Entered...

Robert C. Schenck, to the Dayton bar. He became a prominent community leader.

Dayton Woolen **FACTORY,**
Situated at the Lock on Fifth Street.

D. M. CURTIS

Dealer in Wool and Woolen Goods, and manufacturer of all kinds of Woolen Goods, such as Cloths, Cassimeres, Sattinets, Tweeds, all kinds of Flannel, Blankets, Stocking Yarn, and Yarn for Coverlet and Carpet Weavers.

He is now manufacturing Ladies' Woolen Hose, and Socks for Men, all of the best material, which he will sell low for Cash, at Wholesale or Retail.

Carding, Spinning, Weaving and Fulling done as usual.

Free public education (well, almost)

Taxes supported the opening of Dayton's first public school, but students still had to pay tuition of $1 per quarter. A rented school room on Jefferson Street opened December 5 after the Dayton school district was organized at a meeting at the courthouse May 14.

Changed...

The name of Dayton's first bank, the Dayton Manufacturing Company, to the Dayton Bank, on December 31. Connected with the institution was Valentine Winters, who'd begun his career in Dayton in 1825 earning 10 cents a day.

Arrived...

Robert Conway and family, the first Catholic family in Dayton, from Baltimore.

Above: Early advertising promoted Dayton products.

Below: The head of the Miami Canal in Dayton, as seen by artist Thomas Wharton.

1832

Arrived...

Richard McNemar, on February 10, as the new leader of the Watervliet community of Shakers. He was assigned to get the group onto solid footing again. The community had become the center for Shaker printing in the west.

Appointed...

The area's first board of health, in June, which urged Daytonians to clean up their property or risk deadly cholera. Meanwhile, a canal boat with 25 sick German immigrants arrived from Cincinnati.

We could have become a ghost town

Salesmen pitching stock in the Mad River & Lake Erie Railroad Company, incorporated this year, found virtually no takers in Dayton. The plan: a line from Dayton through Springfield to Sandusky. Folks weren't convinced. Railroads struck some as a passing fad, and the canal had proved its worth — the Miami Extension Canal was under construction, in fact. What did Dayton need with a railroad?

Xenia saw the need and promptly got on the line. (Later, Daytonians who wanted to take the train to New York had to get to Xenia first.) For the next 20 years, towns on the line prospered,

while Dayton continued moving people and products on what it knew best — the stagecoach and canal boat. Dayton's rebuff kept the railroad away until 1851, when a Dayton-Springfield line finally opened. Historically speaking, this episode was a close call.

Seely's folly

It was prime real estate, or so he thought. Bringing a canal to the eastern part of Dayton and linking it with the Ohio canal would surely benefit industries that located along the race. With dollar signs dancing in his head, Morris Seely quickly bought land from Third Street to Wayne Avenue and then southwest to just north of the fairgrounds. But once built, Seely's Basin never brought the yield its creator envisioned. Later, the would-be prime properties on Fifth and Wayne sold for rock-bottom prices — as low

as $5 to $30 per lot. For a long time, the basin was known as "Seely's ditch."

Bookish types

By 1832, literary culture had blossomed in Dayton, which boasted at least six private libraries.

The Dayton Lyceum Association, organized this year, wisely forbade discussions of theology and politics at meetings. Instead, these lovers of literary culture focused on lectures, essays and discussions of every other subject of interest.

The re-election of 'Old Hickory'

Politics was the passion of the day, especially in an election year. The campaign was on for Andrew Jackson's second term, and it was a bitter contest. Daytonians rallied on both sides, with bonfires, processions, banquets at the National Hotel, flag-raisings and speeches. The old general won big against Henry Clay, and life in Dayton went back to normal.

It went to the dogs

Andrew Jackson's victory called for a celebration — and a townwide ox roast seemed just right. The cooking got started, but the chefs soon determined the meat (which had been out of cold storage too long) was unfit to eat. No matter: The dogs of Dayton smelled the cooked meat, gathered at fireside and helped themselves. Jackson's second term, fortunately, went better than the barbecue.

SLICE OF LIFE

A martyr for the cause

Thomas Mitchell, a fugitive slave, was hiding in Dayton when federal officers caught up with him. The night before he was to be returned to his owner, Mitchell made a daring and deadly final dash — leaping from a building, he was killed. Townsfolk, aghast at the tragedy, gathered to hear preachers and orators speak of slavery's injustice. After the Dayton *Journal* announced the first meeting of the Dayton Abolition Society, the town became a hotbed for the anti-slavery movement.

Top: This painting by Thomas Wharton shows Dayton as it appeared in 1832, seen from the southeast.

Right: Volunteer firemen manned the new pumper, 20 to a side, and hand-pumped water from underground fire cisterns located around town.

Safer for travel

Some of Montgomery County's muddy and dangerous country roads, in dire need of improvement, were transformed thanks to three new turnpike companies chartered in February: the Dayton & Covington; the Dayton, Centerville & Lebanon; and the Dayton & Springfield.

Fire concerns

Dayton's newest fire engine, dubbed "Safety," was a $1,250 hand pumper with a suction hose purchased in November. Town Council also bought 500 feet of hose and later organized Safety Fire Engine and Hose Company No. 1. Fire cisterns were built under the streets.

1833

Oddly enough

Montgomery Lodge No. 3 — the first lodge of Odd Fellowship in Dayton — was established May 3.

Celebrated...

The first Mass in Dayton, at a bakery on St. Clair, by a Father Collins, soon after the arrival of Irish and German settlers.

A town in panic

Those 25 sick German immigrants who'd arrived the year before had brought cholera to Dayton, where it thrived in unsanitary conditions: cesspools adjacent to wells; gutters carrying roadway dirt and debris to the river; refuse dumped wherever convenient; open garbage pails at every home's back door. Since victims weren't quarantined, the disease became an epidemic. A doctor and two nurses volunteered to care for patients, who suffered unbearable abdominal cramps and fever. All three caregivers fell sick within 48 hours. Afterward, every mother became a nurse; many patients were taken to Mary "Mother" Hess, who cared for them in her Oregon home. When it was over, at least 33 Daytonians had died.

Sold...

The original Dayton Academy property; a new building was soon constructed at the southwest corner of Fourth and Wilkinson streets. In the meantime, Eliam E. Barney, destined to be principal of the new Dayton Academy, arrived in town.

Benchmarking

Dayton had 1,001 buildings and 4,000 people.

Churches, churches everywhere

The First Reformed Church organized and two congregations built churches: Dayton's first Catholic church, Emmanuel Catholic Church (and school), and the first Episcopal church.

Established...

The Mechanics' Institute, an outgrowth of the Dayton Lyceum Association. Members enjoyed a library, reading rooms and winter lectures.

Nature's fireworks

People were captivated by an extraordinary meteor shower, gazing heavenward as bits of light blazed across the night sky for more than two hours. Old-timers still told of it a quarter-century later.

1834

The law

A marshal and several watchmen made up Dayton's first police department. Town Council passed an ordinance January 3 allowing the appointment of one or more badge-wearing watchmen, charged with protecting the public safety.

If a lawbreaker was particularly feisty, a watchman was permitted to ask nearby townsfolk for assistance.

Paper chase

Dayton's very own *Journal* became Ohio's largest newspaper. Meanwhile, the Democratic *Herald* published its first issue.

Jailbreak

All it took was a cut through the floor and a tunnel up the wall — and four inmates broke out of the old 1813 rubblestone jail. Authorities immediately made plans for a new one, this time of sturdier cut stone.

E.E. Barney: Educator, principal, counselor

The eyes of both teachers and students were opened wide to the world of learning under the tutelage of Eliam E. Barney, elected principal of the Dayton Academy.

Barney's enthusiasm was contagious, and he became one of Dayton's greatest and most influential educators. Texts were closed in favor of time on task; Barney was often found in the country, not in the classroom, studying botany and geology with his students, whom he inspired to plant trees and flowers.

Science wasn't his only focus; he required composition and eloquent oratories. The academy boasted a literary society and library. Many students chose careers only after talking with Barney, who had an uncanny ability to pinpoint a pupil's natural talents and abilities.

He disciplined with an honor system — not by the paddle or switch. His analytical teaching methods made a lasting impact on Dayton's public schools.

He went on to make a significant impact on the city's industrial landscape, as well.

(How did Barney, a New Yorker, wind up in Dayton? He wrote to 50 different postmasters, asking them to write back and describe their towns. He decided Dayton sounded best.)

Above left: E.E. Barney, educator

Above right: William F. Comly, editor of the *Journal* from 1834 to 1862.

Above: Dayton's early Main Street bridge was completed in 1836.

Bridge works
County commissioners earmarked a generous $600 on June 4 for a new covered wooden bridge over the Great Miami River at Main Street. Dayton citizens kicked in pledges, too.

Chartered...
The Firemen's Insurance Company, in the spring.

Auctioned off...
Dayton's first library, which had moved from place to place around town since its incorporation in 1805.

Abandoned...
Dayton's Fifth Street graveyard, which after 30 years was found to be "unsuitable."

Appointed...
Night watchmen, by the marshal.

Founded...
Dayton's first black church, the African Methodist Episcopal Church (now Wayman).

Egg on his face
Not everybody in town was anti-slavery. An angry crowd threw eggs at abolitionist Rev. John Rankin during his lecture at Union Church on February 13. Rankin was the second abolitionist driven from the pulpit since January by a pro-slavery mob, which also vandalized the church and burned the homes of several black Daytonians.

From rodman to bridge man
David H. Morrison — who would someday be known as the best construction engineer in Ohio — began as a rodman (the surveyor's assistant who worked the leveling rod) on the Miami Canal in May, north of St. Mary's reservoir. Morrison, who later organized the Columbia Bridge Works of Dayton, was a respected authority on questions involving alignments, grades, crossings and surveys.

Free schools (really!)
Dayton hosted a school convention in August. Talk of the town: free schools for every child, a notion that spawned the Dayton Public Schools. In attendance: the Rev. William Holmes McGuffey of Oxford, creator of the famous McGuffey readers.

Opened for travel...
The new covered bridge over the Great Miami at Main Street.

Public square
David Z. Cooper, son of Daniel, deeded a public square to the town provided that it was "to be kept forever as a walk for the citizens of Dayton and its visitors." This first public park is today called Cooper Park, adjacent to the downtown library.

Upgrades
Town Council ordered several public works improvements, including the grading, curbing and graveling of streets; the building of canal wharves; and the straightening of the Mad River, and construction of levees along its banks.

Remodeling
The familiar log-cabin look of old Newcom Tavern changed drastically. Dayton's oldest building, at the southwest corner of Main and Water streets, was weather-boarded outside and plastered inside to become the town's first general store.

Passed...
A state law to pay for work on Ohio's roads.

Burned down...
Reid's Inn.

1837

More police protection

In April, two night watchmen were assigned to patrol each ward in Dayton.

The celebration that wasn't

It was billed as a grand affair: the official celebration, on Independence Day, marking the opening of the Miami Canal at Piqua. More than 1,000 people waited patiently for the arrival of Gen. William Henry Harrison in the first canal boat. Neither Harrison nor the boat arrived that day. Not enough water in the canal.

Money troubles

The financial turmoil of the Panic of 1837 left only three banks in the country able to pay their depositors. The Dayton Bank, under James Steele's leadership, was one of them.

Dedicated...

Emmanuel Catholic Church, on Franklin Street.

Community schools

By this time, every neighborhood in town had its own school, with classes conducted in homes or other buildings.

DIED,

In this place, on Sunday last, at the age of 82 years, Mrs. CATHARINE THOMPSON, formerly Mrs. Catharine Van Cleve, mother of the late Benjamin and William Van Cleve. She was the first female resident of this town and county, to which place she came on the 1st of April, 1796. She was also, one of the earliest inhabitants of Cincinnati, having come to that place before its name was changed from Losantiville, when two small hewed-log houses and a few log cabins constituted the whole town. Her first husband, John Van Cleve, to whom she was was married by the Rev. William Tennant, of Monmouth county, N. J. was killed by the Indians, on the first day of June 1791, within the present corporate limits of Cincinnati. Her second husband, Samuel Thompson, was drowned in Mad River near this place, about twenty years since. She was the mother of thirteen children and her grand children have numbered eighty-seven, and her great grand children upwards of ninety. She was a worthy member of the Methodist church for the last twenty years of her life and died in Christian resignation.

Dayton, August 8, 1837.

Top: The Miami Canal's Dayton-Cincinnati section was 67 miles long.

Left: The obituary of Catharine Thompson, who was believed to be the first settler to set foot on the riverbank in Dayton in 1796.

Above: During the panic, banks issued their own currency. The bills were known as "shinplasters."

1838

Formed...

The Third Street Bridge Company, on March 12, created to build the Third Street Bridge.

Road work ahead

Turnpike construction boomed this year. Work on the Dayton & Covington turnpike began soon after March 30; work on the Dayton, Centerville & Lebanon turnpike began on April 16; and work on the Dayton & Springfield turnpike began May 12. The Great Miami Turnpike Company, chartered in 1837, began building a pike from Dayton to West Carrollton and then through Miamisburg, Franklin and Middletown. The turnpike ended at its junction with the Cincinnati Pike in Sharon.

Organized...

The Montgomery County Agricultural Society.

Park planting

Workers began planting trees in the public square now known as Cooper Park.

Industrial power

A dozen mills and factories got power from Cooper Hydraulic, "the old sawmill race," a 50-by-700-foot waterway between Third and Fifth streets.

Schoolhouses

Dayton's first public school buildings — one on Perry Street and the other on East Second — were built for $6,000. One of the most vocal supporters: E.E. Barney, principal of the Dayton Academy.

Get rich quick

For a mulberry tree, a few thousand silkworm cocoons and a bit of time, Daytonians were promised riches beyond their wildest dreams. It was a silk scam, and quite a few businessmen fell for it. After the Dayton Silk Company was incorporated with $100,000 in capital, mulberry trees were purchased and planted and thousands of worms were laid to feed upon the trees. But in the end, folks realized the futility of their investments, and some suffered for years from the loss.

Awarded...
Construction contracts, by the Dayton & Western Pike Company, on July 8.

Held...
The first Montgomery County Fair, October 17-18, in the barnyard of Swaynie's Hotel, at the head of the canal basin.

Divided...
Dayton Township, into election precincts.

Built...
The "new" Presbyterian Church (thanks to James Steele).

Organized...
First English Lutheran Church.

Formed...
An anti-slavery society, in March, by local abolitionists.

Opened...
Swaynie's Hotel, in April, by Alexander Swaynie, who made the First Street establishment a first-class operation.

Swaynie's Hotel was carpeted by the Dayton Carpet Company, which made the first flowered ingrain carpet west of the Alleghenies. Somehow, the company's carpets were marketed and sold in Cincinnati and elsewhere as imports. Buyer beware!

Above: Gen. William Henry Harrison

Dayton: Too big for its britches?

Presidential politics was all the buzz, and Dayton was impassioned about the man they called the "Log Cabin" candidate — none other than war hero Gen. William Henry Harrison, who was running a populist, frontier-style campaign against the aristocratic Martin Van Buren.

Dayton got so stirred up that soon it invited the entire nation to a magnificent, three-day campaign rally and convention — the "Grand Council at Dayton" — featuring Log Cabin candidates Harrison, John Tyler for vice president and Thomas Corwin for Ohio governor. The bold announcement was published in the July 25 issue of the *Log Cabin*, a Whig Party paper, and the rally was set for September 10. But would anyone come?

They came, they saw, he conquered

On September 10, they did come — in droves. In packs. Troops and families came. By stagecoach. By canal. On foot. On horseback. In private coaches. From everywhere they came — 100,000 people in all — and Dayton took care of every last one.

They camped at roadside. They filled the National Hotel and Swaynie's place. They bunked in private homes, straw beds side by side.

Harrison arrived to a hero's welcome at the head of a four-mile parade of floats and carriages that took all morning to reach Dayton from Harshman's Station, where the general had spent the night.

A win and a loss

After an 11 a.m. dinner at Swaynie's, Harrison gave his speech just east of St. Clair Street, where soldiers had camped in 1812. There were cheers, wild cheers. Dayton had done it — it had entertained the nation. In November, Harrison won in a landslide. But the promise of prosperity under his presidency never came to pass. The president got pneumonia just one month after his inauguration. He died on April 4, and Vice President Tyler took his place. ■

Left: The *Log Cabin*, sold to readers for "25¢ in advance," endorsed Gen. William Henry Harrison on June 27.

Organized...

Montgomery County Mutual Fire Insurance Company. Also established: the Oregon volunteer fire company, at Sixth and Tecumseh streets.

Opened...

The Third Street Bridge.

Population:

6,067.

The beginnings of Woodland Cemetery

John Van Cleve dreamed of a rural cemetery — a beautiful resting place outside the town's busy business section. So when farmer Augustus George agreed to sell a large, forested tract just a mile south of town, Van Cleve jumped at it. The price: 40 acres, $60 per acre. Van Cleve led the charge: If he could find 50 subscribers who'd pledge $100 each, he could buy the land and still have enough left to hire workers to clear it. Thus the first steps were taken to establish Dayton's now-renowned Woodland Cemetery.

A third courthouse?

Montgomery was a growing county — one that was outgrowing its second courthouse and adjacent office building. Not only had the county buildings become insufficient, but both jails were outdated (to say nothing of the unsightly old engine house and cannon house nearby). Such facilities were unbecoming of a county on the rise, and folks started thinking about a new courthouse.

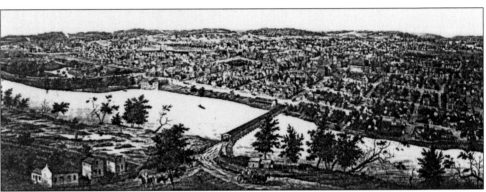

Above: Dayton had expanded by the mid-1800s.

Left: Much housing was still primitive, as this home of the period shows.

Bought...

A lot on Scott Street, by the United Daughters of Zion, a society of black women, on November 17. On this site was built Wesleyan Methodist Church.

The daily news

Daytonians began receiving their first daily paper, the Dayton *Journal*.

Faster travel

Thanks to the stagecoach, travelers got to Cincinnati faster than ever before — in only seven hours — for only $1. (In 1825, Daytonians had paid $2 for the 12-hour trip). Stagecoach trips, however, could be harmful. Potholes pitched coaches side to side, slamming passengers back and forth inside the vehicle. Later, gravel roads made for smoother, safer rides.

Above: The Henry Reese-William Walton House was built at 89 W. Franklin St. in Centerville on a lot valued at $30.

Right: The Dayton City Charter was voted in by a narrow majority, 382 to 378.

This, being the day appointed by the legislature, for the citizens of Dayton to vote "for" or against" the city charter," the judges & clerks of the several wards appeared in the Council Hall, at the hour of 6 o'clock P.M. and made the following report of the polls to wit: For the city charter   Against

		For	Against
The 1st Ward	32 votes		74 vote
2 "	59 "		56 "
3 "	101 "		93 "
4 "	85 "		69 "
5 "	105 "	382	86 " 378

Exhibiting a majority of 4 votes in favor

SLICE OF LIFE

Food, fun and furs

■ The land overflowed with wild turkeys, wild pigeons and deer.

■ Bears were still a common sight, though beaver were gone.

■ Hogs, cattle and fruit were scarce (unless you had a hankerin' for canned berries).

■ A log-rolling party for newcomers resulted in a raised cabin a little later.

■ Indians were still about, eager to trade furs for food.

■ Young boys spent their time trapping raccoons (pelts drew 10 cents) and rabbits (they brought 2 cents each, hide and all).

Smokestacks galore

Dayton boasted 144 "manufactories." Some of the more specialized industries: a hat factory, soap and candle factories, a clock factory, glove factory, and a sash and blind factory.

Extended...

The canal, northward, toward the goal of connecting Dayton with the Great Lakes.

Market rates

By June, flour cost $3.50 a barrel; whiskey 15 cents a gallon.

Stormed...

A black resort in southwest Dayton, called the Paul Pry, by a white mob, on January 26. The incident happened after a light-skinned black woman, thought to be white, moved there. One member of the mob was stabbed and killed. A week later, on February 3, whites retaliated for the stabbing by burning several black-owned homes. Many black residents left town, fearing for their lives.

Lost and found

Dayton got a glimpse of its Indian past when workers found a skeleton, wearing a necklace of 170 copper beads, during excavation of a mound in February. The mound, at the east end of First Street, was cut through as workers prepared to open the street to Springfield Pike. Also found: several arrow and spear heads.

Dayton Inc.

A city charter, subject to referendum, was granted to the former Dayton Township on March 8. After the May 3 election, Dayton officially became a city. The charter was adopted by a slim margin (just four votes, 382 to 378), but it was a victory nonetheless. The new city, which included all of Dayton Township, had a City Council with more power (and more responsibility) than the former Town Council. More officials were elected to manage the greater tasks of a city; one of the first ordinances allowed two constables to be elected, in addition to the marshal.

Chartered...

The Shakertown Pike from Dayton to Xenia, in March.

Ground cover

Hills, ravines and heavy woods made hard work for the men clearing the 40 acres that would become Woodland Cemetery. Work began on May 17, soon after John Van Cleve got the deed from Augustus George.

1842

A new year's resolution, perhaps?

Dayton rang in the new year by hosting a mass Temperance Meeting on January 1.

Incorporated...

Woodland Cemetery, thanks to years of work by John Van Cleve and Robert Steele. Only two other U.S. cities had resting places as beautiful. Van Cleve, who volunteered as superintendent, laid out the site, established the winding roads, and helped plant dogwoods, redbuds, maples and beech. On February 28, the Ohio General Assembly passed the Woodland Charter, adopted by The Woodland Cemetery Association of Dayton on April 10.

Visited...

Former President Martin Van Buren, on June 8.

Waterway

The Mad River's new channel, from the aqueduct straight to the Great Miami River, was completed in the fall. Excavation began in 1841, and by winter 1842, the channel carried water.

Above: Henry Clay visited Dayton on September 29.

Politicking

In the spirit of the 1840 Harrison rally, Daytonians hosted another political convention, this time for Henry Clay, on September 29. Estimates placed the crowd at 120,000 this time. There were military parades, flags, music, meetings, entertainment, speeches and more. The ladies of Montgomery County served dinner at two giant tables, each 800 feet long.

Established...

The *Western Empire*, a daily newspaper, which became the *Dayton Times*, and later the *Dayton Daily News*. (The *Empire,* the organ of the Democratic Party, was called "well-conducted.")

Built...

The turnpike from Dayton through Vandalia to Troy, by the Miami & Montgomery Company.

1843

Chartered...

The Valley Pike, up the north side of the Mad River, in March. The contract for the first 12 miles was let on May 29.

The first of many

The first burial in Woodland Cemetery, which opened its gates on June 7, was for Allen Cullum, originally from Butler County. The cemetery's official dedication was held the first day of summer, June 21.

As superintendent, John Van Cleve kept a beautifully scripted book in his own handwriting, listing burial lot sales and detailed charts of various sections. Also recorded was his meticulous list of 41 tree species, identified by botanical and common names. (Years later, J.C. Kline planted foreign tree varieties, which he brought from abroad.)

'Pity the poor children'

The ladies of Dayton, determined to establish an orphan asylum, held an Independence Day picnic to raise funds.

Graded...

Nine miles of city streets (to date). Only about half were graded from curb to curb.

Visited...

Former President John Quincy Adams, on November 6.

A city without a bank

The Dayton Bank, Dayton's first, closed after its charter expired. For more than two years, from early 1843 to mid-1845, there was no bank in the city.

Keifer and Conover's store

Popular merchant Obadiah Conover teamed up with a Mr. Keifer to run a large grocery and dry goods operation at a shop on Main Street.

Right: Cooper Female Seminary, at the corner of Fourth and Wilkinson.

First children's home

Orphans in the county had their first home, located on Magnolia Street, starting on March 12. The Dayton Female Association for the Benefit of Orphans, incorporated by the legislature in February, ran the home until 1868. The association's charge: to provide for and educate orphans and destitute children.

Authorized...

The purchase of brick, by county commissioners, on August 5. The intended structure: a brand new jail.

Appointed...

A special commission charged with preparing a grand new courthouse, the likes of which had never been seen before in Montgomery County. Leading the committee were John Van Cleve, Samuel Forrer and Horace Pease.

Chartered...

The Wolf Creek Pike, in May. It was built five years later.

Incorporated...

Cooper Female Seminary, for a "thorough education" of the city's daughters.

Initiated...

German schools. (For half the day, lessons were taught in English.)

What's in a name?

The *Western Empire*, a daily newspaper that later became the *Dayton Daily News*, was renamed the *Evening Empire*. Home delivery cost 6 cents a week.

A step up from the rest

One of Dayton's first famous inventors, John Balsley, came to town with 75 cents in his pocket. His invention: the stepladder, in 1865.

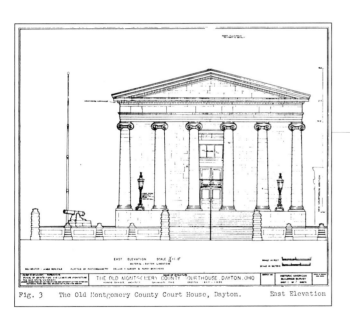

Fig. 3   The Old Montgomery County Court House, Dayton.   East Elevation

Left: An early plan for the courthouse built on Pease's Greek temple design.

Above: Horace Pease, who drew the first plans for a new courthouse.

MILESTONE

On the drawing board: Dayton's Old Court House

They wanted something out of the ordinary. Something romantic. Something grand. Daytonians pined for a marvelous new county courthouse unlike anything else in the city. So the timing was right when Horace Pease — a sophisticated, self-made man, miller by trade and an admirer of classical architecture — proposed a Greek temple of justice based on an engraving of the Thesium of Athens. Pease's initial drawings were rejected in the plans competition, but no matter. The concept was right.

1845

A new plan

County commissioners hired architect Howard Daniels of Cincinnati (and paid him a $500 premium in July) to adapt Pease's pure Greek building to make it work as a modern courtroom. The result: a practical structure in the then-popular Greek Revival tradition. Progress was swift: A construction contract was awarded to John W. Cary on August 23 for $63,000 (the actual cost came to $100,000). The old jail and brick courthouse were auctioned on October 4 for $360 and $300, respectively (the county office building netted only $180). After being moved to the lot's periphery, the buildings served as a temporary home for county officials during construction; court, however, was held at City Hall. ■

It's official: 'The Miami and Erie Canal'

Immediately after the Miami Extension Canal — which ran from Dayton to the junction of the Auglaize and Maumee rivers — was completed, the first canal boat from Lake Erie arrived in Dayton on June 24. The event marked completion of the Miami and Erie Canal, which had been financed by the sale of government land and by bond issues. The final price tag: $8,062,680.

FROM A PORTRAIT DRAWING by
CAROLINE H. VAN BEAN

Left: Charlotte Reeve Conover, local historian

Right: Valentine Winters, prominent banker

Banking days

Jonathan Harshman was president and Valentine Winters was elected cashier on the board of directors of the new, independent Dayton Bank that opened on June 1. This bank, which later became Winters National Bank, traced its origins to Dayton's first bank (the Dayton Manufacturing Company) through $45,000 in silver pieces, which Harshman had been given instead of his stocks and deposits in the original bank. This amount promptly became part of the new Dayton Bank's capital stock. Another institution, the Bank of Dayton, a state bank, opened in July.

Educating the ladies

E.E. Barney was principal of Cooper Female Seminary, which opened September 1 on a lot bought for $2,000. Daughters of only the most affluent Daytonians attended. Two who went on to make a name for themselves were Electra C. Doren, who modernized the city's public library, and Charlotte Reeve Conover, who penned several of the area's history books.

Vital statistics

- Population: 9,792.
- Brick buildings: 880.
- Frame buildings: 1,086.
- Stone homes: six.

1846

SLICE OF LIFE

Literary culture

It cost $3 annually — and $30 for a lifetime membership — to belong to the Dayton Library Association, formed this year and housed in a most elegant room in the Phillips Building. (The association even sold memberships in "perpetuity" — for life and beyond.)

Razed and removed...

The old jail and brick courthouse (auctioned in 1845), in the spring, to make way for the new courthouse. Folks took note as the finest stone around, quarried in Dayton and Centerville, was delivered to Third and Main.

Enlisted...

Soldiers for the Mexican War, which lasted until 1848. Among the first volunteers: German immigrants.

Applicants needed

Dayton recognized early the need for a civil engineering expert to oversee its growing number of public works projects. The city was one of the first in Ohio to create the government post of city engineer. The job eventually went to the obvious choice, bridge-builder and engineering expert David H. Morrison.

A noted papermaker

He was a bookkeeper, so perhaps it was his need for paper that made Col. Daniel E. Mead provide enough capital to join Ells, Claflin & Company, a Dayton firm that ran a paper mill. This marked the founding of today's Mead Corporation.

Chartered...

The Cincinnati & Dayton Railroad, which later became the famed C.H.& D.

'Absolute safety' from future floods

For years, Daytonians who wanted to fill holes in their yards and streets helped themselves to dirt from the levee, originally built by Daniel Cooper and his 1812 war recruits.

At some point, payback was inevitable. It happened in the wee hours of January 2. The weakened levee broke at the Bridge Street bend, the river overflowed, and water filled cellars and lowlands. Supplies in cellars and first-floor carpeting and furniture were ruined, and floating timber and driftwood damaged yards and buildings.

Immediately afterward, the city extended and improved the levees — enough that one local writer praised them as promising "absolute safety" and "long, shaded promenades of beauty and luxury."

As Dayton one day learned, however, there was no such thing as "absolute safety" from the river. ■

Top: Original drawings for the Horace Pease House, eventually built at the northeast corner of Second and Wilkinson streets, were submitted this year.

Bottom: Col. John Gilbert Lowe

Appointed...

John Gilbert Lowe, as one of several directors of the newly formed Dayton Library Association, on January 12. Dayton's new library, chartered this year, was housed on the second floor of the Steele building at 12 N. Main St.

It came over the wires

A Mr. O'Reilly, who helped Dayton get its telegraph office up and running on September 10, sent the first telegraph message received in the city, on September 17. His message: one of sincere congratulations on having the telegraph come to town.

Unlike most cities, Dayton had the telegraph before it had a railroad.

Arrival of a Copperhead

Clement Laird Vallandigham, who later made a name for himself by his intense opposition to the Civil War, came to Dayton and bought the *Western Empire* and a print shop for only $150.

The Whig Party organ

The *Journal and Advocate* became a daily newspaper.

Organized...

The first United Brethren Church, which later became the Evangelical United Brethren Church, in a small room in the Oregon engine house.

Founded...

St. Joseph's Church (and school).

A whole lot of building goin' on

■ Laid: The foundation for Dayton's elegant courthouse.
■ Constructed: The pike from Dayton to Germantown.
■ Erected: Commercial mills, by Daniel Beckel.

1848

Continued...

Construction of the new Montgomery County courthouse. By this time, the city had discovered the limestone it called "Dayton marble," and quarried it for the foundation and pillared facade. It was a choice building material for years, used in the "new" courthouse in 1880, Steele High School in 1893 and other buildings, culverts, bridges, sidewalks, curbs and the steps that led to many a family's front door.

A slippery venture

Incorporated on February 4 was the Dayton Gas Light and Coke Company, which made "Crutchett's patent solar gas" out of grease. Initial plans called for bear grease, but that proved costly and impractical (not enough bears around, for one thing). The company started producing gas from coal, which arrived via canal at a new plant across from where Memorial Hall is today. Chartering the new company: Daniel Beckel, Peter Voorhees, Daniel Stout, I.F. Howells, David Winter, J.D. Loomis, J.D. Phillips, Valentine Winters, John Mills and Daniel W. Weelock. By December 15, Dayton had its first one-mile stretch of gas main.

Above: Construction continued on the new county courthouse.

Changed...

The name of the National Hotel, to the Voorhees House, in January.

Published...

The *Dayton Tri-Weekly Bulletin*, beginning September 1. A subscription cost $3 a year.

Built...

Wesley Chapel, the brick Methodist church at Third and Main.

Taken...

Dayton's first daguerreotype, an early form of photography that used metal plates.

Neck and neck

- Brick buildings in Dayton: 962.
- Frame buildings in Dayton: 925.

1849

MILESTONES

Dayton's first industrial giant

Start a new company — for building railroad cars? Some thought E.E. Barney and Ebenezer Thresher were crazy — Dayton didn't even have a rail line. Things started slowly for the Barney and Thresher Company: It built just two cars in its first year. After that, the venture took off, fueled by Dayton's abundant water power and raw materials. Soon passenger and freight cars in the company's trademark colors — red, burgundy, green, gold and white — were shipped out on the canal and became a familiar sight on U.S. and Canadian lines. The company that became the Barney & Smith Car Works eventually worked more than 2,000 employees on a 54-acre plant. ■

Epidemic proportions

It began with the passing of 19-year-old William Munday on May 22. Cause of death: cholera. In pre-sanitation days, the feces-borne intestinal disease was a killer — and the very word chilled the blood. In just three short weeks, it was epidemic. Dayton looked like a ghost town, with abandoned markets and shuttered stores. Gutters were disinfected with lime, which covered the streets like snow. The sick were taken to a makeshift hospital at the Orphan Asylum (on the site that later became Miami Valley Hospital). After an average of four funerals a day in June and July, the mayor proclaimed the first Friday in August a day of fasting and prayer. At 10:30 a.m., people filled churches to beg for God's mercy. The epidemic finally ran its course; before it was over, 225 Daytonians had died. Afterward, a new Board of Health was appointed and a cholera hospital opened. ■

Above: Ebenezer Thresher partnered with E.E. Barney.

All aglow

Homes were lighted for the first time with Crutchett's natural gas on February 6. "Wet" meters — containing whiskey or alcohol to keep them from freezing — measured home gas consumption. Later, "dry" meters were imported from England.

The ceremonial lighting at City Hall on February 5 was not to be missed: 13 brilliant burners were lit along with a spectacular, eight-burner chandelier.

Formed...

A Benevolent Society, by Dayton's black citizens, on February 22.

Established...

A medical society, by 13 Dayton doctors on September 15, two years after the American Medical Association was established to raise professional standards. Apparently, there was a need: In the first year alone, the Dayton society suspended or expelled four doctors and barred one from membership.

Name games

The brick Voorhees House (once the National Hotel) was renamed the Phoenix House. Later, it became part of the Beckel House.

Authorized...

The sum of $25,000, by the city of Dayton, for the Dayton & Western Railroad.

Purchased...

The 8-year-old *Dayton Transcript* newspaper, by W.C. Howells.

Built...

Xenia Pike and Dayton & Wilmington Pike.

Founded...

Das Deutsche Journal, a weekly Democratic newspaper.

Vital statistics

■ Population: 10,000.
■ Physicians in town: 41 (one for every 268 people).
■ Number of pleasure carriages in Montgomery County: 1,500.

SLICE OF LIFE

Separate and unequal

Dayton gave its black residents their own school system: the Tenth School District for Black Students. Classes were held in the basement of Wesleyan Church, the meeting house for one of Dayton's oldest black congregations.

The Niagara's first (and last) trip

"Better put on your mules if you expect to make Dayton this year." So chided the skeptics who saw the steam-powered canal boat Niagara chugging from Miamisburg to Dayton. Two packet-line owners named Dickey and Doyle outfitted the Niagara with a 10-horsepower engine, thinking steam would make for quicker trips. Their experimental voyage was August 14, with plans to arrive in Dayton at 10 a.m. As always with such events, Dayton was waiting: Crowds lined the canal route, a 20-piece brass band was poised, and a cannon stood ready to salute. Hours and hours passed. But no Niagara. In the end, the trip took a whopping 30 hours. Dickey and Doyle gave up on steam, and stuck with their mules.

1850

First high school

Secondary education arrived in town with the opening of Central High School on April 15.

Standing room only

People jammed the finished courthouse, which was opened and dedicated April 16. Folks admired the flying stone stairway to the visitors' gallery; the stone floors and brick-arched basement; the solid iron doors, shutters and hardware; a dome of interlocking arches; and more of the finest finery.

What they couldn't see was equally impressive: Basement walls six feet thick; limestone foundations nine feet deep; and a roof supported by 30 brick walls and arches in the attic alone. The Greek Revival building, now known affectionately as the Old Court House, is listed today in the National Register of Historic Places and the Historic American Buildings Survey.

Folded...

The *Dayton Tri-Weekly Bulletin*, on April 17, after two years.

Firm, but kind

Catholic boys who wanted a Christian education were welcomed into St. Mary's Institute, which opened on July 1. The school was known for its discipline: "The manner of enforcing the regulations is firm, yet mild and paternal, and appeals to the pupil's conscience." St. Mary's Institute became the University of Dayton.

The Phillips House

J.D. Phillips began construction of a new hotel in honor of his father H.G. Phillips, an early Daytonian. The Phillips House, at the southwest corner of Third and Main, was the town's social center for some 80 years.

Sheltered Shakers

The Watervliet Shakers had minimal contact with outsiders. In fact, it was customary for community elders to scan the Dayton *Journal* and the *New York Tribune* — the only two newspapers the village subscribed to — and share only "appropriate" or "suitable" news with the other members.

Hitting the books

Education became more of a priority for Daytonians. Remarkably, between 1850 and 1870, 90 percent of children aged 7 to 14 attended school. Less than 3 percent of the population was considered illiterate.

City of neighbors

Dayton folk enjoyed horseback or carriage rides to visit friends in such nearby communities as Xenia, Troy, Bear's Creek and Middletown — places where a trip to Dayton was a much-coveted journey to the big city.

Under way...

Construction of Salem Pike and Brandt Pike.

Organized...

The first Hebrew congregation, by 12 men from some of Dayton's first Jewish families.

Top: The Phillips House was named for Daytonian H.G. Phillips.

Above: By 1850, the Miami Valley included a series of flourishing communities, connected by railroad lines, waterways and roads.

RAILROAD ADVERTISEMENT.   253

CINCINNATI, HAMILTON & DAYTON

RAILROAD.

SHORTEST ROUTE BETWEEN

CINCINNATI & CHICAGO,

AND THE NORTH-WEST.

SLICE OF LIFE

Class rank

Ohio ranked Dayton as a second-class city, based on its 10,976 population. (First class required 1,024 more folks.)

They had the time

Dayton told time by the town clock, which City Council bought in July and installed in the tower of the Methodists' Wesley Chapel.

Shear excitement

The Singer sewing machine was exhibited for the first time in Dayton, to great interest, on October 11 by salesman S.N. Shear.

Established...

The Miami Valley Bank.

Steam vs. water

The opening of a steam bakery foretold the eventual change from water power to steam power for Dayton industries.

Constructed...

A new $11,000 plant for the Dayton Gas Light and Coke Company, to replace one destroyed by fire. A Swaynie House banquet on September 16 marked the completion.

Represented...

The United States, by Robert C. Schenck, a Dayton intellectual who was the ambassador to Brazil for six years.

Organized...

The Dayton Insurance Company.

Opened...

A Hebrew cemetery.

MILESTONE

All aboard!

Dayton became a railroad town the day the first locomotive arrived, shortly after the Mad River & Lake Erie Railroad opened on January 27. It connected Dayton to Springfield and Sandusky. The Cincinnati, Hamilton & Dayton started regular service on September 22. A stock issue raised the $200,000 for the line.

Dayton's first railroad station was a brick building at Sixth and Jefferson, on the north side of the tracks.

Cars unsanitary

Early rail travel was far from glamorous. Cars lacked toilets. Engine soot filled the air. Passengers shared ice water in tin cups filled by the brakeman, and thought nothing of discarding lunch papers and other trash on the floor. Moreover, railroads were dangerous. Around 1851, a dapper pedestrian lost a foot when he was struck by a train as he crossed the tracks in Dayton. Placed on a two-wheeled, horse-drawn cart and dragged over gravel roads to a doctor, the poor man could be heard screaming the whole length of the horrible ride.

Coinciding with the arrival of Dayton's first railroad was the peak year of the Miami and Erie Canal, which produced revenues of more than $350,000 from 400 boats. ■

Above: Robert C. Schenck

Above right: Dayton had "arrived" as a railroad destination.

MILESTONE

Dressed to the hilt

The women wore draped and flowing ball gowns, long enough to cover all but the tips of their square-toed slippers. The men wore skirted coats with tails. It was the social event of the year — the October 14 ball celebrating the opening of the three-story Phillips House, the new hotel at the city's center. Guests arrived at the Third Street entrance in horse-drawn carriages, ascended the stairway and saw elegant parlors and a dining-room-turned-ballroom ready for the occasion.

One exquisitely furnished room — complete with Corinthian columns, gilt chandeliers, bookshelves, globes and reading tables — was devoted to use as Dayton's library for many years. ■

1852

Opened...
The New Exchange Bank, on April 5, by Valentine Winters, Jonathan Harshman, R. Dickey and James R. Young. This institution, at the northeast corner of Third and Main, succeeded the Dayton Bank and later became Winters National Bank.

Grand openings
Begun this year:
- The Probate Court of Montgomery County.
- The Dayton & Union Railroad.
- The Greenville & Dayton Railroad.
- The Dayton Asylum for the Insane, southeast of town, which eventually served as many as 600 patients.

Strategy: Diversification
The Barney and Thresher Company hit hard times in the railroad-car business. To get over the slump, it added a department for making farm machinery.

Engineer turned entrepreneur
David H. Morrison stepped down as city engineer, founded the Columbia Bridge Works and opened an office at Fourth and Ludlow streets — the site of today's *Dayton Daily News* building.

A rose by any other name
Neptune, Vigilance, Deluge, Pacific. Greek gods? Canal boats? No — the names of four new fire engines Dayton bought this year.

Left: An unidentified blacksmith reflects the strength and inner dignity of his era.

Identity crisis?
The *Evening Empire* changed its name to the *Daily Empire*. (Later, it became the *Daily Ledger*, then the *Herald and Empire* and then the *Democrat*.)

Swept away...
The unstable Bridge Street bridge, by a December flood that took its toll all along the Great Miami, Stillwater and Mad rivers.

1853

At your service
"Every attention will be paid to customers, and no pain spared to show Goods." This proud announcement in the Dayton *Journal* heralded the opening of a new dry goods store by a Mr. Prugh, a Mr. Joice and a Mr. D.L. Rike, at 17. E. Third St., the former site of Gebhart's Dry Goods Store. It was the start of Dayton's Rike-Kumler Company — later Rike's, and today Lazarus.

As a child, David Rike loved to sell stones, grasses and leaves at his make-believe store at the family's farm near Xenia. As an adult, Rike treated customers and employees alike with deep respect. But he was also obsessed with neatness; at least once, he found a stack of clothes slightly out of line and knocked it over, insisting that it be properly redone.

Arrived...
William P. Callahan. He made a dollar a day at the Ohmer furniture factory and would become a mover in local financial circles.

Moved to Dayton...
The United Brethren Publishing House, founded in 1834 at Circleville.

Held...
The first Ohio State Fair, in Dayton, operated by Robert Steele.

Cosmopolitan Dayton

A city on the upswing needed larger hotels, thought Daniel Beckel, who began building the Beckel House. The new hotel, at the northwest corner of Third and Jefferson, was where William Huffman had built the city's first stone house.

An industry on the move

Thriving again was the Barney and Thresher Company, which by now employed some 150 workers. Weekly production: six freight cars, one passenger car.

More resting places

Over the next seven years, Woodland Cemetery extended its boundaries to Wyoming Street by purchasing city lots and land from the heirs of Augustus George and from Nathaniel Hart.

Died...

Col. George Newcom, one of the famous first Daytonians, at 82. He was buried in Woodland.

Opened...

The Dayton & Western Railroad, running to near Richmond, Indiana.

Barney and Thresher split up

E.E. Barney teamed with Caleb Parker, who bought Ebenezer Thresher's portion of the Barney and Thresher Company.

All aboard

The Dayton & Xenia Railroad opened.

Organized...

First Orthodox Congregational Society.

Above left: Daniel Beckel

Above right: D.L. Rike & Company was located in the old Gebhart block.

Left: U.B. Printing at Fourth and Main streets.

1855

Sherlock Holmes wasn't around yet

The mayor sought 100 detectives, as authorized by City Council on March 16, to stop a rash of burglaries.

A vaguely disgusting place

Dayton made an effort toward public health by creating the Infirmary Board, which nursed the sick and quarantined the contagious. Short-staffed and under-budgeted, the board was never too effective, and unsanitary conditions remained. Some streets were cleaned annually, but many weren't. Cattle roamed wild, and dead rodents were a common sight. (Human scavengers in need of animal fat or other parts had little trouble finding a dead critter or two in the streets.)

Staying afloat

In another slump, the Barney and Thresher Company again turned to farm machinery, filling Cyrus McCormick's order for 400 reapers.

Completed...

The Dayton Asylum for the Insane, which had opened in 1852 on the site of today's 10 Wilmington Place. The asylum was known for its Rococo-style buildings, large trees and ponds. The landscaping was created by German immigrant Joseph B. Heiss, who went on to national renown as a palm grower.

Married...

D.L. Rike, to Salome Kumler. The couple had five children, including Frederick Rike, born in 1867, who later inherited the family's dry goods business.

Above: East Third Street, from Main to Jefferson streets. Neat handwriting on the original invites viewers to "See pig in lower right hand corner."

1856

Founded...

The nation's first black college, Wilberforce University, in the Greene County village of the same name about five miles north of Xenia. It was named for the noted English abolitionist William Wilberforce, and would be a stopping place over the years for such notables as W.E.B. Du Bois and Paul Laurence Dunbar.

Constructed...

Another wooden bridge at Bridge Street, to replace the one swept away in the flood of 1852.

SLICE OF LIFE

Firefighter violence

The rivalry among Dayton's independent volunteer fire companies turned tragic when two of them, the Deluge and the Vigilance, got into a dangerous scuffle during a fire at the Morrison home. Deluge volunteer William Richards was struck in the head by a flying brick and killed. Punishment was swift: The Vigilance Company was disbanded by the mayor.

Right: The home of newly elected Congressman Clement Vallandigham.

A losing proposition

For the first time ever, expenses topped revenues for the Miami and Erie Canal. This year marked the waterway's turning point: It operated in the red until its demise in the early 1900s.

Stone work

David H. Morrison built an unusual stone bridge over the canal on Jefferson Street. Using an odd series of arches underneath, he was able to cross the river diagonally.

The wanderers

Owen Stanley and Harriet Worden Stanley, king and queen of the Dayton gypsies, arrived from England. The Stanley clan became one of the nation's largest gypsy groups.

Built...

Union Station, for Dayton's rail passengers, at Sixth and Ludlow.

Won...

A seat in Congress, by Clement Vallandigham.

Right: Like most cities, Dayton had local breweries. This was one of several in the city.

'New' courthouse beginnings

Another county courthouse? Montgomery County was growing, and its governmental needs grew with it — so the county auditor was authorized on March 3 to bring the matter to voters. Officials envisioned a brick building costing less than $40,000, on the north part of the courthouse lot.

Died...

Harriet Worden Stanley, queen of the Dayton gypsies and wife of Owen Stanley, on August 30 at age 63.

Reduced...

The work force at the Barney and Thresher Company, to about 60 or so, during the Panic of 1857.

A better bridge

Dayton and Montgomery County teamed up to finance a 96-foot suspension bridge — the first designed by David H. Morrison, who became an authority in such designs.

Demolished...

The old Central High School building, to make way for the new Central, at the site of the former Cooper Female Seminary at Fourth and Wilkinson. (Finances were eased a bit with the seminary stockholders' donation of the land to the Dayton Board of Education.)

A banking family

Jonathan H. Winters, son of Valentine Winters, joined the New Exchange Bank, which was renamed V. Winters and Son. The bank was regarded as one of the best in the country.

1858

Bring out the troops

Artillery, cavalry and infantry troops — 22 companies in all — paraded down Main Street at 10 a.m. July 3 in the largest military demonstration the city had seen. Ohio Gov. Salmon P. Chase reviewed the troops, who were accompanied by six brass bands and other bands playing field music.

Died...

John Van Cleve, on September 6. His work at Woodland was assumed by a man with the same love for the cemetery — Robert Steele.

Opened...

Dayton's first city jail, between Fifth and Sixth streets, in December. (Previously, the county jail had done the job.)

Corporate changeover

Ells, Claflin & Company, which ran a paper mill, became Mead & Weston, forerunner of today's Mead Corporation.

Re-elected...

Daytonian Clement Vallandigham, to Congress.

1859

MILESTONE

A visit from a would-be president

Abraham Lincoln, the Illinois lawyer and noted speechmaker, visited Ohio in September on a speaking tour arranged by his Republican Party. It was Lincoln's idea to stop in Dayton before proceeding on to Cincinnati. A local reception committee took care of Lincoln's every need, even seeing to entertainment at the Phillips House before his courthouse speech on September 17.

The Hon. Lewis B. Gunckel of Dayton was a bit surprised when he knocked on Lincoln's door at the Phillips House, was told to come in, and found Lincoln sitting in a chair without his collar or cravat, with his wife brushing his hair. Gunckel later remarked that Lincoln felt no need to apologize for his less-than-presentable appearance.

During the day, Congressman Robert C. Schenck of Dayton proposed Lincoln as a presidential candidate for the fledgling Republican Party. It seemed unlikely then, but Lincoln was elected in 1860.

Lincoln's Dayton address

Lincoln's two-hour oration — delivered from the steps of the Old Court House — focused on

Left: Abraham Lincoln, as he appeared about the time of his Dayton visit.

slavery and the conflict under way between the free and slave states. But was it eloquent? Stirring? We'll never know for sure. Since each party-aligned newspaper in those days made it a point to harass the opposition, accounts of the speech vary dramatically. For example, the Republican *Journal* reported Lincoln's crowd at 5,000; the Democratic *Empire*, however, reported only 200 present, estimated that half were curious Democrats (and not Lincoln

supporters) and accused Lincoln of fallacies and false assumptions.

According to one account: "He is not a very pleasant speaker. He cannot long retain a Dayton audience. The people look at him, listen a few minutes, and then walk off."

Gunckel's account, however, marveled at Lincoln's clarity and called the speech intensely interesting.

Portrait opportunity

Artist Charles W. Nickum had little time to paint a portrait of Lincoln, who was set to leave Dayton on the 4 p.m. train.

Lincoln, apparently amused by the young man's efforts, agreed to sit for a spell and reportedly said to Nickum: "You may make a good picture, but you'll never make a pretty one." What resulted is a now-famous painting of the still beardless Lincoln, which has been reproduced through the decades. ■

Another strong comeback

The Barney and Thresher Company bounced back from the Panic of 1857 with 160 employees and an annual payroll of $78,000. The company was becoming a Dayton giant, feeding local foundries and lumber companies and creating spinoff service industries. Company employees had the means to buy land and build homes; in fact, as many as 100 employees were homeowners — a significant number for the time.

Arrived...

Numerous runaway slaves and free blacks, during Dayton's railroad construction boom in the late 1850s. Slaves were drawn to Dayton because of the city's well-known abolitionists and its Underground Railroad stations. Free blacks believed they could avoid capture by coming to the city.

Right: Dr. Rose, in the doorway to his "office."

Below: Horses were hitched in front of Main Street and City Hall.

SLICE OF LIFE

Read all about it

Miami Valley folks who read the *Cincinnati Enquirer* got it from the memorable Billy Wolf, a legendary carrier who handed (not threw) his subscribers their morning paper. He was short and quick, always in a hurry to finish his 30-mile route.

The wanderers lay down to rest

As unlikely as it may seem, it's possible that Dayton was the site of the country's first-ever gypsy cemetery burial. More than 60 members of the Stanley clan — one of the United States' largest gypsy tribes — were buried at Woodland Cemetery starting in 1878. King Owen, 67, who died on February 21, 1860, was laid alongside Queen Harriet, his wife, who died in 1857. On their tombstone is a long verse. One stanza:

Owen Stanley was his name,
England was his oration,
Anywood was his dwelling place,
And Christ his salvation.

The Stanleys were succeeded by their son Levi and his wife Matilda Joles. In north Dayton we now have Stanley Avenue and Gipsey Drive.

The doctor imposter

Dayton's own Dr. Rose — who was not an M.D. at all — was determined to keep his fellow citizens from the hands of real physicians, whom he felt tortured, poisoned, burned and dissected the living. He claimed to have a cure for everything, from toothache to fits. His "office" was his home on Jefferson Street, between Fifth Street and the railroad crossing. It was marked by signs such as "Slaughter pens further up. No one has died under my treatment in 25 years." Passing funeral processions saw a sign that read: "Not my patient!"

1860

Torches, flags and speeches
The faithful held a huge rally and reception at the Old Court House, on May 19, for Clement Vallandigham, who was running for Congress again this year from the Third Ohio District.

Captured...
1.6 percent of the U.S. market for railroad cars, by the Barney and Thresher Company.

Returned...
Brother Maximin Zehler, to head St. Mary's Institute, today the University of Dayton.

Formed...
The Montgomery County Democratic Committee, on June 9.

Down to business
E.D. Babbitt, famous for the Babbittonian system of penmanship, established Miami Commercial College, many of whose graduates went on to find their fortunes in larger cities. Today the school is Miami-Jacobs College.

What they didn't know was hurting them
Open sewers, unsanitary milk, mosquitoes — even decayed teeth — led many to an early grave. (Some families even exposed their children to measles, chicken pox and whooping cough just to "get it over with.")

Shoo!
With backyard manure piles, open garbage pails and no window screens, flies were a persistent nuisance, swarming on kitchens, bakeries and dining rooms. Folks might fan the pests away with newspapers tied to broomsticks, but they always came back. A later innovation that foiled the flies: protecting cakes and pies under metal dome screens — a solution that likely gave somebody the idea to use screens on doors and windows.

Still growing
Dayton's population had nearly doubled in 10 years to 20,081. Three of every five Dayton residents were immigrants. The city's illiteracy rate was about 7.5 percent.

Above: The Pony House Hotel and Restaurant on South Jefferson Street.

Left: Canal boats were slow-moving, ungainly craft.

Wartime politics
As war clouds gathered, Dayton was divided. Lincoln was the city's choice for president — but only by 300 votes. And Clement Vallandigham won re-election to Congress, where he was by now nationally known as a Peace Democrat and Southern sympathizer who stood solidly against Lincoln.

MILESTONE

War!

"Sumter fired on!" blared the headline in the newspaper extra April 13.

Word spread quickly: The war of rebellion had been declared the day before over slavery and states' rights. The South wanted slavery at any cost — even if it meant breaking away. The North believed the Union had to be saved. And so began the Civil War. On April 15, Daytonians raised flags and made speeches in support of the Union. President Abraham Lincoln had called for 75,000 volunteers; Montgomery County needed to supply less than 500. By April 17, young men who had volunteered for Dayton's Light Guards, Lafayette Guards and Montgomery Guards left the Sixth Street depot, bound for Columbus and cheered on by well-wishers. On April 19, Ohio's soldiers left Camp Jackson for Washington, D.C.

A terrible toll

No one imagined the dreadful, four-year struggle that was to come. By the time it was over, Montgomery County would supply nearly 6,000 soldiers, 3,664 of them from Dayton.

Blacks believed that fighting for the Union would eventually produce freedom. But they weren't allowed to join — at least in the beginning. Later, bled by heavy casualties, the Union accepted black troops but still paid them less than white soldiers and only reluctantly let them see action.

In all, 86 blacks from Montgomery County joined the Union forces. The Army's first black officer, Maj. Martin Dilaney, came from nearby Wilberforce, in Greene County.

Supporting families and soldiers

Back home, Dayton took care of its own. City Council appointed a relief committee and $10,000 in aid to wives and children; Montgomery County offered a similar amount. Funds were raised at bazaars, musicals, drama fairs and festivals. Clothing and supplies, including bandages and nearly 1,000 blankets, were sewn, collected and given to soldiers at Camp Corwin, 2.5 miles east of Dayton, thanks to Dayton's Soldiers' Aid Society.

The press took sides

Public sentiment on both sides intensified with editorials from the Democratic *Empire*, which opposed the war, and the Republican *Journal*, which supported it. Clement Vallandigham continued to speak out against the conflict, predicting the public would soon turn against the "madness." ■

Planned...

A theater, by two West Carrollton brewers, William M. and Joseph M. Turner, who would build the Turner Opera House (today the Victoria Theatre).

Emerged full-force...

The era of steam power, as demand for war materiel increased.

Quit the canal?

With the boom in railroads came murmuring about abandonment of the canal. Still, the manmade waterways had produced $7 million in net revenue for Ohio over the years. Serious talk of closing the system didn't emerge until the 1870s.

Above: Col. Hiram Strong (top) and Luther Bruen lost their lives early in the war, fighting for the Union.

Right: The railroad was becoming dominant as the means of transportation and transport of goods.

LITTLE MIAMI & COLUMBUS & XENIA

RAILROAD,

BETWEEN CINCINNATI AND COLUMBUS.

THREE DAILY EXPRESS TRAINS.

Exclusively an Eastern Route for

COLUMBUS, STEUBENV'LE, CRESTLINE,

Wheeling,	Baltimore,	Pittsburgh,
Washington City,	Philadelphia,	Cleveland,
Dunkirk,	Buffalo,	Albany,
Niagara Falls,	New York,	Boston,

AND PLACES IN NEW ENGLAND.

SLEEPING CARS ON ALL NIGHT TRAINS.

Trains run by Columbus Time, which is 7 Minutes Faster than Cincinnati Time.

BAGGAGE CHECKED from Cincinnati to New York, Boston, Philadelphia, Baltimore, Washington City, Buffalo, Dunkirk, Pittsburgh, Wheeling, Cleveland, &c.

FOR THROUGH TICKETS

And all information, please apply at the old Office, south-east corner of Broadway and Front Streets, diagonally opposite the Spencer House ; and Burnet House Office, south-west corner of Vine and Baker Streets, opposite the Custom House ; and at Cincinnati, Hamilton & Dayton, and Little Miami Depots.

P. W. STRADER, Gen'l Ticket Agent.

1862

Assassination

J.F. Bollmeyer, editor of the *Dayton Empire*, was slain on November 1. Henry M. Brown killed the outspoken Southern sympathizer, shooting him in the head on Second Street near Jefferson as the editor walked to market. Brown was caught and the jail was stormed by Bollmeyer's supporters, who demanded an immediate trial. Brown was indicted for murder.

The original inscription on Bollmeyer's Woodland Cemetery gravestone, erected by his wife, read: "He fell by the hand of an assassin, a Martyr to the cause of freedom of speech and of the press."

Cemetery trustees, at odds with the wording, had the marker removed. Mrs. Bollmeyer agreed to change the inscription, which now reads: "He fell by the hand of violence, a Friend to the cause of freedom of speech and the press."

Founded...

Lowe Brothers' paint factory.

Casualty count

As the Civil War ground on, names of killed or wounded Daytonians were listed on a daily bulletin at the *Journal* office. High school boys stopped by the newspaper at noon, almost afraid to look for fear they'd find their father or brother on the dreaded list.

'God bless the Dayton people'

The ladies of Dayton served plenty of coffee and lunches to blue-coated soldiers as trains of 1,200 or 1,500 troops passed through the city via the Sixth Street depot.

December 31

Blacks in town celebrated the reading of the Emancipation Proclamation, which went into effect the next day.

Above: This wagon works and blacksmith shop was photographed in a rare moment of leisure.

1863

Far left: Clement Vallandigham

Left: William D. Bickham

MILESTONE

Vallandigham: 'Traitor, secessionist, blackguard'

It was 3 a.m. May 5 when Union soldiers from Cincinnati arrested Clement Vallandigham at his Dayton home for showing sympathy toward the enemy. For two years, Vallandigham had warned of a shattered Union unless the conflict was ended and compromise reached. His oratories hurt the government's recruiting efforts, which now involved handsome bounties to attract enlistees. During a May 1 speech, Vallandigham had even called for "King Lincoln" to be dashed from his throne. Finally, federal authorities had had enough of him.

Vallandigham's supporters were outraged by his arrest, claiming the Peace Democrat's free-speech rights had been violated. But no matter: After the vocal Vallandigham was found guilty of "uttering disloyal sentiments" under General Order No. 38, he was banished to the Confederacy. The Peace Democrats — "Copperheads," they were called — avenged Vallandigham by storming and burning the printing plant and offices of the Republican *Journal*, on Main Street just south of Third, on May 5. The $10,000 loss included a rare collection of books and other important works. The rioters were never charged. ■

Quick comeback

Dayton citizens donated $6,000 to rebuild the burned-out *Journal*. On May 11, Maj. William D. Bickham arrived in town to get the paper on solid footing and accepted the money as a three-year loan. Until he could train a new staff, Bickham wore every hat — business manager, editor, reporter and ad man.

Pitched...

A tent, May 27, on the Old Court House lot, which served as recruiting headquarters for four companies of Ohio militia. On June 26, men signed up to serve in the cavalry for six months.

Bought...

Wilberforce University, the historically black college in Greene County, by the African Methodist Episcopal Church, which has run it ever since. Asking price: $10,000. This year also saw the arrival of the college's first black teacher, Sara Jane Woodson, whose family claimed to have evidence that they were descendants of Thomas Jefferson and one of his female slaves.

Grand 'bazar'

A whopping $20,000 was raised for soldiers and their families thanks to a grand "bazar" held at the Beckel House from December 23 to January 4, 1864. The Soldiers Fair and Bazar, organized by the city's Soldiers' Aid Societies, featured international booths and the sale of jewelry, fruits and flowers.

Christmas presents (belated)

Soldiers' families benefited from the "Grand Wood and Provision Procession" on December 30, which included 142 loads of wood from Montgomery County farmers.

Established...

First National Bank. The Second National Bank was also chartered.

Organized...

The Miami Valley Insurance Company.

Opened...

The Dayton & Michigan Railroad.

'Glory to God in the highest;
Ohio has saved the Union'

So telegraphed President Abraham Lincoln upon hearing that his tireless antagonist, Clement Vallandigham, had been defeated in his bid for Ohio governor on October 13. (Vallandigham later gave up politics in favor of practicing law.)

Top: An early political cartoon depicted Abraham Lincoln and Jefferson Davis trying to keep Clement Vallandigham out of their courts.

Above: Early advertisements promoted printing.

Right: Fund-raisers for the troops were common. This handbill promoted the program.

1864

End of an era

The excitement and charm of "running with the engine" ceased on March 1 after a paid fire department and steam engines replaced Dayton's volunteer force and hand-pumpers. What sparked the change? The destructive *Journal* fire in 1863.

They'd had enough

Fifteen drunken Union soldiers, tired of local Peace Democrats and their opinions, invaded the *Empire* office on March 3. They scattered type, tossed the place and then left.

Drafted!

People were worried. The war was in its third year, and casualties were high. What would come next? The draft. By July, President Abraham Lincoln had called for 500,000 men. No one was exempt (unless of course, you had the $400 or $500 it took to pay a substitute recruit to take your place). Meanwhile, local societies, individuals and clubs kept funneling supplies to Union soldiers. On November 26, a day proclaimed by Ohio's governor for making contributions to soldiers' families, Dayton pledged $10,000 plus provisions. Lincoln called for another 300,000 men on December 21, and the Miami Valley responded. Montgomery County met its quota of 598 soldiers, and Dayton supplied its required 200 men.

Changed...

The name of the Barney and Thresher Company, to the Barney & Smith Car Company, after Preserved Smith bought out Caleb Parker's interest in the firm. By this time, the company was getting $1,250 for every railroad car it built. Daytonians had great affection for the industrial giant, known around town as the "Car Works."

Paid...

Money, to Dayton families who qualified for local aid because of the war. Most got $1.50 a week (as long as funds were available).

Proposed...

A Civil War monument, by Gen. Robert C. Schenck.

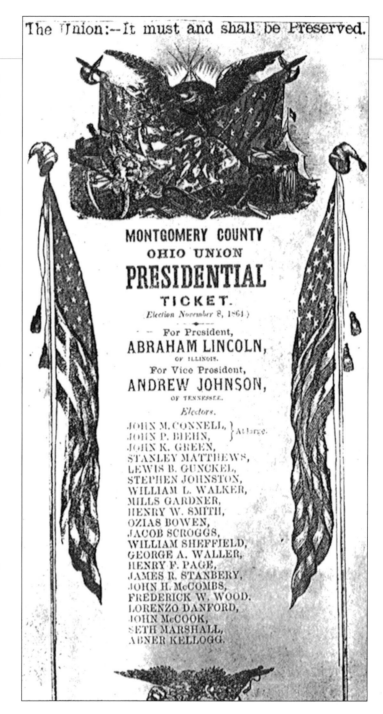

The Union:—It must and shall be Preserved.

MONTGOMERY COUNTY OHIO UNION PRESIDENTIAL TICKET.
(Election November 8, 1864.)
For President, ABRAHAM LINCOLN, OF ILLINOIS.
For Vice President, ANDREW JOHNSON, OF TENNESSEE.
Electors.
JOHN M. CONNELL, } At large.
JOHN P. BIEHN,
JOHN K. GREEN,
STANLEY MATTHEWS,
LEWIS B. GUNCKEL,
STEPHEN JOHNSTON,
WILLIAM L. WALKER,
MILLS GARDNER,
HENRY W. SMITH,
OZIAS BOWEN,
JACOB SCROGGS,
WILLIAM SHEFFIELD,
GEORGE A. WALLER,
HENRY F. PAGE,
JAMES R. STANBERY,
JOHN H. McCOMBS,
FREDERICK W. WOOD,
LORENZO DANFORD,
JOHN McCOOK,
SETH MARSHALL,
ABNER KELLOGG.

Above: The Lincoln/Johnson ticket, appearing on the presidential ballot for Montgomery County, promised to preserve the nation.

Left: Local dentists stayed busy trying to preserve — or replace — their patients' teeth.

Passed...

An act of Congress calling for permanent national homes to care for disabled soldiers and sailors. Federally financed, the homes would offer chapels, lecture and music halls, hospitals, libraries, reading rooms, a post office and telegraph office, stores and workshops to provide a decent quality of life for the maimed veterans who had served so gallantly and given so much.

Invented...

The stepladder, by John Balsley.

Consolidated...

Several railroads, to form the Atlantic & Great Western Railroad, which later became the New York, Pennsylvania & Ohio.

Established...

The Miami Valley Boiler Works, the Teutonia Insurance Company and the Ohio Insurance Company.

MILESTONE

The end of the war!

Doorbells rang and church bells chimed at 2 a.m. when the news arrived on April 9: Gen. Robert E. Lee had surrendered to Ohio's own Gen. Ulysses S. Grant. Daytonians marched, sang and danced in the streets. April 14 was a day of celebration and thanksgiving. War heroes carried tattered flags as they passed in review down Main Street amid cheers and rejoicing.

Festivities cut short

After the grand celebration, everyone took April 15 off, including newspapermen; the *Journal* offices were closed. Manning the telegraph office was one operator, the first to see the ominous message creep across the wires: "President Lincoln assassinated." Within an hour, the *Journal* had issued an extra. People were stricken with grief and mourning. On April 19, business ceased from 10 a.m. until 2 p.m. as Dayton's churches held services in Lincoln's memory. ■

SLICE OF LIFE

Burgeoning industry

Dayton, "the valley city of the Miami," had become a community of factories — turning out tables, chairs, cupboards, farm tools, buggies, carriages and wheel works (hubs and spokes).

Getting around

Traffic was light, as there were typically only two buggies per block. Drays — two-wheeled, low-riding carts — were used to carry freight, and were abundant.

What things cost

■ For $1, you could choose between a Sunday roast, or butter and eggs for the week.
■ For $3 a week, you could hire a girl to do your housework (laundry included).
■ For $5, you could pay the doctor for helping deliver a baby ... or engage musicians to play at a private party.
■ For $20 a month, you could rent a nice house on a residential street.

Street conditions: Deplorable

Because the middle of the street was often higher than the gutters, carriages teetered along at an angle. Rain turned streets into limestone mortar beds; dust irritated noses and throats. A common sight: roaming pigs, cows and geese. A puddle at Fourth and Jefferson streets provided a comfortable spot for a mother pig and her brood.

What they ate

■ Meat, three times a day (fried whenever possible).
■ Green vegetables (often bought from nearby market gardens).
■ Occasional oranges (rarely, though; they were luxuries, this far north).
Such diets, along with a lack of fresh air and water, brought on upset stomachs and sick headaches and sent everyone to bed now and then. Typical treatments: Violent purgatives and quinine.

Below: The Main Street (far left) and Third Street bridges were the main routes into the city. Landmarks of the day included the Turner Opera House (near the left) and the train station (on the right).

1866

Culture in the city

"The finest west of Philadelphia." That's what patrons said about Turner's Opera House, which opened New Year's Day with the drama *Virginius*, starring famous actor Edwin Forrest. The best seats in the house ran as much as $10 to $12; general admission was $1. Over the years Turner's Opera House, known today as the Victoria, featured everything from burlesque and vaudeville to symphonies, plays and dance recitals.

Opened...

The Wayne Street market house, in March.

Authorized...

The creation of children's homes, by the state legislature, on March 20. For Montgomery County commissioners, the law meant planning a new facility for the Dayton Orphan Asylum.

The $250,000 flood

It happened again — rising waters spilling into town, dirty water filling Dayton cellars and homes. The current swallowed pigpens, logs, fences, haystacks and even some houses, which splintered along with runaway canal boats against the Main Street bridge. The September 19 flood caused some $250,000 in damage, and sent people scavenging through the muddy remains to save what they could.

Some kids found a silver lining: A few were seen playing Robinson Crusoe during the flood, floating along in a washtub.

Founded...

Dayton Malleable Iron Works, by Charles Newbold and Peter Loeb, for making carriage hardware and malleable iron castings. By the late 1800s, it was a leading Dayton industry.

Furnished and finished...

The Beckel House, as a hotel. (Until this year, it had been used only for meetings and other gatherings.)

Reincorporated and located in Dayton...

The Christian Publishing Association, established in 1843.

Top: The rushing water had left Water Street (later Monument Avenue), but damage from the flood remained. The boat Diadem lay stranded near the canal.

Above right: Turner's Opera House opened New Year's Day to great acclaim, with *Virginius*, starring Edwin Forrest (above).

SLICE OF LIFE

Cheaper by the dozen

Lucius D. Reynolds was a thrifty printer: Why couldn't the Gardner & Reynolds print shop outsmart its competitors by printing large quantities of standard business forms — and then sell them in small quantities to local businesses? The concept was right. Business took off, and the print shop near First and Main became Reynolds and Reynolds. Today it's North America's fifth-largest supplier of stock continuous forms.

Welcome, weary soldiers

Established on March 26 was the National Asylum for Disabled Volunteer Soldiers, Central Branch. It was the third such home established in the country at that point. Why Dayton? The city proved its interest by donating $20,000 toward the $46,800 purchase price of 400 acres three miles west of town. The site was attractive, too: on high ground, accessible via railroad. Instrumental in attracting the home were Rep. Lewis B. Gunckel and *Journal* editor William D. Bickham. The first veterans moved in September 2; that winter, 750 disabled veterans were cared for. For 50 years a must-see for visitors to Dayton, the old Soldiers' Home is now the Veterans Affairs Medical Center.

They cleaned up their act

A new Board of Health established on June 3 went to work creating sewers, to eliminate well-water contamination from cesspools.

Born...

Wilbur Wright, on a farm in Millville, Indiana, April 16.

SLICE OF LIFE

Never on Sunday

Couples and families who enjoyed Sunday afternoon walks at Woodland Cemetery were startled to find themselves locked out.

Cemetery officials had gotten complaints about crowds, damaged landscaping and general disorder. The new rule: Only lot owners, their families or funeral attendees were allowed on Sundays, and everyone needed a ticket to get in.

Sometime later, the Sunday strolling ban was lifted.

Incorporated...

The Barney & Smith Car Company. A work force of 350 was producing 20 freight cars and 2.5 passenger cars weekly.

Passed...

An act, by the state legislature, allowing Montgomery County to build a new courthouse.

Mobbed and destroyed...

Wayman African Methodist Episcopal (AME) Church, which served Dayton's oldest black congregation.

A bowstring bridge

Ever-inventive local engineer David H. Morrison patented his wrought-iron arch bridge design, popular for highway bridges for nearly 40 years.

Organized...

Dayton Building Association No. 1, the first organized under state charter, which preceded modern-day building and loan associations.

Above: By the late 1860s, the covered Main Street bridge had fallen into disrepair. It would be replaced in 1871 with an iron span.

Dawn, May 30

Guns boomed at the Soldiers' Home. It was the nation's first Memorial Day celebration, and Montgomery County marked it with 12,000 marchers in a 1 p.m. parade down Dayton's Main Street and ceremonies at the county's 38 cemeteries, where the graves of Civil War dead were decorated.

Law and order

Organized in May was the metropolitan police force, consisting of a chief, second lieutenant and 20 "regulars." After only nine months, Dayton returned to its previous system of a city marshal and constables.

Dry goods, anyone?

Henry Perrine had Dayton's leading dry goods store, in the Phillips House.

1868

Church and state

Erected this year was the Protestant Chapel at the Soldiers' Home — said to be the first permanent place of worship built by the U.S. government. Records say a New York foundry melted down Confederate cannon to form the chapel bell.

Annexed...

The area north and west of the rivers — including what came to be known as Riverdale, Dayton View and Edgemont.

Opened...

The Montgomery County Children's Home, 528 S. Summit St. White children got dorm rooms; black children were housed in the back.

Erected...

A brick meter house/superintendent's office and a purifying house/engine room for the Dayton Gas Light and Coke Company, on Water Street between St. Clair and Mill.

SLICE OF LIFE

Street greetings

On Easter during the '60s, "Professor Brooks," a well-known black Daytonian, could be found strolling down Ludlow Street, adorned in a fine coat and boutonniere and carrying a green parasol. His salutations were melodic. Two common ones: "How does your corporosity sagashiate this morning?" and "A lovely morning for pergrinations, madam."

Above: "Professor Brooks"

Left: Milton Wright

1869

Wright arrival

It was a new job that brought the Rev. Milton Wright, his wife Susan and their children to Dayton in June. Wright was hired to edit *The Religious Telescope*, a weekly published by the Church of the United Brethren in Christ. The Rev. Wright this year also introduced a resolution leading to the founding of Union Biblical Seminary in 1871.

Singing His praises

It was winter and there was a fever — of the religious kind. Dayton jumped on the church-revival bandwagon during the winters of 1869 and 1870; once spring arrived, the faithful held camp meetings in the woods just off the Great Miami River near what's now Triangle Park.

Disaster!

Ruins, ashes, dust and a blackened facade. That's all that remained after the $500,000 Turner Opera House fire — Dayton's costliest to that time. The May 16 disaster was one in a long string of arsons set by one or more dastardly Dayton firebugs in the late 1860s. Insurance covered a loss of only $128,000.

Opened...

A "normal school," a sort of teacher's institute, for instructing Dayton teachers.

Purchased...

Land on Ziegler Street, by the Board of Education, for building a school for Dayton's black children.

Chartered...

The Dayton Street Railroad Company, for running horse-drawn cars, by William P. Huffman and H.S. Williams. (Passed this year: a city ordinance regulating the up-and-coming street railways.)

To be replaced?

Was the heyday of the Old Court House past? Quite possibly. The firm of Kellogg & Burrows won an $800 contract from Montgomery County commissioners and began to draw plans for a new courthouse.

SLICE OF LIFE

'If I were a rich man...'

A millionaire by today's standards might have made $30,493 a year in 1869 — the income of Dayton's richest man as reported in the *Journal* on May 3. Who was he? We don't know for sure, but it's a safe bet he wasn't a doctor. One of Dayton's most prominent physicians made just over $3,000 — and still managed to send his four children to schools back east or in Europe.

That's the way it was

■ If you were a Dayton businessman in 1870, you most likely operated on Main Street, between Second and Fourth, or on Third Street. Elsewhere downtown were churches and homes. Beyond downtown was bounteous farm and pasture land.

■ Dayton's population this year: 30,473. Nearly half its citizens were foreign-born.

Top: A new Main Street bridge made of iron replaced the old covered bridge.

Right: Valentine Winters' home at 130 W. Third St., where the city parking garage is now.

MILESTONE

Riding the line

Dayton's first street railway was the Third Street Railroad, which ran 3.75 miles along the length of that street. Speed limit: 6 mph. Lots of folks considered it far from perfect, and griped in the Dayton *Journal*. Some said the tracks had made Third Street "a perfect bed of slush and mud." Others complained of rude drivers, or of having to ride with women carrying oversized market baskets. Still others said service was undependable — which was true; a driver might pass a group of waiting passengers if he thought his horses wouldn't be in the mood to continue on.

Before word got around, a farmer spent time on a snowy morning digging up what he thought was a lost strip of metal buried in Third Street. When a passerby told him he was digging up the streetcar rail, he called the fellow's story pure hogwash. ■

The new Main Street bridge

The elaborate gingerbread design of engineer David H. Morrison's iron, four-span Main Street bridge became a familiar sight. This famous bridge, started this year and completed in 1871, replaced the old wooden structure and spanned the Great Miami until 1892.

Celebrated...

The right to vote, by blacks in Montgomery County, who organized "Colored First Voters" shortly after ratification of the Fifteenth Amendment on February 3. The group encouraged other blacks to exercise their newly won voting rights.

$10,000 a plate

It's been said that sons and daughters of Dayton banker Valentine Winters, attending a dinner celebrating their father's birthday, found hefty $10,000 checks under their plates.

Visited...

The Soldiers' Home, by Gen. William Tecumseh Sherman, Union hero and Ohio boy.

1870

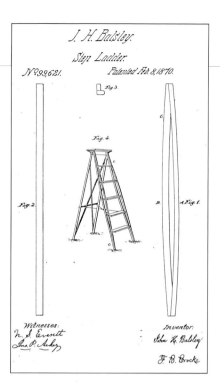

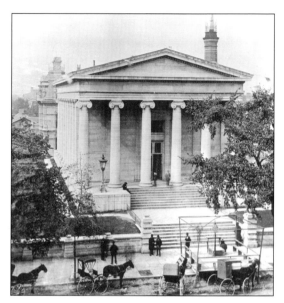

Think tank

They were book lovers and intellectuals — lawyers, teachers, doctors and businessmen who gathered as the Saturday Club for the first time on January 8 to discuss serious topics and opine on public matters of the day. Members were free to question or challenge presenters, who gave formal papers, essays or adventure stories. The club met for more than 30 years.

Organized...

The Young Men's Christian Association in Dayton, on March 2. A women's society, called "The Womans' Christian Association, of Dayton, Ohio, for the Support of Widows and Destitute Women," was organized November 26.

On the way: Fresh water

Work began on the city's first water system, the Holly Water Works, on March 16. The Board of Water Works was organized on April 13, and the first pump installed later this year.

Born...

James Middleton Cox, on March 31, in Jacksonburg, Ohio. Cox went on to be editor and publisher of the *Dayton Daily News*, a three-term Ohio governor and a candidate for President.

A less-than-stellar showing

Dayton's Gem City Team made a miserable showing against the Cincinnati Red Stockings on May 26. The home team lost 104-9 at Binam's Park off Keowee Street.

Zehler's folly?

Too large to be practical — that's what some said about Dayton's largest building, located not downtown but at St. Mary's Institute. St. Mary's Hall, which could be seen from anywhere around town, was ordered by Brother Maximin Zehler, who was much pooh-poohed for the massive structure. The hall, which still stands in defiance of those nay-sayers, now houses the University of Dayton's administration.

Donated...

Lot 3, Section 108, to the Grand Army of the Republic, by Woodland Cemetery trustees. The plots were set aside for Civil War veterans.

Organized...
The Zion Baptist Church.

Six and one
By this year, Dayton had six school districts and a central high school.

Built...
Grace Methodist Episcopal Church, at Fourth and Ludlow. Most Methodists in Dayton congregated here until the building of Grace United Methodist Church in 1921.

Issued...
A patent, to Daytonian John Balsley, for a wooden stepladder.

Top left: A drawing from John Balsley's stepladder patent.

Top right: The Old Court House was the centerpiece of downtown life.

Above left: St. Mary's Hall was Dayton's largest building.

Above right: John Gates Doren, editor of the *Dayton Democrat* from 1870 to 1889.

Above: Railway companies flourished in the Dayton area.

Right: Winter travel brought horse-drawn sleighs to Dayton streets.

Always make sure it isn't loaded

Clement Vallandigham, the notorious Dayton war protester and leader of the Peace Democrats in the 1860s, was mortally wounded June 16. While defending a man accused of murder, attorney Vallandigham used a loaded gun to show how the crime might have occurred — and accidentally shot himself in the head. Vallandigham died the next day. His client was found not guilty.

Born...

Orville Wright, at 7 Hawthorn St. in Dayton, on August 19.

Both Orville and Wilbur had a mechanical mindset, which they credited not to their father, Milton, but to their mother, Susan, who once built a sled for her children that was passed down through the family. Milton Wright taught his sons the value and rewards of hard work.

Visited...

Residents at the Soldiers' Home, by President and Ohio native Ulysses S. Grant, on October 3.

Bible belting

Union Biblical Seminary was opened by the Church of the United Brethren in Christ on five acres at West First Street and Euclid Avenue. First-year enrollment: 11 students. It was later renamed Bonebrake, and became the United Theological Seminary in 1954.

The seminary's three-story main building was not always dedicated strictly to religious instruction. In the 1940s, Monsanto Chemical Company rented it for secret research on the first atomic bomb.

Street railways flourish

Chartered this year were the Wayne and Fifth Street Railway and the Dayton View Street Railway. Also begun: the Oakwood Street Railway Company, with 11 drivers, 13 cars and 30 horses.

Incorporated...

Merchants National Bank.

They didn't travel very light

Heavy bustles and trains trailed the era's women, who needed special luggage to preserve the fancy puffs and loops of their elaborate dresses. These Saratoga trunks stood 30 inches tall and held four to six dresses in special trays. They were cumbersome for baggage men — often called "baggage smashers" — who grumbled about the vanities of women traveling with four or five trunks.

Dashing through the snow

After a good snow, First Street became a raceway for horse-drawn sleighs, and a sleighing carnival was held each winter through the 1870s. Crowds cheered John S. Lytle, one of the fastest drivers, who could goad his two black horses to a three-minute mile.

1872

A more pleasant ride

Unlike some local streetcar companies, the Wayne and Fifth Street Railway, which began operations in June, was well-regarded for its clean tracks and modern, roomy cars. Daytonians called the line the "Water Works and Asylum Route."

Awarded...

A $154,000 contract to build a new county jail, on July 30, to Marcus Bossler.

Born...

Paul Laurence Dunbar, on June 27 at 311 Howard St., to former slaves Joshua and Matilda Dunbar. Dunbar became Dayton's most noted man of letters, internationally famous as a poet and author.

Opened...

Calvary Cemetery Association, on July 9.

Painting the town

One of the first mixed paints was marketed by Dayton's Lowe Brothers Company, founded by Henry C. and Houston Lowe on September 1 after they bought Stoddard & Company.

Caregivers

The property and endowment of the Dayton Female Orphan Asylum was transferred to "The Womans' Christian Association, of Dayton, Ohio, for the Support of Widows and Destitute Women," which opened a home three years later.

Incorporated...

Mead & Weston, the paper company, as Mead & Nixon Paper Company.

Moved...

Dayton Malleable Iron Company, from East Dayton to West Third Street.

A gay old time

For a little outdoor music and a lot of fun, you might board the Home Avenue Railway on Third Street and head to the Soldiers' Home. It was Dayton's favorite summer recreation spot.

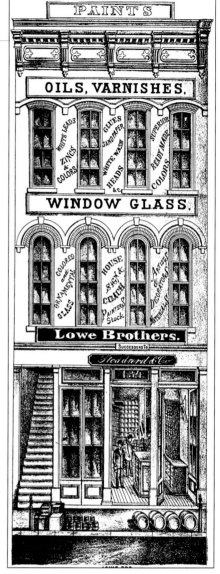

Top left: Paul Laurence Dunbar

Top right: Lowe Brothers, a prominent Dayton business, offered an extensive line of paints.

Above left: The Washington Street bridge spanned the river between stone supports.

Above: The Home Avenue Railway took riders to the Soldiers' Home.

Thank God for 'Holly Water'

With its waterworks completed, the Holly Manufacturing Company supplied fresh "Holly water," as the locals called it, from wells near Keowee Street and the Mad River. That meant no more dangerous drinks from cesspool-fouled private wells.

Established...

The Metropolitan Police Force, created by state law to handle the city's growing need for law enforcement and the recent rise in crime. The 35-member force included a chief, two lieutenants, 26 patrolmen, three roundsmen and three turnkeys.

Dayton's force made an astonishing 1,502 arrests in the first seven months.

Opened...

The Mutual Home and Savings Association.

Win some, lose some

Dayton residents, who knew how to raise money for a cause, had $15,000 in a kitty for a state fair, which was under consideration by the legislature. After Columbus was selected for the site, Dayton was down but not out its money, which it promptly put toward a fairground of its own.

Keep your hands on your wallet, if you can

Ohioans, along with everyone else, endured the Panic of 1873 and the rampant inflation that followed.

Founded...

The Dayton Exchange, on December 1, to promote the growing city's industry, retail trade and financial operations. On December 23, the civic association met in the Beckel House to plan a new railroad to the Jackson County coal fields.

An aggressive storeowner

F. Gebhart, landlord to D.L. Rike's dry goods house, was more than skeptical when Rike came to him with expansion plans.

Expand? In a panic year? It seemed crazy. Gebhart asked that the partition between Rike's store and store room be left in place. "It will be easier to rent two rooms if you fail," Gebhart told Rike.

Nevertheless, the partition was removed, the store grew and Rike's enjoyed steady success and many more expansions over the years.

Below: The east side of North Main Street, seen near First Street.

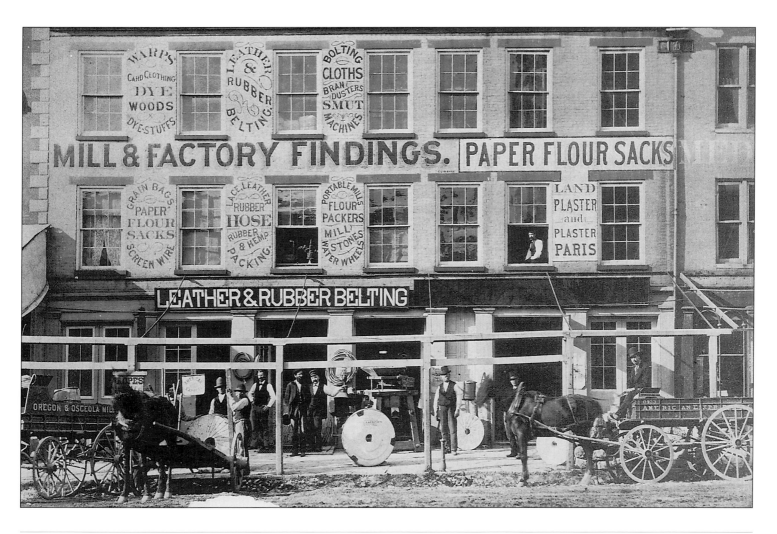

1874

See how she runs

Not to be outdone by Columbus, the site of Ohio's new state fair, Dayton promoted the first Southern Ohio Fair, held September 29 to October 2 at the fairgrounds south of downtown. Getting ready was a huge chore that summer and fall, as folks from all over Montgomery County put up buildings, barns and stalls, enlarged the race track and raised a new exposition hall. Finally, everything was ready. The fair was a great success, with the main attraction on the final day: the running of Goldsmith Maid, "the world's fastest racehorse." The Maid drew 75,000 wide-eyed fans and didn't disappoint, breaking a world trotting-horse record with a 2.18-minute mile. The race was the most talked-about event of the fair, which became an annual event.

Awarded...

A contract for a monument honoring Civil War soldiers.

Organized...

The Philharmonic Society, by Dayton vocalists, who met for the first time on August 25.

A most venerable spot

Christ Episcopal Church on West First Street opened on March 22. It's thought to be the city's oldest brick church still in use.

Soldiers at home

By this year, the Soldiers' Home housed 2,000 veterans.

Above: Horse races were among the highlights of the Southern Ohio Fair.

1875

Accepted...

The new stone jail, on West Third Street behind the Old Court House, on February 8. The jail, completed the year before, cost $190,000 and included a home and office for the sheriff. (Saddled with a thankless job was the sheriff's wife, charged with feeding the prisoners.)

For women only

Widows and poor women had a place to go thanks to "The Womans' Christian Association, of Dayton, Ohio, for the Support of Widows and Destitute Women," which opened a home on February 8 and dedicated it May 11. Invitation, however, was not without a price: "Any widow of good moral character

over 60 years of age, belonging to Dayton, can be admitted to this home upon the payment of $100 to the endowment fund, furnishing her own room, clothing and paying funeral expenses, but females destitute of funds, friends and home will also be admitted temporarily. Every inmate is required to pay for her board, either in money or work, and those who have employment outside of the home may enjoy its benefits by paying $2 per week."

Home away from home

Dedicated on May 3 was the YMCA's new home at 32 E. Fourth St., the former Dunlevy residence. John Dodds and C.V. Osborn raised the $24,000 purchase price.

Another respected Dayton operation

Established this year was the J.W. Stoddard Company, a maker of agricultural implements such as grain drills, seeders, hay rakes and harrows. (The firm, which later produced bicycles and automobiles, was renamed the Stoddard-Dayton Company and became a key player in early motor-car manufacturing.)

Awarded...

Another patent, to Dayton stepladder inventor John Balsley, for an adjustable table leg.

Added...

Another school for black children, on Baxter Street, upon request from parents on West Third Street.

Mine eyes hath seen the glory...
In remembrance of the Civil War and its heroes, the Ohio National Guard performed concerts at the Old Court House.

A very busy guy
Yet another patent was awarded to Dayton stepladder inventor John Balsley, this time for a paper bag machine.

Founded...
Amos Press Inc.

SLICE OF LIFE

The pleasure principle
Operating in a saloon across from the fairgrounds was "back room entertainment," managed by Elizabeth Richter (also known as notorious Dayton madam Lib Hedges).

An old-fashioned Christmas
While most Christmas gifts in the 1870s were homemade, lots of folks visited Payne and Holden's, Dayton's leading bookstore, to find something to place beneath the tree. A volume of poetry, perhaps? An ink stand or paper cutter?

Two building novelties
It was a sprinkler system inside, and sheet–metal ornamentation outside, that raised eyebrows on opening night of the Gebhart Opera House March 12. Two weeks later, the opera house hosted Dayton's first baby show, and in June Daytonians gathered there to see and hear a "talking machine" invented by Thomas Edison. Admission was $1 to stand, or $1.50 if you wanted a seat; those with more to spend could get private box seats for $8 each. Gebhart's Opera House was on the south side of Fifth between Main and Jefferson.

Top: Trolley tracks cut through the intersection of Third and Main streets.

Above: The Gebhart Opera House, as it appeared in later years.

Given...

Ten band concerts at the fairgrounds this summer.

They burned the midnight oil

A free public night industrial school was established — and much welcomed in a city with a growing manufacturing base. A school of freehand drawing opened December 17 in the Gebhart building on Third Street.

It died a slow death

The deteriorating Miami and Erie Canal finally lost favor with the state, which moved to stop supporting operations on the waterway. Still, the canal saw some use until the early 1900s, and ceremonies marking its abandonment happened as late as 1929.

John H. Patterson, future founder of the National Cash Register Company, was once a canal toll collector at Third Street. Seeing receipts decline, he predicted the demise.

Opened...

The Dayton & Southeastern Railroad, later to become the Cincinnati, Dayton & Ironton.

Goodbye, Dayton

The Wright children — Reuchlin, Lorin, Wilbur, Katharine and especially Orville — were sad to leave their beloved Dayton for Cedar Rapids, Iowa, in June. The move came when their father, the Rev. Milton Wright, was elected a bishop of the Church of the United Brethren in Christ.

In those days Wilbur, 11, and Orville, 7, might have been seen playing with "the bat," a toy whirligig of paper, bamboo, cork and rubber bands. They made a larger version that wouldn't fly — but at least they were trying.

Above left: Wilbur Wright

Above: Orville Wright

Below left: John Patterson

Below: The 1878 telephone directory advised: "The following parties are already connected with the Exchange may be talked to through our office."

THE DAYTON
BELL
Telephonic Exchange,
NO. 118 E. THIRD STREET.

The following parties are already connected with the Exchange and may be talked to through our office.

Kiefaber & Bro., Fruits &c., 118 E. 3d St.
Geo L Phillips, No. 29 W. 4th St,
American Express Office, 37 E. 3d St.
Beckel House.
Geo. F. Rohr, Hardware, 19 E. 3d St.
J. K. McIntire, Wholesale Grocers, 125 E. Third Street.
Wm. Sander, Wine House, 136 E. 3d St.
Charles A Phillips, 28 W. 4th St.
J W Johnston, Printer, 32 N. Jefferson St,
T A Phillips & Sons, Cotton Factory.
1878

Right: The grounds of the Soldiers' Home

Hail to the queen

Some 45,000 people attended the funeral of gypsy queen Matilda Stanley, buried in Woodland Cemetery in the family plot marked by a tall, angel-crowned monument. The crowds were almost unmanageable, forcing the minister to conduct the service by standing on a plank above the vault. Newspapers called the funeral procession an unbelievable sight, stretching from the cemetery to the junction of the Mad and Great Miami rivers.

A Dunbar teacher

Louise Troy, the daughter of former slaves, began teaching elementary school in Dayton. One of her students during a 42-year career: Paul Laurence Dunbar. Named after her is the Louise Troy Structured Magnet School on Richley Avenue.

Hello?

Kiefaber & Brothers became Dayton's first subscriber to the Dayton Bell Telephone Exchange, installed at 118 E. Third St. above the fruit store. Dayton's first phone directory was a single sheet with 10 names.

Dayton's first hospital

Two Cincinnati nuns, Franciscan Sisters of the Poor, approached Dayton doctor John C. Reeve and said they wanted to help him start a hospital. He agreed.

By July 2, the two were busy scrubbing and disinfecting the rooms of a two-story brick structure at Franklin and Ludlow streets. By July 25 they admitted their first patient — a railroad brakeman with a crushed arm.

St. Elizabeth's Hospital, which accepted the indigent sick, was dedicated August 15. The sisters cared for 187 patients that first year, nearly 1,000 after three years. St. Elizabeth soon had seven physicians, and Dr. Reeve remained chief of staff for 30 years.

SLICE OF LIFE

All in a day's work

The Metropolitan Police Force caught three masked robbers who'd used force and threats to steal $30,000 in notes and cash from the Daniel Frantz family near Trotwood. Mr. Frantz got his money back, and the robbers got long terms in the penitentiary.

Above left: James Ritty

Above right: The Dayton Metropolitan Police Force

He tried to keep them honest

Where was the money going? Into his bartenders' pockets, that's where. Restaurant owner James Ritty needed a way to keep his workers from pilfering money, so he invented a mechanical counter that tallied food and drink sales of the day. By November, Ritty had a patent for his device, called the cash register.

A heavy lady

A 500-pound Goddess of Liberty statue was raised and placed atop the Gebhart Opera House during the city's July Fourth festivities. Today the statue is a keepsake of the Dayton Art Institute.

Received...

A permit from the city, by the Dayton Bell Telephone Exchange, on August 15.

Approved...

Leon Beaver's plans for a new courthouse, on November 21.

Subscribers wanted

The Montgomery County Soldier's Monument Association was established August 29 by 70 citizens determined to raise money for a Civil War monument honoring county veterans.

1880

Awarded...

Construction contracts for the new courthouse at 15 N. Main St., on June 2. Construction began that summer.

Fit as fiddles

Ten Dayton men interested in their "moral and physical welfare" organized the Dayton Gymnastic Club on March 7.

Raised...

$200 for the Civil War monument, from entertainment at the fairgrounds July 4. Another $200 was raised in the fall with a local production of *The Drummer Boy of Shiloh* at Turner's Opera House. Fund-raising tapered off after that. The Soldiers' Monument, now at the head of Main Street downtown, wasn't erected and dedicated until 1884 — nearly 20 years after the war.

Silent lines

No telephone calls could be made in Dayton from 2 to 4 p.m. Thanksgiving Day, when the exchange closed so that company employees could enjoy Thanksgiving dinner.

Died...

E.E. Barney, the prominent educator and industrialist. His Barney & Smith Car Company had captured 5.4 percent of the national market in railroad coaches, up from 1.6 percent in 1860.

Constructed...

A Memorial Hall on the grounds of the Soldiers' Home, where veterans could enjoy local entertainment and such celebrities as Sarah Bernhardt, the famous French actress, and Edward H. Sothern, who appeared in Shakespearean productions.

Incorporated...

The Fifth Street Railway Company.

An unpopular way of life

Celibacy had become a tough sell for the Shaker community, which had started its slow decline in Montgomery County. Tenant farmers worked the Shaker land that hadn't already been sold; only 46 believers were left at Watervliet, most of them 60 or older.

Top: This section of Main Street was tree-lined and peaceful.

Above: The firehouse at Fifth and Brown streets boasted an observation tower.

Reorganized...

Dayton's fire department. The new board of commissioners hired Daniel C. Larkin as chief.

Kin to Daniel Boone

At 312 Wayne Ave. was a pump shop run by a descendant of the famous Kentucky pioneer Daniel Boone. Dayton's Daniel Boone first sold wooden well and cistern pumps, later switching to metal.

Above: Daniel C. Larkin (left), shown with an associate in this 1902 photograph, was named chief of Dayton's reorganized fire department.

SLICE OF LIFE

Growing, growing

Dayton's population, 38,678, had grown nearly 27 percent since 1870, up from 30,473.

Where were the children?

Plenty of them weren't in school. Truancy rates hit 30 percent.

Liberated women

Only about a half-dozen Dayton women dared to venture beyond their place in the home and into the business world. While the very few who did make the leap typically worked as stenographers, the trickle of women into the work force was not without controversy. At least one attorney predicted disaster if working women became commonplace. (Surely, women were not capable enough to sell stockings or operate a typewriter.)

A friend to their customers

The Fifth Street Railway Company, which installed tracks this year, was known for letting children ride free on the first Sunday of the month and for taking Children's Home residents to and from the theater.

On Sunday night, there'd be three whistles — and they'd be loud. It was the driver of the Fifth Street line, warning young boys out courting in East Dayton that it was time to bid their sweethearts adieu (or miss the ride home).

Dayton amenities

A prominent Montgomery County history published in the early 1880s noted the following about the up-and-coming city of Dayton:

- The city was attracting the attention of people from abroad.
- "Few drones" lived in Dayton.
- Dayton's wealth was distributed fairly equally among its citizens, compared to other cities its size.
- Most Daytonians were churchgoers.
- "Dayton marble" — both beautiful and durable — was an abundant building material.
- Dayton was the hub for nine railroads.
- Unsightly or unkempt tenement houses were virtually nonexistent.
- Dayton's manufacturing and shipping facilities offered opportunities to capitalists and manufacturers alike.
- And finally: "... her educational, moral, social and sanitary advantages render Dayton a most desirable place for residence."

Above: Winters Bank

Nightly news

The new "paper of the people" was the Dayton *Evening Herald*, published February 7 as the city's first evening daily. Cost: 10 cents a week.

Ring, ring, ring

The first long-distance telephone call in Dayton came from Indianapolis in October.

By now Dayton, West Milton, Piqua, Xenia and Miamisburg were connected by telephone. But not everyone saw the value in what was still regarded as experimental; some investors worried that phone service would never expand to the point that it was profitable. (Even little boys grumbled about the telephone, complaining that the wires got in the way of their kites.)

Authorized...

The opening of Winters National Bank, by the U.S. Treasury Department on December 21.

It served its purpose

Built this year was the Southeastern Railroad, from Dayton to the Jackson County coal fields in southeast Ohio, thanks to the Dayton Exchange. (Afterward, the civic association dissolved.)

Paper baron

Daniel Mead renamed the Mead & Nixon Paper Company to the Mead Paper Company after becoming sole owner.

Passed...

A bill by the Ohio legislature authorizing taxes for a Civil War monument in Dayton.

Pledged...

$10,733 by Daytonians for building a new Widows' Home.

Moved...

The Wright family, from Cedar Rapids, Iowa, to Richmond, Indiana, in June.

1882

A rise in status

The bank known as V. Winters & Son officially became Winters National Bank on January 1. Its first president: Jonathan Winters I.

Gas lamps: Flickering out

The *Journal* was the site of the first formal demonstration of an electric light in Dayton, on February 13. Less than two weeks later, on February 25, The Brush Electric Light and Motor Company of Montgomery County prepared to supply the area with electric light and power and to sell or rent electric equipment.

On the horizon: A Civil War monument

The fund for a Soldiers' Monument in Dayton began growing after the first tax installment netted $5,850.

A thriving industry

Sales hit $100,000 annually for Dayton Malleable, which was producing farm equipment and bicycle parts.

Career change

Stepladder inventor John Balsley became a real estate investor after selling his stepladder company.

A weathered look

Temperatures? Rainfall? Barometric pressure? These were the concerns of Edith Longstreth Boyer, the city's first meteorologist, who began a weather observatory this year. Ms. Boyer, who continued meteorological operations from her Huffman Hill home for the next 57 years, provided valuable local weather statistics after U.S. government data from area weather stations was destroyed in the 1913 flood.

Died...

Prominent Dayton engineer and bridge designer David H. Morrison, founder of the Columbia Bridge Works and builder of several local spans.

Above: The new St. Elizabeth Hospital building was dedicated on November 19. It stood on the west side of the Great Miami River at Hopeland Street, and replaced the hospital's rented quarters on Franklin Street.

1883

A power house

Merged on January 12 was The Brush Electric Light and Motor Company and The Dayton Gas Light and Coke Company, forming The Dayton Electric Light Company. The plant, near Forest and Riverview, included a one-story brick generator room, a two-story brick boiler house and a one-story turbine room or wheelhouse.

Flooded...

Points along the rivers, yet again, on February 3 and 4.

Illuminated...

The city's streets, by 50 arc lamps on February 16. Dayton was one of the first cities in Ohio to light its streets with electricity.

Welcome, customers

The Boston Drygoods Store, which would become Elder-Beerman Stores Corporation, opened March 30 at 114 E. Third St. Elder's was the first department store in Dayton to have an elevator, escalator and drinking fountains.

Thomas Elder, who ran the first store, showed his shrewd business sense by the way he handled an early merchandising mishap. He meant to order a dozen horse blankets, a popular item back then. When a dozen cases arrived, a shocked Elder promptly set up a sidewalk display, since there wasn't enough room inside the store for so many blankets. His newspaper advertisement featuring the 98-cent blankets suggested that ladies consider using them as capes.

Purchased...

50 shares of new-issue stock in the National Manufacturing Company, by brothers John H. and Frank Patterson, May 8. Later, John bought controlling interest in the company for $6,500 and went on to establish the National Cash Register Company in 1884.

He had the last laugh

John Patterson had a few second thoughts about making cash registers after sharing his plans with his Dayton Club colleagues, who snickered and teased him in October about his crazy idea. Patterson ignored them and went ahead anyway.

Many of Dayton's social events took place at the Dayton Club, at the southwest corner of First and Main streets. Famous architect Charles Insco Williams designed the structure, which featured a ballroom and stage, billiard rooms and bowling alleys.

At last — let the carving begin

Daytonian George Washington Fair, who'd been a Union Army private, was the model for the Soldiers' Monument. Sculptors in Carrara, Italy, worked from photographs of Pvt. Fair when they began carving the Italian marble on September 19.

Early plans called for Miss Columbia, rather than Fair. Veterans argued that a woman didn't belong at the top of a war monument. Harumph!

Bought...

Dayton's first patrol wagons. The Metropolitan Police Force used them for the first time on December 12.

Organized...

The Dayton Corps of the Salvation Army, on December 7.

Founded...

The Montgomery County Bar Association.

Above: Looking north along Main Street from Fifth Street, the Soldiers' Monument could be seen in the distance in this early downtown photograph.

MILESTONE

One moment in time

The statue of Pvt. George Washington Fair, to grace the top of the Soldiers' Monument, landed in New York from Cararra, Italy, on June 20. Then it was on to Dayton.

Meanwhile, Montgomery County officials sealed a time capsule inside the monument's base on July 15.

The capsule included:
- A Bible.
- City directories for 1883 and 1884.
- Recent annual reports from the city clerk, workhouse, fire, police, health, infirmary and wastewater departments and the Dayton Women's Christian Temperance Union.
- Constitution, bylaws and membership list of the Old Guard Association.
- A newspaper from May 30, 1884.
- A list of officials of the E.G. King Post, Grand Army of the Republic.
- The story of the Soldiers' Home.

A monumental celebration

With some 70,000 people watching, Montgomery County dedicated the long-awaited monument at Main and Water streets on July 31.

The affair was festive and grand. Decorations included 250 tattered battleflags said to be stained with the blood of Dayton veterans. There were banners, cannon salutes, a parade, visits to the Soldiers' Home and, of course, the unveiling — which didn't come off quite as planned.

1884

To the rescue

The sheet concealing the noble statue wouldn't budge, no matter how hard the ropes were pulled. Clarence E. Ward, a nimble chimney sweep (some say a steeplejack), was asked to scoot up the pillar and release the bothersome shroud. By the time he did, rain had soaked the onlookers — who, in spite of it all, erupted in thunderous applause.

Fittingly, Water Street was renamed Monument Avenue on August 1. ■

The graduate

Wilbur Wright made it through his Richmond, Indiana, high school but missed his June commencement. (He was one of eight graduates.) The Wright family returned to Dayton later in 1884.

Home grown

Local professionals — from the architect to the woodworker to the ironworker — completed the new courthouse, a fortress-like, 33-room stone structure that cost $174,945. It so pleased the community that some recommended tearing down the Old Court House because "it has no further purpose to fill." (Ironically, the new one was the one razed, in 1972.)

The founding of 'The Cash'

Businessmen had to be sold on the idea: Replace a penny pencil — with a $125 cash register? At first, business was slow. But John H. Patterson, who established the National Cash Register Company this year, was not easily defeated. With 13 employees and a 3,200-square-foot factory, he began manufacturing and marketing the new device to businesses. His meticulous training of the NCR sales force — Patterson told them exactly how to dress, how to sell and when — produced great returns, as did his genuine attention to the needs of his factory workers.

Patterson never lost any sleep worrying about business matters. But he did awaken at 5:45 a.m. every day — without an alarm clock — so he could be at his office by 6:30 a.m.

Left: The Patterson family was photographed at home.

Below: Looking west on Franklin Street, at the corner of Ludlow.

Chartered...

The Bicycle Club, by Dayton men who enjoyed bicycling as a hobby. Today the club, at 131 W. Third St., is the city's oldest active private men's club.

Incorporated...

The Ohio Rake Company.

Established...

The new Widows' Home, on Findlay Street, by the Woman's Christian Association of Dayton. It had 30 residents.

Right: Signs at Third and Jefferson let potential customers know that real estate was the business of W.R. Nevin & Company.

A multinational corporation

His company had sold only 64 cash registers by now, but that didn't keep John H. Patterson from looking to the future. He took National Cash Register international by establishing a distributorship in Liverpool, England.

An inside job

More than $2,500 was embezzled from the police department — by Police Secretary J.H. Ensign, of all people.

Busy signal

Subscribers to the Dayton Bell Telephone Exchange numbered 495.

SLICE OF LIFE

A charming river drive

Recognizing the value of riverfront land, E.R. Stilwell saw great possibilities in building up the Great Miami River levee from Monument Avenue to First Street. And Professor James A. Robert, former principal of the old Cooper Seminary, endorsed developing the former pasture land and gypsy campground between the river and the old levee, between the Third Street and Dayton View bridges. Their vision led to Robert Boulevard, a charming street of 96 lots that became home to many of Dayton's most prominent families in the 1890s. Today it's Robert Drive, skirting Sinclair Community College.

Right: The staff of the Dayton YMCA.

SLICE OF LIFE

Not fit to print

It was page three of issue No.1 of *The Midget* that raised the ire of Orville Wright's father, Milton. The paper was printed by 15-year-old Orville and his friend Edward Sines for their schoolmates, but the elder Wright refused to let them distribute it when he turned to the third page and saw it entirely blank, save for the words "Sines & Wright," printed twice. Perhaps the job had overwhelmed the boys, who hand-set all the type and printed one page at a time on their small press. Whatever the reason, the bishop was not amused. Said he: "(Readers) might get the impression that the publishers were lazy or shiftless."

Strike!

Not a horse car could be found on Dayton's streets during the city's first major streetcar strike in mid-March. Drivers griped mostly about wages (they wanted $12.25 a week instead of $10) and hours (they wanted to work 12 hours a day, not 16). And why should they have to deposit $9.40 of their own cash for making change? It took two weeks to reach an amicable settlement.

Sold...

Another 73 cash registers by NCR, from April 1885 to April 1886.

Flooded...

Dayton, on May 12, with major damage to the west side.

Opened...

Notre Dame Academy, at Franklin and Ludlow streets, by the Sisters of Notre Dame, for training Christian women.

1887

Incorporated...

The Gem City Building and Loan Association, on October 27. Its office was in the Callahan block at Third and Main.

Cash registers catch on (finally!)

After three years of sluggish sales, the National Cash Register Company hit the jackpot — selling 5,400 machines.

Founded...

A night school for men, by David Sinclair of the Dayton YMCA, with 55 students. This became Sinclair Community College.

Enrolled...

Orville Wright, into Central High School. He never graduated.

Removed...

The stone bridge over the canal on Jefferson Street, built in 1856 by the late David H. Morrison.

Established...

The Board of Trade, with 336 members, for developing a new railway station.

MILESTONE
Progress, or not?

Dayton wasn't ready to write off its horse cars yet — even after the White Line Street Railroad Company announced in May it would run electric cars from the top of North Main south to Third, Ludlow, Washington, Germantown, Eaton, King and Roseyard streets. Even as the 25-foot iron poles for trolley wires were installed, folks were skeptical. Certainly these electric cars couldn't run in rain or snow. Wouldn't watch wearers find their timepieces adversely magnetized? And what about parades, with all those overhead wires in the way?

Before regular runs began in 1888, the line had its share of troubles. A competitor, the Oakwood Street Railway, wanted to stop White Line from using its downtown tracks and building adjacent to its horse-car tracks. The companies battled all the way to the Ohio Supreme Court, which ruled in White Line's favor. ■

Above and below: New energy sources were on the way, but horses still powered public transportation and fire engines.

Left: The canal wasn't all business. Some Daytonians had the advantage of recreational boating in their back yards.

The daylight factory

Would it even stand? Daytonians wondered about the large number of windows John H. Patterson and his brother Frank included in the Cash's new factory, built on part of the Patterson family homestead and occupied in June. All that sunlight, and the distractions! But they worried less when the factory's 115 employees began producing 25 cash registers a day — up by one-fourth over previous productivity records. Perhaps there was something to this daylight thing?

Patterson: 'What more than wages do we owe our employees?'

A bright, sunny workplace was only the beginning of the revolutionary ideas Patterson brought to NCR. Employees soon enjoyed unheard-of pleasantries — such as fine landscaping and ventilated machines to remove dust — and benefits such as health education, evening classes, lunchrooms and a recreational facility. Compared to what factory workers were used to in those days, this was nirvana. ∎

Above: Pvt. George Washington Fair died just four years after the monument bearing his statue was erected. Flanking the monument are the Main Street bridge (left) and the fire house (right).

Right: the Public Library, shown here in later years, was built in Cooper Park.

Died...

Pvt. George Washington Fair, the Civil War veteran who modeled for the Soldiers' Monument, on January 23. He was buried in Woodland Cemetery.

Black, white and read all over

It was the biggest and best in the state. That's the billing Dayton's new library received during dedication ceremonies on January 24. The new structure, centered in Cooper Park and memorable for its French Gothic Romanesque style, featured Dayton limestone and Marquette red sandstone trim. It housed 26,647 volumes and 1,000 pamphlets.

Was there browsing in the stacks? Not likely. Patrons had to request books from the librarian, who retrieved them as needed. For faster service, written requests were a must.

1888

Up and running...

The city's first electric trolley car, operated by the White Line Street Railroad Company, on August 8. Daytonians who at first had frowned upon the newfangled contraption quickly saw the benefits of clean, fast, comfortable electric cars over the old horse-drawn vehicles. Competitors scrambled to follow suit, and by 1900, horse cars were a faded memory.

Dayton's early electric cars featured electric lights, ventilated roofs, fare-conveyor tubes and lengthwise seats. The system's overhead lines were powered by two 2,000-horsepower engines, three dynamos and boilers.

Formed...

The Mozart Club, on October 15, by serious musicians of all talent levels. The club performed 13 recitals per season.

Head count

The Dayton Asylum for the Insane determined in November it had "cured" 2,785 of the 6,463 patients served since it opened in 1852.

Moved...

The Davis Sewing Machine Company, to Dayton. The Gem City's George P. Huffman bought the company, founded in Watertown, New York. He remained president until his death in 1896.

Incorporated...

Fourth National Bank.

Laid...

Granite blocks on East Fifth Street, between Main and Jefferson. It was Dayton's first paved street.

SLICE OF LIFE

Big brother was watching

A bigger and better printing press — that's all Orville Wright wanted, but it was easier said than done. After watching his little brother struggle a bit, Wilbur stepped in to help, moving this piece here, that piece there, this other piece over here. The result? A working press. The young men put it to good use.

1889

The club movement

The Woman's Literary Club, established March 30, was Dayton's first official "women's club." Some discussion topics:
- "What is meant by culture?"
- "Is it desirable that women should speak in public?"
- "What is the best course to pursue in the study of literature?"
- "Distinctive features of woman's work."

Eventually, members chose to focus on English authors and the classics. At a time when such clubs were springing up across the United States, the Woman's Literary Club opened doors for Dayton women by advocating self-culture, philanthropy and community service; members promoted summer band concerts, juvenile court, public playgrounds and vacation schools — and even helped the city's first police matron get appointed in 1894.

A 'Y' for black women

Established: the Eaker Street AME Church Sewing Club, which later became the Women's Association No. 2 — the nation's first black YWCA branch. It was later renamed the West Side YWCA.

Left: The *West Side News* listed Wilbur Wright as editor and his brother Orville as publisher.

Printed and published...

The first edition of *West Side News*, a four-page weekly, by 17-year-old Orville Wright on March 1. After April 13, business was conducted at 1210 W. Third St., with Orville as publisher, Wilbur Wright as editor and Orville's friend Edward Sines as keeper of the cash book. The brothers ran a press of their own making that could produce 1,200 impressions an hour. Subscriptions: 40 cents a year (or 10 cents for 10 weeks).

The Dayton Club

"To maintain a place for social entertainment of members of the club and their families, friends, and visitors from abroad." Such was the sole purpose of the Dayton Club, established earlier this decade by prominent, wealthy Dayton men.

The club held a reception May 28 in its new rented quarters, the Peter P. Lowe residence on North Main Street.

Adopted...
The meter system, in March, by the Dayton Electric Light Company.

Beat Springfield!
That was the mission of the Dayton Reds, a baseball team formed by Dayton's street railway companies and six businessmen. The team's fame, however, was fleeting. When few fans showed up at the Williams Street grandstands, the backers cut their losses — to $2,000 — and permanently benched the team. So long, Reds. We hardly knew ye.

Arrived...
Shakers, from the shut-down North Union Village near Cleveland, to Montgomery County's Watervliet community of the sect.

Renamed...
The Gebhart Opera House, to The Park Theater.

Introduced...
Natural gas for fuel.

Incorporated...
Reynolds and Reynolds.

SLICE OF LIFE

Economic health and well-being
Dayton's 700-plus factories, with access to nine railroad lines, were producing $20 million in products annually. Diversity kept the economy healthy. Said one report: "(The manufactories) are so varied in character that each extends the other aid, and never is dullness of trade generally felt."

Don't drink the milk
Dirty stables? Dirty cows? Dirty hands? Dirty milk cans? The city's milk supply was in bad shape, and folks began calling for safe, pure milk.

Top left: The Montgomery County Jail

Top right: The Dayton Widows' Home

Middle: Residents of the Dayton Widows' Home were photographed on the front porch.

Left: The Kuhns Building, at Fourth and Main, is prominent in this view looking northwest across downtown.

1890

Wanted and needed: A new hospital

Malaria, diphtheria, typhoid, pneumonia, fevers. Would it ever end? Dayton needed more medical care, and the Protestant Deaconess Society, formed August 21, responded by opening a temporary hospital in 1891. This became Miami Valley Hospital.

How business was done in the good old days

The Gem City Building and Loan Association gave a Dayton housewife $1,700 in September to buy a piece of property. Loan terms: $30 a month and free board — at her husband's livery stable — for horses owned by two of the association's directors.

News boys?

Their weekly was a success. So why not publish every day? The ambitious Wright brothers turned the *West Side News* into a daily, *The Evening Item*. They ran wire stories, local news and an editorial page. The established press proved too much for the fledgling *Item*, which quietly folded after three months. But the Wrights weren't finished with printing. Wright and Wright Job Printers operated on the second floor of the Hoover Block at the southeast corner of West Third and South Williams streets. On December 13, they printed the inaugural issue of the *Dayton Tattler*, published by their friend Paul Laurence Dunbar and his associate, Preston Finley. Dunbar and Orville Wright, incidentally, were classmates at Central High, where Dunbar was the only black student.

Installed...

City sanitary sewers, starting in the center of town. Discovered during the excavation was a floor of walnut logs, laid by early Daytonian Obadiah Conover in 1811 for his blacksmithing business.

Ticket-punching

Ticketing and pricetagging became automatic with Fred Kohnle's invention of a pin-ticketing machine. The company, originally the Climax Tag Company, later became the Automatic Pin Ticketing Company. Today, it's Monarch Marking.

Above: From Main Street, the view of East Third Street showed unpaved streets and trolley lines.

Left: This outbuilding behind the Wright brothers' workshop was rustic but functioned as storage space.

Yes, it's the Buzfuz Club

The young men, most fresh out of college, who established the prestigious Buzfuz Club in a law office this year were interested in discussing literature, the sciences and such topics as the history of European nations. After two years, they abandoned their original cause in pursuit of more "social" interests. (The name, by the way, came from Sgt. Buzfuz in Dickens' *The Pickwick Papers*.)

Invented...

The electric dental gold annealer, by Dr. Luzern Custer of Dayton.

Subscribed...

760 citizens, to the Dayton Bell Telephone Exchange.

Opened...

Lorenz & Company, music publishers.

More people

Dayton's population was 61,220, up from 38,678 in 1880, an increase of 58 percent.

Free wheelin' (and dressed for the occasion)

Bicycling was in vogue, and Dayton women didn't want to miss out. But how to pedal with those skirts? Thus was born the wheeling skirt: a circular, divided frock perfect for pedaling. Ladies took well to the new fashion, but many men didn't. Ministers and editors got on their respective soapboxes: Was this womanly behavior? Was it decent? What was next?

Night out

Thousands of visitors from miles around flocked to the Soldiers' Home to hear outdoor summer-evening concerts by the home's official band (which was uniformed, well-practiced and well-paid). They could also watch deer roaming in Deer Park along with a black bear, raccoons, prairie dogs and other animals.

MILESTONE

A gifted poet

At Central High School, he not only wrote the class poem but edited the school paper. He was president of the School Society and the Philomethean Society. He even published six issues of a black-oriented newspaper, the *Dayton Tattler*, during his senior year. He was Dayton's beloved poet, Paul Laurence Dunbar. Confident and armed with a diploma this year, Dunbar tried to find a job suitable for a high school graduate. But because Dayton employers discriminated against blacks, Dunbar was forced to take a job as an elevator operator and moonlight as a groundskeeper for the Rike family. In the meantime, Dunbar wrote and wrote. By the time he died in 1906, he was famous for such works as *Lyrics of Lowly Life*, one of several volumes of popular poetry, and *The Sport of the Gods*, one of three novels. ■

Above: Paul Laurence Dunbar (back left) was the only black student at Central High School. His classmate was Orville Wright (back center).

Right: The *Dayton Tattler* was published by Dunbar and printed by the Wrights.

SLICE OF LIFE

Dayton leaders

■ With 280 rooms and steam heat, the Beckel House was Dayton's leading hotel.
■ The *Dayton Daily and Weekly Journal* was the area's leading — and oldest — Republican newspaper.
■ With its 800 families, St. John's Evangelical Lutheran Church was likely Dayton's largest church.
■ The Davis Sewing Machine Company, the country's second-largest sewing machine plant, was producing 400 machines a day in a factory a mile long.
■ Farmers knew the "Tiger" brand of farm implements, produced by Stoddard Manufacturing Company, recognized worldwide for its quality products.

Organized...

The Helen Hunt Club, Dayton's second women's club, on February 21. This club for teachers focused on studying literature and reading papers and plays aloud.

In memoriam

Robert Steele, a Dayton leader throughout most of the 1800s, died September 24. His contributions to Dayton's schools, the library, Woodland Cemetery and other civic organizations, such as the county fair board, the sanitary commission and the YMCA, earned him a prominent place in Dayton's history. Steele High School, which opened in 1894, was named in his honor.

Opened...

Protestant Deaconess Hospital, which became Miami Valley Hospital, at Pritz House on East Fourth Street October 18. This temporary hospital had 37 beds and seven physicians.

Straight and narrow

Street paving continued on parts of Wayne Avenue, Washington, Germantown, North Main, Fifth and other Dayton streets.

1892

Sold!

A Cincinnati investors group bought the Barney & Smith Car Company in May for $4.5 million. The company had 40 buildings on 28 acres.

Held...

Dayton's first Columbus Day parade, on October 21.

They peddled bikes

The Wright brothers capitalized on the bicycling craze by opening their first bicycle repair shop and showroom at 1005 W. Third St. The young entrepreneurs (Wilbur was 25, Orville was 21) had a five-tiered price structure:

- Boys' machines: $40 to $50.
- Good adult machines: $50.
- Fine machines: $60.
- Excellent machines: $80.
- Best bicycles built: $100.

The West Third store was one of six bicycle shops the Wrights operated over the years.

Added...

The Dayton Bicycle, to the line of products manufactured by George P. Huffman's Davis Sewing Machine Company. Also produced by the company: motorwheels, motorcycles and washing machines.

It grew up

Erected this year was Dayton's first skyscraper, the five-story Callahan Bank Building at Third and Main, which eventually grew to nine stories. First tenants: Winters National Bank and City National Bank.

Paved...

All streets in central Dayton (except for Third Street).

Top: The Columbus Day parade

Above: Fishing on the Great Miami River.

One man's junk

It was an argument with his daughter that led "Kayser the Miser," Dayton's best-known scavenger, to hang himself on August 3 at age 80. Fritz Kayser, who drove a skinny horse and battered wagon, was Dayton's own pack rat. His sole aim in life: collecting as much junk and garbage as he could find, which he stored in five outhouses on his Cass Street property near Wayne Avenue. Kayser's main haunt was the city dump. Bottles? Jugs? Hats? Shoes? Rags? Broken china? Kayser the Miser wanted it all. If he wasn't happy, he at least died rich. His net worth, including property and real estate, totaled more than $200,000. And what became of the old man's treasures? They ended up back where most of them started: the city dump.

Sophisticated and cosmopolitan

The men were handsome and the ladies lovely, adorned in lace-and-ribbon gowns and flamboyant hats (many with ostrich plumes). It was the Gay '90s, and social engagements were the order of the day. Taking the lead was the Dayton Club, which organized dinner parties, private entertainment and jaunts to the Soldiers' Home for its 138 local members (seven members were from New York, Columbus, Middletown and the Soldiers' Home). All this fashion-consciousness made for well-to-do dressmakers and milliners in town.

Top: "Nut" the elephant led the Charity Circus parade.

Right: Canal boats docked near the Armory.

Below: Shoppers in Rike's.

The Armory

A many-cultured city
The Dayton Museum of Natural History opened September 15 on the second floor of the public library building in Cooper Park.

Panic of 1893
The dollar plunged to a value of 60 cents by December 31, ruining 600 banks, 74 railroads and 15,000 businesses across the country. Hard times were on their way to Dayton.

New Rike's store: 'Ultimate in elegance'
After the D.L. Rike Dry Goods House was incorporated this year as the Rike Dry Goods Company, David Rike moved the entire store to a new stone building at Fourth and Main that was modeled after a structure at the Chicago World's Fair. Back then, Rike's employed 100 dressmakers and 25 tailors.

Serving Dayton cyclists
Dayton had 14 bike shops. The Wright brothers' second one, rented for part of this year, was at 1015 W. Third St.; their third shop, rented until 1894, was at 1034 W. Third St. The brothers called their business the Wright Cycle Exchange, and later The Wright Cycle Company.

In print
Paul Laurence Dunbar published his first book of poems: *Oak and Ivy*.

Consolidated...
Many local street railway companies, to form the more efficient City Railway Company.

Opened...
Thresher Electrical Company.

1894

MILESTONE

NCR: A well-oiled machine

John H. Patterson insisted that NCR salesmen go strictly by a manual called *The Primer*. Here's why:

"An agent may be ever so well informed on Cash Registers, yet if he attempts to convince a purchaser by his own impromptu arguments, he will find himself floundering in a sea of words.... Some Salesmen think it is belittling to their ability to sell by *The Primer*.... There is no gainsaying the fact, that *The Primer* arguments are stronger, by far, than any that can emanate from the salesman's brain on the spur of the moment, no matter how bright he may be."

Patterson expected customers to put $30 down and pay $25 a month on their new cash registers. But, acknowledged the company: "... where an agent can do no better, we accept $30.00 cash and $15.00 monthly."

From *The NCR*, a company publication: "Just think of it! We employ over 1,300 people and are running day and night to keep up with our orders, while other manufacturing plants are running small forces and at half time. Why is this? It is because the National Cash Register is an article of true merit, without which no storekeeper can become successful." ■

They saved it

Charles Insco Williams knew what he wanted: an apartment house at the southwest corner of Main and Monument. The prominent architect was ready to work. First, he had to raze Shafor's Grocery, the ugly old clapboard building in his way. And what did he find beneath the siding? Logs — lots of them. Williams had stumbled across the original Newcom Tavern. Later, John H. Patterson moved the cabin to Van Cleve Park, and the Daughters of the American Revolution raised pledges for its renovation. Williams eventually got his upscale apartment house, and called it Newcom Manor.

Left: John H. Patterson provided his employees with a bright, well-ventilated workplace in which to assemble NCR's increasingly popular cash registers.

Below: Patterson also placed high value on employee education, and made this reading room available.

SLICE OF LIFE

The hooker with a heart of gold, and a purse to match

Perhaps it was her Sunday parade of the women in her employ that caught the eyes of Dayton lawyers, judges and politicians. Whatever it was, Lib Hedges' prostitution business boomed. She moved her concern to Pearl Street and ended up owning more than 100 pieces of Dayton real estate. Incidentally, Hedges gave back to the community that had been so good to her: She was a big supporter of the YMCA, YWCA and local charities.

Above: Streetcars paused for this photograph at the corner of Third and Jefferson streets.

Right: Steele High School was at the corner of Main and Monument streets.

Below: Summer brought outdoor dancing to the NCR Sugar Camp.

Speed demon

A rocking chair was the second-place prize won by Orville Wright in the 1-Mile Novice Class A Race during the Dayton Bicycle Club-sponsored meet at the fairgrounds on June 30. He went on to win three bicycle racing medals July 4 in races sponsored by the YMCA Wheelmen Club of Dayton at the YMCA Athletic Park (at what's now Riverside and Ridge). And on September 3, Orville won the gold medal in the mile championship and the silver in the half-mile. Wilbur, who suffered from a hockey-stick injury to the jaw, didn't race bikes. Instead, he was Orville's starter, charged with giving his brother's bike a shove at the starting line.

An advertising vehicle

The Wright brothers advertised their bicycles in *Snap-Shots at Current Events*, a weekly magazine printed by Wright & Wright Printers from October 20 until April 1896.

Completed and opened...

Steele High School, which replaced Central High. All high-schoolers in Dayton attended Steele until Stivers opened in 1906 as a general high school.

Buzz, buzz, buzz

The Water Works Board of Trustees was warned about the dangers of electric current for streetcars, which was believed to be corroding underground water and gas pipes. But what to do? It took until 1911 to find a solution.

Hard times at Barney & Smith

Aftershocks from the Panic of 1893 rolled through Dayton, striking hard at the Barney & Smith Car Company. It stayed barely afloat by cutting jobs and closing up shop as needed through 1896.

Completed and dedicated...

Deaconess Hospital, on Charity Hill overlooking Dayton.

Growing

The Soldiers' Home now encompassed 578 acres.

1895

Electrified...
All but one of Dayton's street railways.

At lightning speed
Development began on the interurban electric railroad, built to run high-speed electric cars between Miami Valley cities. Hourly interurban runs promised the speediest-ever transport of passengers and freight, with cars capable of nearly 100 mph.

Moving up and on
The Wrights cut overhead by combining their printing and booming bicycle businesses under one roof, The Wright Cycle Company, at 22 S. Williams St. A downtown branch store at 23 W. Second St. stayed open for about a year.

Chatty
The Dayton Bell Telephone Exchange had 1,013 subscribers.

Published...
Majors and Minors, by Paul Laurence Dunbar. It was his second book of poems.

Invented...
A register for recording and printing taxicab fares, by John Ohmer. He later established the Ohmer Fare Register Company.

Opened...
The Adler and Childs Department Store, by M.L. Adler and Albert Childs.

Organized...
The Young Women's League.

Hired...
The Rev. DeSoto Bass, as pastor of Wesleyan Church. He later helped form the Colored Ministerial Alliance.

SLICE OF LIFE

Something for everyone
This year the Soldiers' Home drew 350,000 visitors, who enjoyed shady woods, exotic plants, a bubbling spring with tin dippers for drinking, goldfish in a lily pond and an alligator pool. The grand military band played concerts from beneath a blue-roofed bandstand. And when the home finally closed in the evening, folks continued merrymaking and amusement at nearby Lakeside Park.

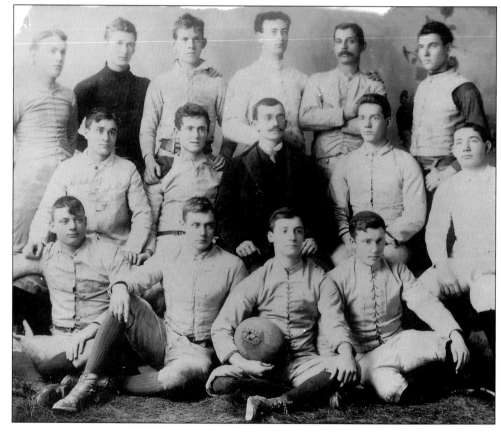

Left: Early street advertising promoted cheap power, coffee and carpeting — all at the same time.

Below: The YMCA football team meant business.

Bottom: The electric interurban trains reached speeds approaching 100 mph.

Propelled to prominence

Influential critic William Dean Howells' review of Paul Laurence Dunbar's *Majors and Minors* in the national magazine *Harper's Weekly* on June 27 earned the young writer widespread acclaim as America's leading black poet, and one of the very few to be published at this time. Publishers urged Dunbar to produce more pieces in black dialect after Howells praised the way Dunbar had captured what he called the lyrical qualities of black life. Dunbar, however, fought the Negro-poet image, insisting he was, quite simply, a poet.

Howells, himself a native Buckeye, wrote the introduction to *Lyrics of Lowly Life*, a collection of Dunbar's best poems published this year.

Eager for interurbans

An early entrant into the interurban market, Dayton became one of the largest interurban centers in the country, second only to Indianapolis. By July 1, residents could get to Miamisburg via the interurban, also called the "electric traction railway."

She made books more inviting

Browsers were welcome soon after head librarian Electra C. Doren reorganized the public library to allow open shelving. Doren was head librarian through 1905 and then again from 1913 until she died in 1927.

Bona-fide doctors

Enforcement of the State Medical Practice Act began this year. Those professing to be doctors had to pass an exam — after graduating from high school and an approved medical college — before being allowed to practice.

Charity prevailed

Since its founding in 1878, St. Elizabeth Hospital had seen 15,000 patients (many of them unable to pay).

MILESTONE

A birthday party for Dayton?

The idea was planted by Mary Davies Steele, daughter of the late great Robert Steele, on her sickbed. And the notion stuck. With Newcom Tavern saved and restored, Daytonians got nostalgic with centennial fever. Folks scoured their attics in search of antiques to furnish the historic home. They found spinning wheels, beds and cradles, Dutch ovens, candle molds, hominy mills, pewter candlesticks and cider presses. A grand celebration was in the works.

Looking ahead

Addressing citizens on Dayton's future was John H. Patterson, who on March 19 boldly proposed a new form of municipal government grounded in business methods and organization. (The commission-manager form of government began in 1914.)

Kickoff

The centennial celebration officially opened with a grand jubilee that started at dusk on March 31 and culminated at midnight with rockets and clamor lasting an hour. On April 1 schools hosted special programs and citizens heard regular ringing of the old Newcom Tavern bell (by then located in Steele High School).

'Daytonia'

The celebration's highlight was the locally produced pageant *Daytonia*, held May 18-23 in the Grand Opera House, which told Dayton's story from the days of Newcom Tavern and beyond. To pull it off, locals of every religion, organization and affiliation worked together under the direction of producer Harry E. Feicht. (Pageant proceeds went to St. Elizabeth and Deaconess hospitals.) Forefathers were reverently recalled by Harriet M. King in her essay on "Dayton of the Past," which appeared in the *Souvenir of Daytonia*: "It is pleasant to stop in our whirling life and recall their quiet, earnest personality, their independence and kindliness."

A last hurrah

The three-day celebration starting September 14 included speeches, banners, a parade and poetry readings by Paul Laurence Dunbar. In 100 years, Dayton had been transformed from a wooded frontier settlement into a thriving, bustling modern city. Indeed, it was something to celebrate. ■

Above: The Callahan Bank Building stood at the northeast corner of Third and Main streets.

House brand

Experienced sellers of ready-made bicycles, the Wright brothers decided they could build better bikes themselves. And that they did. Their top-of-the-line was the Van Cleve, named after their great-great grandmother Catharine Van Cleve Thompson, thought to be the first to set foot on the Great Miami riverbank in 1796. Another offering: the St. Clair, named after Gen. Arthur St. Clair, one of Dayton's founders. Samples were ready in April, with production beginning May 15.

And still growing

The Soldiers' Home covered 625 acres and housed 6,000 veterans.

Consolidated...

The White Line and the Wayne Avenue Company, street railways that became the People's Railway Company.

More folk

Dayton's population was about 80,000.

Ran...

Sixty-four passenger trains a day through Dayton.

'Only forty-eight germs'

Dayton was proud of its water, according to this 1896 report: "The quality of the water, by recent analysis, has been found to be first-class. It is clear, cold, and remarkably free from injurious matter. In a recent analysis an average of only forty-eight germs to the cubic centimeter were found in the samples examined. The average temperature in the pipes is about 50."

Printer's ink

Headquartered at Fourth and Main was the United Brethren Publishing House, home to writers, editors and artists producing religious literature. Dayton was becoming known for its printing industry.

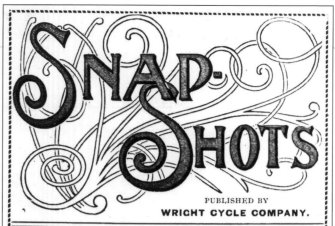

SNAP-SHOTS

PUBLISHED BY
WRIGHT CYCLE COMPANY.

VOL. II.   DAYTON, O., APRIL 17, 1896.   No. 6.

With all the Democrats and half the Republicans opposed to the Bosler Ripper bill, it would be a waste of money to submit it to a popular vote next Fall.

※

It is lucky that President Cleveland's little children were not in Dayton when they took the measles. They might now be convalescing in the pest house.

※

A delirious man hanging on to a bar is a sad sight of course; but it has its mitigating circumstances when, delirious with joy, he hangs to the bar of a WRIGHT SPECIAL bicycle.

※

For a number of months, Wright Cycle Co. have been making preparations to manufacture bicycles. After more delay than we expected, we are at last ready to announce that we will have several samples out in a week or ten days and will be ready to fill orders before the middle of next month. The WRIGHT SPECIAL will contain nothing but high grade material throughout, although we shall put it on the market at the exceedingly low price of $60. It will have large tubing, high frame, tool steel bearings, needle wire spokes, narrow tread and every feature of an up-to-date bicycle. Its weight will be about 22 pounds. We are very certain that no wheel on the market will run easier or wear longer than this one, and we will guarantee it in the most unqualified manner. When you have seen the machine you will appreciate how exceedingly low the price is.

Left: *Snap-Shots* was published weekly by the Wright brothers between 1894 and 1896. Shown here is the publication's last edition.

Below: Part of Dayton's centennial celebration centered around the recently rediscovered Newcom Tavern.

Right: The Wright Cycle Company, hard at work.

Below: What is now the Victoria Theatre was the site of the first international NCR sales agent convention.

Organized...

The Dayton Historical Society, on April 10. Newcom Tavern, which had become a public museum in Van Cleve Park, was its first home.

Abandoned...

The Dayton Electric Light Company's original plant from the early 1880s, near Forest and Riverview.

Invited...

Paul Laurence Dunbar, to London, to recite his poems at Queen Victoria's Diamond Jubilee.

Printers, riders, gliders

At their last bike shop — 1127 W. Third St. — the Wright brothers did more than build, repair and sell bikes. They tinkered with gliders, too.

SLICE OF LIFE

They hit the greens

Golf, anyone? It was the newest sport, but where to play? At first, cow pastures seemed to work well (except for the cows). Once the Dayton Golf Club was organized this year, members took their clubs and balls to Rubicon farm, the old Patterson Homestead.

On sale

Popular at the Elder and Johnston Department Store this year were Scottish tweeds, English cashmeres and serges. Dolls with moving arms cost a quarter. (The week before Christmas, Elder and Johnston delivered 3,000 packages to local residents.)

Another flood?

The water damage was serious — but not enough to get Daytonians really worried about flood protection. The 1898 flood was a forerunner to the 1913 disaster that crippled the city.

Newspaper mogul

The *Dayton Evening News* was purchased this year by James M. Cox for $26,000. It later became the *Dayton Daily News*.

Coming: A classy place to stay

Construction began on The Algonquin Hotel, designed by Dayton architect Charles Insco Williams for J. Elliott Pierce.

Married...

Paul Laurence Dunbar, to Alice Moore, a New Orleans schoolteacher and writer. The ceremony took place in Washington, D.C., where Dunbar worked as an assistant in the Reading Room of the Library of Congress.

Built...

A factory, by Reynolds and Reynolds, at 800 Germantown St., which later became its corporate headquarters.

Came and went...

The Spanish-American War, in about five months. U.S. soldiers in this Cuban conflict were later recognized with a statue at Memorial Hall.

1899

Printers no more

With their sights set skyward, the Wright brothers sold their printing business to printers Thomas R. and Marion Stevens. They kept making bicycles, though, until 1904.

Hitting the books

Wilbur Wright wrote to the Smithsonian Institution requesting information on aeronautics. It marked the brothers' first attempt to get serious about flight.

Kites, kites, everywhere kites. The Wrights collected scientific flight data by building and flying regular and box kites of all types, shapes and sizes at or near Dayton's Riverview Park. Watching the Wrights was James E. Salts, nephew to Charles Webbert, the Wrights' bike shop landlord. A year or so later, when the second floor of the bike shop was overrun with kites, Orville and Wilbur set a huge bonfire to rid themselves of those they no longer needed. Young Salts couldn't bear to watch. Could they spare him one? Wilbur gave a kite to the excited youngster, who took off running and bumped into his uncle nearby. Webbert doubted the boy's story, ordering him to return the kite to the Wrights. It — like the rest — went up in flames.

The secret of flight

In their quest to build a flying, winged glider, the brothers had run into a few snags. But something clicked when Wilbur, alone inside the bike shop, picked up an oblong innertube box and twisted it. The left side went up and the right side went down. Could a glider wing be made this way? And could the pressures on each wing be balanced as needed in a similar way? ■

Left: Wilbur Wright used a lathe to turn bicycle components.

Below: A hard freeze and thick ice on the Great Miami River brought out skaters and horse-drawn sleighs.

April fool!

A local practical joker grabbed his crystal ball and printed *The Dayton Globe* newspaper on April 1 after predicting what would be news in Dayton on April 1, 1946. Readers chuckled at the thought of an aerial landing field on top of a skyscraper, motorized delivery trucks at NCR, a loudspeaker, and an ice-making machine for the home. Here's how the April Fool sheet described "the newer woman" of 1946: "The 'newer woman' is as strong in her morals and methods as she is in her commercial and business pursuits.... She knows a hawk from a handsaw, and is an authority on the habits of each. She wastes no dimes on cigarets or politics, intrigues or lovers. She has grandly graduated past such follies. In these procreant days of 1946 she picks her man, not his pockets."

Above: Among the improvements Patterson brought to the NCR factory environment: an elegant dining room.

Below: The corner of Third and Ludlow has long been a hotel site. The Algonquin, shown here, was built in 1899.

Held...

The Dayton Street Fair and Midway, for a week starting June 26, to raise money for St. Elizabeth and Deaconess hospitals. Attractions and features — there were as many as 1,000 — included an opening parade, open house at an NCR factory, children's day, a wedding, ladies' day and Montgomery County day. Two interesting attractions: Millie Christine, a two-headed girl, and Chiquita, 26, the smallest woman in the world at 17.5 pounds.

Strike!

Employees of the Dayton Manufacturing Company rebelled after 17 of their co-workers at the railroad-car hardware plant were discharged. The city contended with violence and picketing during its first major strike.

NCR stats

■ Male employees: 1,668. Each worked 9.5 hours a day but got paid for 10.
■ Female employees: 264. Each worked 8.5 hours a day, got paid for 10, received a hot lunch at noon and got two 10-minute breaks.
■ Weekly company payroll: $27,000.

Sued...

The People's Railway, the City Railway and the Oakwood Street Railway, by the city of Dayton — which alleged underground water line damage from the trains' electric current.

Opened...

The Algonquin Hotel, a modern, first-class hotel at Third and Ludlow, which drew water from its own private well. In its place today: the downtown Radisson.

Established...

The Miami Valley Hospital School of Nursing, Dayton's first, by Lillian S. Clayton and Ella Phillips Crandall.

Married...

Frederick Rike, son of D.L. Rike, to Ethel Long. One of their three children, David L. Rike, went on to lead the Rike family business.

Founded...

Price Brothers Company, by Harry S. Price Sr., to manufacture concrete products for the construction and pipe industries.

1900

MILESTONE

The great First Street fire

The blaze began in the back of the J.P. Wolf & Son tobacco warehouse at First and Foundry streets at 6:25 a.m. on February 1. It spread quickly, fueled by tons of leaf tobacco. An estimated 10,000 spectators watched ice-caked Dayton firefighters struggle against the inferno. Chief Daniel C. Larkin called aid from Springfield, Cincinnati and Columbus. By noon, firefighters managed to get the blaze, Dayton's biggest ever, under control. The damage: a whopping $600,000. The next evening, City Council got a $78,000 wish list: five steam fire engines, a chemical engine, two new firehouses, 15 more firefighters, 10 horses and more hose — plus a list of water system improvements that would cost $170,000.

Firefighter George Coy was injured when a burning wall fell on him. Unconscious for hours, he was asked how he felt when he awoke. Said Coy: "Better than 10 dead men." ∎

Below: Members of the Dayton Camera Club strike poses during a club picnic.

Pedal to the metal

Dayton attorney Carl Baumann drove the first auto on Dayton's streets. The one-cylinder contraption ran down Main Street in March, frightening man and beast alike. Daytonians, who at first called the crazy carriages "benzine buggies" or "devil wagons," didn't take long to embrace the auto. By 1910, six auto factories were up and running in town.

Fresh produce

If you were a farmer with produce to sell, you didn't pass up the chance for curb space at Dayton's Street Market, which opened this year. Spaces for rent were auctioned at $50 to $100 a year.

Opened...

Dayton's first maternity ward, at what would become Miami Valley Hospital.

Market-driven

Bad times befell the Barney & Smith Car Company. Wooden cars became dinosaurs overnight as the railroads called for steel freight cars to haul ore. New companies sprang up to meet the new demand, and Barney & Smith, which built wooden cars, lost ground. E.J. Barney, son of founder E.E. Barney, resigned.

An arcade idea

It worked in London, so why not Dayton? E.J. Barney and Michael J. Gibbons formed the Arcade company to establish an arcade structure, complete with arches, a dome and a covered area for shops and a market.

Sabbath? What Sabbath?

Profit-minded saloon keepers appeared to comply with city laws by locking their front doors on Sundays — but plenty invited back-door business on the Sabbath. Police cracked down this year.

Electrified...

All 32 miles of Dayton's streetcar lines.

Subscribed...

1,955 citizens, to the Dayton Bell Telephone Exchange. Automatic dialing was unknown. Callers on the large, wooden, boxy telephones connected by first ringing "central."

Built...

The Conover building, a 13-story structure at Third and Main.

Ranked...

Dayton, No. 1 in Ohio in the number of patents issued. Ohio's fifth-largest city, Dayton was also ranked third in the state in capital investments.

A viable industry

Foundries and machine shops provided many Daytonians — more than 3,000 — with a good living at the turn of the century. One of the most well-known foundries: Dayton Malleable, which employed 700 to 800 men.

Bought...

The building at 800 W. Fifth St., for the West Side YWCA.

MILESTONE
A winged man

With plenty of kite-flying experiments under their belts, Wilbur and Orville Wright were ready to try flying their $15 glider, made of wood and covered with cotton sateen. But they needed steady winds of at least 15 to 20 mph. Where to find them?

Kitty Hawk, North Carolina, the weather bureau advised.

So off they went. Wilbur arrived on September 13, Orville about 10 days later; they set up camp and reassembled their crated glider, which had a 17-foot wingspan. The brothers passed their evenings at camp making music — Wilbur on his harmonica and Orville on his mandolin. They spent their days flying the glider like a kite, taking tests and measurements, making adjustments and minor repairs (which would have been major without sand-dune landings). It was time for their first manned glider flight. Orville laid out straight, face down, gliding down a long, sandy hill.

He did it again. And again. When he was lucky, he was airborne for 15 to 20 seconds on Kill Devil Hills, covering 300 to 400 feet each time. After a dozen flights — and a total of two minutes in the air — the Wrights were satisfied that their control system worked, and that they'd found errors in commonly accepted aeronautical data.

After three weeks, they headed back to Dayton. Time for a bigger and better glider.

The fate of that famous first glider? Kitty Hawk's Postmaster Bill Tate, who'd housed the brothers until they set up camp, took it apart and gave the sateen wing covering to his wife, who made new dresses for their two little girls. ∎

Top: An early glider at Kitty Hawk.

Above: The Conover Building at Third and Main still stands, now as the American Building.

Above right: Living conditions for the Wrights at Kitty Hawk were primitive.

Dayton statistics:

- Population: 85,000.
- Territory: 11.12 square miles.
- Reputation: A center of precision tool manufacturing (thanks to companies like National Cash Register, Ohmer Fare Register and Davis Sewing Machine).
- Industrial firms: 350.
- Retail establishments: 500-plus.
- Average work week: 55 to 60 hours.
- Average factory wage: $9 per week.
- Labor union members: 5,300.
- National banks: Seven.
- Rent for a typical seven-room home: $12.50 a month.

1901

Testing the wind

Their 1900 Kitty Hawk experiments had convinced the Wrights that accepted aerodynamic data was wrong. Back at the bike shop, they put their two-wheelers to work on aerodynamic experiments: By quickly pedaling an air-pressure test bike, they could simulate wind. When that wasn't enough, the brothers built the first wind tunnel to test the behavior of a model glider. Meanwhile, the Wrights corresponded regularly with Octave Chanute, the country's great glider expert. Chanute visited Wilbur and Orville in June.

South for the summer

Armed with new theories — and a bigger and better glider (which weighed 100 pounds and had a 22-foot wingspan) — the Wrights returned to Kitty Hawk on July 10, gliding 100 times over distances of 300 to 400 feet. In spite of the glider's "sled-runner" skids, the brothers found their new machine was far from perfect and was unprotected during wayward landings. (In fact, this new glider seemed more difficult to control than their 1900 model.)

The Wrights' last manned flight this year ended in a crash that cut Wilbur's face, bruised his nose and blackened his eye. But the pair persisted, flying the glider again — this time like a kite. They controlled wing warping from the ground, but the glider simply would not behave. They still had a long way to go.

Wilbur, disappointed, wrote: "At this time I made the prediction that man would sometime fly, but that it would not be in our lifetime." ■

Top left: The Wrights built nearly all of the gear they used to test aerodynamic concepts, including this early wind tunnel.

Top right: Ice skaters welcomed cold weather when the surface of the Great Miami froze solid.

Above: NCR posters stressed simplicity and time savings.

Tried...

The first "electrolysis" case in Dayton. Cities across the country watched *City of Dayton vs. The City Railway* with interest, since electrolysis problems — in which railway current damaged underground water and gas lines — had sprung up elsewhere, too. A verdict came in 1902, with the railway ordered to make changes to contain its electrical current.

Dedicated and opened...

Dayton's Union Station, on July 27.

Strength in numbers

Machinists at the National Cash Register Company, 2,300 in all, banded together and threatened a strike, betting that John H. Patterson would give in to their demands. Patterson, bitter and disenchanted, felt betrayed but accepted some of their demands.

Won...

The Western League pennant, by the Dayton Vets baseball team.

Trial balloons

Transportation was changing, and the canal — if it were to survive — had to change with the times. If it was speed people wanted, then how about steam-powered paddle boats? Why not tow boats with an electric mule? Alas, the steam-powered paddles tore up the banks. And the company formed to build tracks for the proposed "mule" was accused of really just trying to get a right-of-way for building a railroad. The Miami and Erie Canal simply refused to die quietly.

Eureka!

Data the Wright brothers collected during their Dayton wind-tunnel experiments didn't disappoint. The brothers flew their third glider, the biggest yet, about 1,000 times at Kitty Hawk in September and October. Flights went some 600 feet and lasted about a minute each. Confident they had confirmed their newly developed principles of flight — which included a tail that moved vertically like a bird's, preventing tailspins — the Wrights returned to Dayton in October. The next step: developing the engine and propellers needed to keep their machine in the air.

Running full tilt

The efficient Corliss engine, named in honor of inventor George H. Corliss, was moved to NCR's power house to provide electricity and steam heat for the company. The 210-ton engine, which took up 950 square feet of floor space, produced 800 kilowatts of power at full tilt. NCR used two Corliss engines until 1948.

The city's crown jewel

Construction started on Dayton's Arcade. The Third Street facade, designed by architect Frank Andrews, was presumably inspired by an Amsterdam guild hall.

ID, please

Mugshots were never the same after Dayton police adopted the Bertillon system for photographing criminals. In addition to shooting front and side photos of a thug, they recorded 11 precise body measurements — including the "width of cheeks" and the "length of right ear." The next step, according to police, was "... to note the bodily shape and all mental and moral qualities that may be exhibited. Lastly, all marks and scars are carefully measured and fully recorded."

They dabbled in art

Budding artists could carve wood, make jewelry and do other crafts with the Dayton Society of Arts and Crafts, the city's first organized arts group. It was, sadly, short-lived.

Formed...

The Dayton Teachers' Club.

Pictured in later years, the Arcade was a showplace, with a grand entrance off Third Street (above), a vast market with unusual food items (right) and a series of specialty shops (below). It was designed by architect Frank Andrews.

1903

Motor power

Efficient motors — light but powerful — were hard to come by, so the Wrights worked with bicycle mechanic Charlie Taylor to build and test their own 12-horsepower, 179-pound motor for their flyer. To avoid disturbing neighbors, the courteous brothers ran daytime tests, when most folks were at work.

Some assembly required

The first Wright Flyer was so big that it couldn't be fully assembled in the bicycle shop workroom on West Third. (In fact, the flyer's center section prevented the brothers from getting to the front of the shop. Customers had to wait patiently while one of the Wrights slipped out the side door and came around front.) Orville and Wilbur assembled the entire flyer after they returned to Kitty Hawk on September 25. They used bike parts — such as oversized chains, sprockets, spoke wire, tubular steel, ball bearings and modified wheel hubs — to build the aeroplanes flown from 1903 to 1905.

Who should fly first?

The brothers flipped a coin. Orville won. It was December 17.

First in flight

The first Wright Flyer was a clumsy-looking, 750-pound machine in which the pilot lay on his stomach. The weather cooperated that day: With winds ranging from 24 to 27 mph, Orville and Wilbur made four flights:
- 10:35 a.m.: Orville flew for 12 seconds, covering 120 feet.
- 11 a.m.: Wilbur flew for 12 seconds, covering 175 feet.
- 11:40 a.m.: Orville flew for 15 seconds, covering 200 feet.
- Noon: Wilbur flew for 59 seconds, covering 852 feet.

No glory

The nation — and Dayton, surprisingly enough — were slow to grasp the accomplishment. The Dayton *Evening Herald* ran a brief story on December 18 touting the brothers' achievements with perhaps a bit of embellishment: "Machine Makes High Speed in the Teeth of a Gale and Lands at the Point Selected" (actually, the Wrights were at the wind's mercy for their landings). The *Dayton Daily News* was ahead in breaking the story in its second edition on December 18. It included portraits of the Wright brothers and the headline: "Dayton Boys Emulate Great Santos-Dumont."

Cost-effective

After spending only $5,000, the Wrights had achieved successful powered flight. (Other would-be pilots had spent much more without success: Sir Hiram Maxim spent $200,000 and Samuel Pierpont Langley spent $100,000.) ■

Top: The footprints of careful assistants follow the path of the Wright Flyer. They supported the wings during early test runs.

Middle and above: Kitty Hawk provided nearly ideal conditions for testing the Wrights' aircraft. It also provided spartan living conditions.

WRIGHT FLYER.

Clever Device of Bishop Wright's Sons.

REMARKABLE ACCOMPLISHMENT OF TWO OF DAYTON'S INDUSTRIOUS YOUNG MEN.

Gratifying Success Reported With Excellent Prospects of Achieving Complete Success With Their New Flying Machine.

Bishop Milton Wright of this city has received a telegram from his sons, Wilbur and Orville Wright, who are at Kitty Hawks, North Carolina, the fourth autumn, experimenting in gliding through the air on aeroplane of their own make, and regulated by devices of their own invention. The telegram says that they have had gratifying success with their flying machine, built the present year by them in this city. The Wright Flyer, as they call it, is a double-decked, curved aeroplane, driven by a small but powerful gasoline motor with aerial screw propellers. The telegram is as follows:

Kitty Hawk, N. C., Dec. 17.

Bishop M. Wright, 7 Hawthorn street.—We have made four successful flights this morning, all against a 11-mile wind. We started from level, with engine power alone. Our average speed through the air was 31 miles. Our longest time in the air was 57 seconds.

ORVILLE WRIGHT.

A telegram from Wilbur Wright, received by his father the 15th inst., stated that success was assured, but some misjudgment at the start had retarded their first flight, and limited

Women physicians

The first two women to practice medicine in Dayton were Gertrude Felker and Eleanora S. Everhard, who worked jointly for more than 40 years.

They got him back

John H. Patterson persuaded Col. E. A. Deeds, 29, a former NCR employee, to return to Dayton to manage engineering and construction for the Cash. Deeds had been in Niagara Falls supervising the building of a model shredded-wheat factory.

Retired: Canal boats

The state, pressured by a public fed up with the canal, decided not to renew its lease with a company that used mules to pull barges. The canal slowly faded away.

Constructed...

One of the first concrete bridges in the United States, over the Great Miami River at Main Street, for $128,000.

Above: Veterans at the Soldiers' Home.

Right: News of the Wrights' first flight reached members of the local press, who at first were unimpressed. This story in the *Evening Herald* ran on page 12.

Below: An aerial photograph — made from a balloon — shows Steele High School (lower right) and buggies crossing the Main Street bridge. A small clearing near the center of the river basin is believed to have been the balloon's launching site.

1904

Huffman Prairie: The world's first flying field

Torrence Huffman loaned his 68-acre cow pasture eight miles east of Dayton to the Wrights for flight experiments. (Huffman's only request: Could the aviators shoo the cows before takeoffs?)

They shrugged it off

The first successful flight of the new 1903 Wright Flyer came on May 26 after a two-day weather postponement. Reporters invited to watch weren't impressed with the 60-foot jaunt. In fact, they remained unimpressed for two years, though the Wrights flew practice flights about every day.

Developed...

A new catapult launching device, which let the Wrights take off in light winds. On September 15 Wilbur made a half-circle, which was followed by the first complete circle on September 20. The longest flight to date was on November 9, when Wilbur circled Huffman Prairie four times in five minutes. (In spite of these achievements, short flights and accidents remained the norm.)

'The grandest sight of my life'

Amos Ives Root, a Medina, Ohio beekeeper, saw Wilbur's September 20 flight, wrote a magazine article about the men and their magnificent flying machine, and fired it off to *Scientific American* and other publications, which promptly dismissed the story as false. Root published the article he called "What Hath God Wrought" in his own magazine, *Gleanings in Bee Culture*. It was the first eyewitness account of an aeroplane in flight:

"The machine is held until ready to start by a sort of trap to be sprung when all is ready; then with a tremendous flapping and snapping of the four-cylinder engine, the huge machine springs aloft. When it first turned that circle, and came near the starting-point, I was right in front of it; and I said then, and I believe still, it was ... the grandest sight of my life. Imagine a locomotive that has left its track and is climbing up in the air right toward you — a locomotive without any wheels, we will say, but with white wings instead ... coming right toward you with a tremendous flap of its propellers, and you will have something like what I saw. The younger brother bade me move to one side for fear it might come down suddenly; but I tell you friends, the sensation one feels in such a crisis is something hard to describe. When Columbus discovered America he did not know what the outcome would be, and no one at that time knew.... In a like manner these two brothers have probably not even a faint glimpse of what their discovery is going to bring to the children of men."

Top: The Wrights continued their flying experiments at home, on Huffman Prairie.

Above: The Dayton Lighting Company's promotional sign lit up the corner of Fifth and Ludlow.

Name change

Protestant Deaconess Hospital, renamed Miami Valley Hospital, moved to its current location south of downtown.

An opening gala — Arcade-style

Dayton celebrated the completion of part one of the Arcade by hosting a grand, three-day festival starting March 4. People loved the domed archway and the "super" market, which featured unusual fruits and vegetables, seafood, baked goods, specialty foods, meats, fresh flowers and other luxury items in specialty shops. A band played as shoppers enjoyed palm and orange trees, exotic decorations and caged animals from the Cincinnati Zoo — even an alligator. Said one account: "... it is a fairyland of life and color."

Little time for bicycles

Obsessed by their aeroplane, the Wrights moved out of the bicycle business, building no new bikes after 1904.

R&R

National Cash Register's recreation program began after John H. Patterson allowed employees to use part of his Hills and Dales estate.

Constructed...

Another addition to the Algonquin Hotel, which brought its room total to 300. Still a bustle of activity were Dayton's two other prominent hotels: the Phillips House and Beckel House.

Hired...

Charles F. Kettering, by Col. E.A. Deeds, to electrify the cash register.

Subscribed...

4,094 citizens, to the Dayton Bell Telephone Exchange.

Organized...

The Dayton Breweries Company, with Adam Schantz as president. At one point, Dayton was quite a brewing center, with nearly 30 local breweries in operation.

Top left: The Dayton YMCA became the Auditorium Theater, and later the State Theater.

Top right: The Callahan Bank building

Above: Miami Valley Hospital

1905

MILESTONE

Third time's a charm

Wilbur and Orville got to work May 23 on their third powered flying machine, and by June 23, she was ready to go.

One of the brothers controlled the aeroplane by laying on the lower wing, left of the engine, and moving his hips from side to side to operate the wing-warping system. But despite the improvements, this flyer was no better than last year's. Every day brought wrecks and damage. The worst was on July 14, when the flyer slammed to the ground, requiring considerable repairs (Orville walked away with only bumps and bruises).

By August 24, the Wrights were back in the air with the rebuilt flyer, which this time performed beautifully: Flights lasted several minutes, accidents disappeared, landings were smooth. By September 26, Wilbur remained airborne for 18 minutes. After that, each flight outlasted the one before. For more than 39 minutes on October 5, Wilbur circled Huffman Prairie 30 times in the Wright Flyer III, covering 24.5 miles, landing only when he ran out of fuel. It was the longest flight to date.

World's first practical aeroplane

After one kite (1899), three manned gliders (1900, 1901 and 1902), and three powered airplanes (1903, 1904 and 1905), the Wrights had finally, really, learned to fly. Their aeroplane could remain in flight for an extended time — controlled completely by the pilot — and then land without crashing. And by this time, the word was out. The *Dayton Daily News* reported on October 5 that the Wrights were flying daily.

(One reporter offered a Wright family friend $50 for word of the next flight date.) Suddenly, there was a scramble to watch the machine in action, take photographs and talk to the inventors — who just as suddenly grew gun-shy. Everything they had worked for, including the potential for great financial rewards, could be lost if too many details of their work were disclosed before they got a patent.

So the Wrights put away their aeroplane — and didn't fly again until 1908. ■

Left: This early photo captured the first practical airplane. By 1905, routine, controlled flight was a reality.

SLICE OF LIFE

The great divide

The Barney & Smith Car Company produced its first steel railroad car this year; workmen skilled in crafting the elegant wooden cars of yesteryear were left by the wayside.

Unskilled workers had to be found. The company turned to J.D. Moskowitz — a foreign-labor contractor who had created a successful colony of Hungarian workers for Dayton Malleable on the west side — to establish a similar work force.

Moskowitz's Kossuth Colony, a self-contained, walled community of Hungarian immigrants, covered four blocks north of Dayton on Leo Street. It included 40 five-room doubles, a clubhouse and huge bar, bank, grocery, general store and even a travel agency so residents could bring their Hungarian relatives to Dayton. Kossuth dwellers who bought products outside the colony risked firing and expulsion. While their weekly wage was less than the U.S. average — $9 for a 55-hour work week — residents paid only $8 to $10 monthly for board and laundry.

Arrived...

Frank M. Tait, from Pennsylvania, to run what would become the Dayton Power and Light Company, starting January 1. Tait's legacy includes working with Thomas A. Edison and extending high-tension lines to nearby towns.

For their own good

Light? Air? Safety? These basics were all but ignored in the construction of many new buildings in Dayton, and physicians protested to City Council that a building code was needed. But between scarce funds and a complacent public, the code wasn't adopted until 1916.

Established...

The Dayton Steel Foundry Company, in a cornfield, by George Walther. It made small steel castings for cars.

A big, red fire truck

It was a "bright red contraption, complete with brass trimmings, lamps and gong" that Fire Chief Daniel C. Larkin brought to Dayton in September. It could hit 25 mph.

Reorganized...

The Mead Paper Company, to avoid bankruptcy. Later, manufacturing was consolidated in Chillicothe, with a small office in Dayton's Reibold building.

Dayton-made autos

Charles Stoddard went to Europe to study auto manufacturing, and returned to join his father, John, in establishing the Dayton Motor Car Company in the Stoddard Manufacturing plant, which had stopped making farm equipment in 1904. By fall, they'd sold three Stoddard-Dayton autos. Few things were considered "standard," with extras including the windshield ($75), solar lamps ($150 per set), speedometer ($75) and a mohair top ($150).

Granted...

A patent, on May 22, protecting the control system on the Wrights' aeroplane. Meanwhile, the brothers sought buyers, meeting for two years with financiers and government purchasing agents. No contract until 1908.

An opulent church

Dedicated: St. Mary's Church, a richly grand, Romanesque building with colored windows from Germany, carved marble altars from Italy, and an inlaid marble mosaic sanctuary floor.

Entered...

The first class at Stivers High School.

Held...

The first service in the First Lutheran Church, at First and Wilkinson streets.

Renamed...

The Park Theater (the old Gebhart Opera House), to The Lyric Theater.

Above left: Paul Laurence Dunbar died in Dayton on February 9, at age 33. His grave is in Woodland Cemetery.

Above: Dunbar, who was a heavy drinker, is believed to have suffered with tuberculosis.

1907

Utility competitors

It was a war of utilities: Dayton Citizens Electric Company, a Dayton Lighting Company rival, built another coal-fired steam and power plant. In 1907, customers paid 15 cents per kilowatt hour of electricity.

Useless sinkhole?

More and more folks were getting sick of the canal — not the least of whom was John H. Patterson, who organized the Anti-Canal Association to get rid of the thing. He believed the dirty waterway threatened the public health, and was also a "useless sinkhole for the people's money."

New Dayton carmaker

Dayton's Speedwell Motor Car Company, which began making the Speedwell this year, turned out 25 cars in 1907.

Strength in numbers

The Dayton Federation of Clubs, spearheaded by Marie J. Kumler, united women's clubs when members realized they could be more effective by banding together. (Also organized: the Dayton College Women's Club.)

Joined...

The Dayton-Springfield-Urbana electric interurban railway, to the Ohio Electric Railway System. Locals called the DSU the "Damned Slow and Uncertain."

Named...

Frederick H. Rike, born in 1867 to David and Salome Rike, as president of the Rike Dry Goods Company.

Purchased...

Battery-powered buses by the National Cash Register Company to ferry employees to and from work, in response to poor service by the Oakwood trolley.

Experimented...

The Wrights, with a hydroplane, on the Great Miami River.

Dedicated...

First Lutheran Church, at the southeast corner of First and Wilkinson streets, a year after the first service was held.

Above: Orville Wright (left) conducted experiments with a hydroplane on the Great Miami River.

Below: The entrance to Woodland Cemetery.

SLICE OF LIFE

Purest of the pure

A committee formed to demand pure milk for Dayton's children — after which milk had to be "certified" according to the law: Cows were milked by electric machines, and had to be healthy, clean and well-cared-for in sanitary barns by white-uniformed attendants. The public willingly paid the higher prices for certified milk in exchange for peace of mind.

A well-known reputation

Dayton was known throughout the country for its "variety of manufactories" for a city of its size.

In memoriam

Funds were appropriated for downtown's Memorial Hall, built to honor the area's Civil War veterans, and construction got under way.

Top: Wilbur Wright directed the setup of his demonstration airplane in Le Mans, France.

Middle: Orville Wright demonstrated a Wright Type A airplane in Fort Myer, Virginia.

Above: Orville was injured and his passenger killed in a crash during a demonstration.

MILESTONE

At last — a dotted line to sign on

The Wrights won their first contract February 10, agreeing to deliver and demonstrate to the U.S. Signal Corps an airplane — flying with a pilot and passenger — before August 28. The demo had to last one hour and cover 125 miles, flying at 40 mph or faster. In March, a French syndicate contracted to produce and sell Wright airplanes. Part of the agreement: a demonstration in France, with a flight speed of at least 50 kilometers per hour.

Hauling out the old Flyer

Wilbur and Orville got to work immediately. For the machine to accommodate a passenger, changes were in order for the 1905 Wright Flyer III, which needed upright seating, a new engine and hand controls. Final test flights were made in secret at Kitty Hawk on May 6-14. On the last day of testing, the Wrights' machinist and mechanic, Charley Furnas, made history as the world's first airplane passenger.

Arrived...

Wilbur, in France, in August, where he demonstrated the Wright Type A airplane at the Hunaudieres race course near Le Mans. Wilbur made 113 flights — 60 with passengers — logging 26 hours in the air between August 1908 and January 1909.

The first female airplane passenger was Madame Hart O. Berg from France. After making the historic flight with Wilbur, Madame hobbled off the airplane. The reason: Her husband had tied a cord around her skirt, just above her ankles, to keep it from flapping immodestly in the wind.

Arrived...

Orville, at Fort Myer, Virginia, in September, where he demonstrated another Wright Type A airplane for the U.S. Signal Corps beginning September 3. ■

SLICE OF LIFE

Disaster

During demonstrations on September 17, Orville's right propeller blade broke when the plane was 100 feet in the air. The crash killed passenger Lt. Thomas E. Selfridge and injured Orville, who suffered a fractured thigh, broken ribs, scalp wounds and back injuries. Selfridge's death was the first military aviation casualty. Tending to Orville, hospitalized in Washington for seven weeks, was his sister, Katharine Wright.

World records

Shortly after the accident, which disturbed Orville greatly, Wilbur flew for 90 minutes, a world record. (Said Wilbur: "This will cheer Orville up.") Later that year Wilbur flew for 2 hours and 20 minutes, another world record, winning the Michelin prize of $4,000.

1908

Enter the 'barn gang'

Behind the home of Col. E.A. Deeds at 319 Central Ave., in an old barn, there was a meeting of great minds. Deeds and his NCR co-worker Charles F. Kettering believed great fortunes could be had in the automobile industry. The two began tinkering in Deeds' barn in their spare time, experimenting with a car they called "Suburban Sixty." Soon the two had developed the first auto ignition system, which led to the invention of the electric self-starter in 1912. Later, NCR employee William A. Chryst, who dubbed Kettering "Boss," joined the "barn gang."

A feather in Dayton's cap

The world's second-largest YMCA building was built in Dayton at Third and Ludlow on a site donated by Mary Bell Eaker. Later, it became Dayton City Hall. The old YMCA building at 32 E. Fourth St. became the State Theater.

Merged...

The Dayton Exchange, the Board of Trade, the Boosters Club and the Commercial Club, to form the Dayton Chamber of Commerce.

Won...

A seat in the U.S. House of Representatives, by Ohio Democrat and newspaper publisher James M. Cox. He served the state's Third District until 1913.

Manufactured...

600 sewing machines and 600 bicycles a day, by the Davis Sewing Machine Company.

Name change

The Rike Dry Goods Company became the Rike-Kumler Company.

Established...

The Dayton Pump and Manufacturing Company, by Frank M. Tait.

Produced...

100 Speedwell autos this year, by the Speedwell Motor Car Company.

Subscribed...

9,003 citizens, to the Dayton Bell Telephone Exchange.

Above: Walton, Anderson and Chryst worked in Deeds' barn.

Left: Kettering's drawing for the first auto ignition system. Witnesses' signatures are in the lower-right corner.

Below: Deeds' barn has been moved from its original site to the Kettering-Moraine Museum.

They got a free lunch

Thomas Elder celebrated the 25th anniversary of the Boston Dry Goods store by giving women free lunches. His promotion attracted so many customers that Elder continued the practice.

A French excursion

Orville and Katharine Wright sailed in January to Pau, France, where Wilbur trained three French pilots and flew for dignitaries.

She cheered them on

Katharine Wright flew with Wilbur for seven minutes, four seconds on February 15 at Pau. It was her first airplane ride. She and her brothers went to Rome, where Wilbur trained two Italian pilots and flew for King Victor Emmanuel. Katharine had become her brothers' confidante and counselor, hostess and cook, press agent and official correspondent.

Welcome home

The trio returned to Dayton on May 13, arriving by train to the sound of church bells, factory whistles and cannonfire. They were driven home in a carriage drawn by four white horses.

Model A is No. 1

The Army's Aeronautical Division accepted the Wright Model A, the first U.S. military aircraft, on August 2. Dubbed Signal Corps Airplane No. 1, the $30,000 craft could fly 47 mph for more than an hour and carry a pilot and passenger upright.

Flew...

Wilbur, around the Statue of Liberty, on September 29. Under the airplane was tied a canoe, just in case. On October 4, New Yorkers gawked as he flew 10 miles along the Hudson River, providing most with their first sight of an airplane in flight.

A company is born

The brothers created the Wright Company on November 22 to manage production and distribution. A factory was established in Dayton with corporate headquarters in New York. Orville ran daily operations while Wilbur fought patent infringers in court. ■

The real celebration

The inventors were honored at the Wright Brothers' Home Celebration June 17-18. Thousands assembled to show their pride for Dayton's hometown heroes. After a Main Street parade came a reception at the YMCA and fireworks over the Great Miami. The next day the Wrights received three gold medals — from Congress, the Ohio General Assembly and the city of Dayton — in a ceremony before 75,000 at the fairgrounds. Behind the stage, 5,000 children dressed in red, white and blue formed a huge American flag.

Top: When Katherine Wright (also pictured above left) flew with her brother Wilbur at Pau, France, she tied her skirts to protect against the wind — and to be modest.

Above: Orville and Wilbur Wright with King Edward III.

1909

Inventors establish Delco

Dayton Engineering Laboratories Company was founded in July, after Cadillac's Henry Leland ordered 5,000 ignition systems from barn gang members E.A. Deeds and Charles F. Kettering. Deeds became Delco's president and Kettering vice president. Both were on the threshold of industrial greatness. "Boss Kett" quit the Cash this year, eager to produce an electric ignition system.

Property exchanges

Ohio paid $80,000 for the Shaker community farm. The State Mental Hospital used the buildings and land until the 1940s. The state continued farming the land until 1981, when it was turned into the Miami Valley Research Park.

Dayton winner

The winner of the first car race at Indianapolis was a Stoddard-Dayton auto, with an average speed of 57.3 mph.

Completed...

Construction of Memorial Hall, begun in 1907.

Trolley days

Dayton had 100 miles of street railway tracks.

Renamed...

Union Biblical Seminary, to Bonebrake, four years after John M. Bonebrake donated 3,840 acres of Kansas farmland to the seminary.

Manufactured...

The Courier auto, by the Courier Car Company.

Above: Wheeler Lovell and Charles Kettering worked together on the auto ignition system.

Women helping women

Female employees at Aull Brothers and Kinnard's regularly enjoyed hot lunches provided by the Young Women's League, which prepared 20,000 such meals annually. The league's purpose: to help "business and wage-earning women." Its 818 members taught 11,000 local women sewing, millinery, embroidery, cooking, stenography, bookkeeping, English literature, gymnastics and other skills. To pay off a $23,500 debt on its West Fourth Street headquarters, the league sponsored numerous fund-raisers. One of those allowed the league to be publisher-for-a-day of the *Dayton Daily News*, with proceeds from that day's paper sales going to the club. League members printed copy from Teddy Roosevelt, Mark Twain, the late Paul Laurence Dunbar and Booker T. Washington.

City statistics

Dayton's 1,200 factories had an annual output of $45 million. According to one account: "Dayton HAS — Good health, cheap fuel, progressive spirit and modern methods. "Dayton LEADS — The cities of the world in the output of autographic registers, automatic indicating, recording and printing cash registers, automatic toys, diversity of automobile parts, bookbinders' machinery, building and loan associations, cash registers, cast iron fittings, clay-working machinery, computing scales, cast iron vases, and cement tools, duck clothing, filters, fine-cut tobacco-cutting machinery, hoisting jacks, railway cars, sewing machines, shoe lasts and golf clubs, US stamped envelopes and US stamped envelope paper." Dayton was also dubbed a "City of Homes" because of its top national ranking in the number of people who owned homes.

Some famous firsts

The world's first commercial cargo flight left Dayton November 7. Phillip O. Parmalee, with $800 worth of silk strapped in the passenger seat, took off from Huffman Prairie and headed for the Morehouse-Martens Company in Columbus. Flight time: about an hour. Enroute, Parmalee enjoyed a sack lunch Orville gave him — the first in-flight meal. Parmalee's flight and subsequent air show cost Columbus merchant Max Morehouse $5,000. Morehouse cashed in by selling the famous silk, and peddling postcards of the flight with a bit of the cloth attached.

From here to there

Built this year was Dayton's largest interurban station, across from the library at Third and Kenton streets, by the Ohio Electric Railway. Later, it became the station for the Cincinnati and Lake Erie Bus Company. Interurban coaches — which traveled from 6 a.m. to 11 p.m. at 75 mph or more — were quite cozy, complete with overhead luggage racks, warm wooden interiors, brass hardware, leather seats and fancy ceiling lights. Farm wives liked to ride to town on the interurban, shop for the day and make it home in time to cook supper; traveling salesmen liked it, too. Besides passengers, the interurbans carried light packages, mail and produce. (On Halloween, the motorman and the conductor had to be on the lookout for pranksters who liked to pull the trolley off the wire, killing its power.)

Groundbreaking...

In January, at 2701 Home Road in Dayton, for the new Wright Company factory.

Founded...

Mike-Sell's Potato Chip Company.

Above: Main Street, looking north.

1910

A meeting place is born

Memorial Hall was dedicated January 5. It cost $250,000 to build.

Extended...

Electric service, in December, to West Carrollton, making it the first Dayton suburb to have the modern-day convenience.

They PAYEd up

Dishonest street railway conductors could no longer pocket spare change once PAYE cars came into use. The "Pay As You Enter" system let customers drop their money into a fare box before taking their seats.

The loan that Winters rejected

"Because newspapers don't make money, that's why," explained Valentine Winters to James M. Cox, who desperately wanted a loan to build a larger *Dayton Daily News* building. But Winters wouldn't budge. Cox, as the story goes, was outraged. He stormed off, somehow got the money he needed and told his architect: "Build me a damned bank." The result: an ornate, pillared, Italianate bank-like structure — more elegant than even Winters' bank itself — at the corner of Fourth and Ludlow.

Opened...

The West Dayton YMCA, to serve black Daytonians.

Standard equipment

Those able to afford a 1910 model Cadillac found their machine equipped with a new convenience: the single-spark ignition system, invented by Charles F. Kettering.

A knack for selling

It seemed John H. Patterson's sales methods had begun to pay off for NCR. The Cash had 95 percent of the cash register market.

Introduced...

The Wright Baby Grand Racer, at America's first international air show (the Belmont Park Flying Meet in New York). The racer's top speed: 80 mph. By now, Orville was training exhibition pilots, and the brothers opened the Wright School of Aviation in a hangar on Huffman Prairie.

**Top:
Memorial Hall**

Middle: Phillip Parmalee (right) dressed for the cold conditions he would encounter on his flight from Dayton to Columbus. It was the first commercial flight. Orville Wright is on the left, holding an oil can.

Below: Third Street took on a ghostly glow in this photograph made through the entrance to the Arcade.

Above: No longer used commercially, the canal had fallen into disrepair. This boat was abandoned behind the fairgrounds.

Below: The Wright School of Aviation was training pilots. Orville is third from the left.

Bottom: Students at the school learned balance aboard a tipping cart. Harry Atwood held a weighted board to simulate wings.

From New York to California

After 12 major accidents, two sprained ankles, a twisted back and a concussion, pilot Calbraith Rodgers — trained at the Wright School of Aviation — arrived December 10 in Long Beach, California, after an 84-day flight from Long Island, New York. It was the nation's first coast-to-coast flight. Rodgers flew 4,231 miles in 82 hours and 4 minutes in the airplane called VIN FIZ, after his soft-drink sponsor.

Frederick's folly

A department store with its own power plant? Other businessmen laughed at Frederick Rike, who was building a monstrous seven-story structure, complete with an elevator and dining room, at Second and Main. Bankers in Dayton and New York had denied Rike's request for a loan, which he finally won from an insurance company. The building's cost: $1 million. Nevertheless, the Rike-Kumler Company was beloved in Dayton. Said a *Dayton Daily News* editorial March 11: "There is no single firm that more typifies Dayton.... It has been essentially a Dayton enterprise. The people connected with it have helped to make the city."

Changed...

The name of The Hills and Dales Railway Company, to the Dayton Power and Light Company, on May 5. Frank M. Tait became the company's first president in October.

Parts of the whole

Orville Wright found bits and pieces of the 1905 Wright Flyer at the Kill Devil Hills campsite, where he had returned to test a new unpowered glider in October. He saw no value in the remains, which, he said, "were so badly damaged by the weather and the field mice that have made an abode of them." In November, the remains were shipped to a Pittsfield, Massachusetts, museum with Orville's permission. When museum proprietor Zenas Crane asked Orville for the remaining parts so the museum could reconstruct the plane, Orville refused, convinced Crane's workers could not get it right. Reluctantly, Crane stored the remnants in the basement.

Orville, meanwhile, set a world record at Kill Devil Hills by gliding for 9 minutes and 45 seconds on October 24.

Manufactured...

The Dayton electric auto, by the Dayton Electric Car Company.

Accepted...

Solutions, proposed by the railway companies to the city of Dayton, for stopping electrolysis, which was damaging underground water and gas lines. Two of these solutions required the railway companies to maintain the system.

1912

Death of a great inventor

It was a sad day for Dayton when Wilbur Wright died of typhoid fever, a common disease at the time, on May 30. He was 45.

From publisher to governor

Newspaper publisher James M. Cox, a Democrat, won the Ohio gubernatorial election. Under his leadership was passed a landslide of humanist legislation: a workmen's compensation act, mothers' pension law, children's code and penal-system changes.

Indicted...

John H. Patterson and 29 other NCR officials, in February by a federal grand jury. The charge: restraint of trade. The trial began November 20.

Opened...

The new Rike-Kumler store at Second and Main, in March. It was, the *Evening Herald* proclaimed, "a splendid commercial palace to give Dayton rank with greatest cities."

Out with the crank

At last, "Boss Kett" had done it. He had started a car without cranking. The electric self-starter — Charles F. Kettering's greatest invention — debuted on 1912 Cadillacs.

Yeah, well — so much for quality control

The Dayton Motor Car Company turned out a Stoddard-Dayton-Knight car only after giving it 28 coats of paint (each sanded and buffed), making initial test drives and then disassembling and checking the car for problems. Each car was reassembled and then test-driven again before being sold. All that work may have been too much for the company, though — United States Motors, which acquired it, failed by 1913.

Built and dedicated...

The first known memorial to the Wrights, at Camp d'Auvours near Le Mans, France, where Wilbur flew in 1908. The black granite boulder says simply: "WILBUR ET ORVILLE WRIGHT, KITTY HAWK, 1903."

Above: James M. Cox was voted in as governor.

Left: The 1912 Cadillac was the first car to have a Delco self-starter ignition and lighting.

Below: Charles Kettering (at the wheel) and assistants tested the ignition system.

Right: The U.B. building, now known as the Centre City building, loomed over Main Street and the city jail.

Below: The Hoover Block (right) and the Setzer Building (second from right) were seen looking toward downtown. Both buildings are now part of Dayton's Aviation Trail.

Tragedy at the flying field

Frank J. Southard was killed in the first fatal Huffman Prairie air crash on May 21. Dayton photographer William Mayfield captured it on film.

Began...

Construction of Hawthorn Hill, the Wright family's Oakwood mansion named in honor of their Hawthorn Street home.

Organized...

The Montgomery County Art Association, by Miss Linda Clatworthy, to spark interest in art. The association (directed by Mrs. Henry Stoddard, president) organized lectures, exhibits and loans of pictures.

Opened...

■ Dayton's first emergency room, at Miami Valley Hospital.

■ NCR Auditorium, which brought culture to many.

Renamed...

■ The Automatic Pin Ticketing Company, founded in 1890, to Monarch Marking.

■ St. Mary's Institute, to St. Mary's College, which became the University of Dayton.

Elected...

Col. W.J. White, as governor of the Soldiers' Home.

Abandoned...

The Miami and Erie Canal. Finally.

SLICE OF LIFE

They wanted a say

Members of the Women's Suffrage Association of Dayton gave speeches and marched through town as they fought for the right to vote. Their leader was Jessie Leech Davisson.

1913

Rising water

The rain began on Easter Sunday, March 23. A severe flood seemed imminent by 7 a.m. Tuesday, March 25, when the gauge at the Great Miami River hit 24 feet. Wolf Creek and the Great Miami, Stillwater and Mad rivers, overpowered by constant, heavy rains, overflowed with a vengeance. Water burst levees, overran gutters, rose in the streets and marooned people for days on attics, rooftops and the upper floors of buildings. Nearly 4 trillion gallons of rain — the amount that cascades over Niagara Falls in a month — fell on the Dayton area on March 23-27. In downtown Dayton, the water was 12 feet deep.

Despite the many floods Dayton had suffered over the years, the 1913 disaster still took the city by surprise. People had convinced themselves such devastation could never happen.

Who took charge

John H. Patterson called a 6:45 a.m. emergency meeting with his top executives on March 25. He mobilized NCR to collect food, medicine, drinking water and the supplies needed to feed, shelter and care for the city's waterlogged residents. Patterson's meeting took 15 minutes. By noon, NCR was building flat-bottomed boats in assembly-line fashion, one every eight minutes. In an instant, the company became Dayton's flood-relief headquarters.

How some survived

■ As whirlpools swirled violently below, families crawled along phone wires to get to higher ground.

■ Dayton's librarian and her staff, marooned in the library's upper-floor museum, wrapped up in exotic animal hides to keep from freezing.

■ For four days, a Dayton Power and Light Company crew grabbed floating fruit and vegetables from the floodwaters and drank rainwater to survive.

■ At Union Station, 300 stranded passengers subsisted on a single box of chocolate creams.

Above: Photographer William Mayfield captured this view of the original Newcom Tavern building from the fire tower nearby. "I hurried down and the water was over my ankles up on the levee," he said. "By the time I could get down to the *News* building the water was over my knees as I went through the door."

Below: Boats replaced other means of transportation as flood waters covered East Fifth Street in the Oregon District.

Above: As the water continued to rise, people came out onto balconies and roofs to watch. This photograph was made from Gov. James M. Cox's office in the *Dayton Daily News* building, looking east on Fourth Street. Water was almost up to the second floor of some buildings.

1913

Babies were born

Mrs. Forrest Kuntz delivered twins in a boat sent to rescue her family. The rescuer-turned-midwife: Harry Schenck.

And then things got worse

After the waters came the explosions, and the fire. Had the city's gas been turned off early enough, Dayton may have been spared the $2 million in fire damage that followed. But the fire spread. Paint, turpentine and other volatile fluids fueled blast after blast at Lowe Brothers Paint Store.

Men at the Beaver Power Building, fearing the worst as the fire crept closer, formed a bucket brigade on the building's stairways from the first floor to the roof. They passed and tossed an estimated 10,000 pails of water in a last-ditch effort to keep the fire from the power building. Miraculously, it worked.

In the meantime, power company employee Edward W. Hanley dove deep into the water and swam to the valve room in an attempt to turn off the gas. Five times he resurfaced, gasping for air. Finally, he managed to shut the valve, and Dayton was spared from further explosions and fires.

Among the losers:

■ The Barney & Smith Car Company, whose shops were filled with 14 feet of water. The flood was the last straw for Dayton's first giant industry, which soon went into receivership.

■ Professor August Foerste, a nationally recognized scientist at Steele High School, who had researched the U.S. coastal structure for 20 years. His charts, maps, records, data and massive manuscript were swept from his office into the murky waters, lost forever.

■ Dayton's library, which lost 46,000 volumes.

■ Dayton Power and Light Company, with virtually all its overhead transmission and distribution lines destroyed downtown — a $300,000 loss.

■ Newsalt's jewelry store, which lost its inventory after entire jewelry cases smashed through store windows.

Above: Central High School was under about 10 feet of water in this view looking east on Fourth Street toward Wilkinson.

Also hit hard...

■ The Rike-Kumler Company, after eight feet of water crashed through its storefront. Frederick Rike refused to be daunted by his $200,000 loss, shoveling mud himself and resolving to come back. A commercial paper house loaned him enough money to rebuild and restock. (Rike's sole collateral: his reputation.) Rike-Kumler became one of the first Dayton businesses to reopen.

■ The Elder and Johnston Company, which lost $250,000 in merchandise recently moved to the first floor so the second floor could be remodeled. Like Rike, Elder appeared ruined, but he wasn't a quitter. Elder's friends from Boston pooled their resources and loaned him $100,000 to reopen. Included in Elder's remodeled store was an electric elevator, an ice plant — even an interior decorating service.

■ Farmers in the Miami Valley, whose fields were stripped of rich topsoil or covered with gravel and debris. They, too, got to work.

Rescued...

10,000 men, women and children, by the NCR boats. Before it was over, the Cash had built 300 of the boats, sent to pluck refugees from roofs and trees and remove them to safety. The refugees were cold, hungry, scared and in shock from watching family members and friends fall victim to the waters. Many stayed at the NCR factory, which served 2,750 meals daily, or in a tent city built by the National Guard on NCR property. Others were housed and fed in school buildings or private homes.

Extent of disaster slowly sinks in

After surveying the damage, George F. Burba, secretary to Ohio Gov. James M. Cox, telegraphed his boss: "Famine and sickness likely to ensue if extensive relief does not come promptly." Declaring his hometown a major disaster area, Cox told the Associated Press: "This is the greatest emergency this country has had to face since the Civil War."

Above: Debris filled the street at the corner of Fifth and Ludlow, looking east toward Main.

Declared...

Martial law, on Wednesday, March 26. Armed sentries patrolled the streets.

After the waters receded

Dayton was unrecognizable. Where there had been a booming city there was now mud, filth and destruction. Wrecked streetcars, pianos, autos, lumber, trash, pavement chunks and dead horses had been tossed haphazardly. Homes were in splinters. Scattered everywhere were timber, stray poles and tangled wires. (Miraculously, old Newcom Tavern — which stood in Van Cleve Park on Monument Avenue right in the path of the wave that burst forth from the levee — survived.)

The cleanup

Residents worked 12-hour days in the massive cleanup led by Patterson, whom Cox had named president of the Citizen's Relief Organization. Some 50,000 curiosity-seekers came from the outskirts to view the destruction, and Patterson angrily threatened to put them to work: "Those men carrying a camera on one arm and a female on the other are evidently not intending to work and will be questioned."

Who helped

More than $2 million came in from across the country; one donation ($5) came from as far away as Kennicott, Alaska. Army sanitary officers helped restore sewage, water and gas service. The government provided dry bread and bologna; men who had been millionaires stood in food lines with the common folk.

'It happened here'

Appearing in Dayton after the flood were postcards showing drowned horses, stiffened in grotesque positions.

Printed...

The *Dayton Daily News*, on presses at NCR, until operations downtown could be restored.

Found...

Teak and mahogany, from the Barney & Smith Car Company, as far downriver as New Orleans.

Damaged...

$100 million in land and buildings; 1,000 homes were destroyed.

Death toll

More than 300 lives were lost. Some said many more would have died had NCR not initiated its massive rescue effort in time.

1913

On April 20, Patterson called a community meeting to propose a $2 million flood-prevention fund, saying the city must do whatever it took to prevent another such catastrophe. Some scoffed at the effort, given the $100 million loss the city had just suffered. Nevertheless, Patterson and other pledge-takers appealed to people's sense of civic duty. Pledges were taken and recorded on a three-story cash register raised on the Old Court House lawn. Driving the campaign was the slogan, "Remember the promises made in the attic!"

When subscriptions closed May 25, the giant cash register said it all: Dayton had raised a whopping $2.15 million.

Patterson's committee took quick action, hiring the Morgan Engineering Company of Memphis to develop an extensive flood-control system for the Miami Valley. The brains behind it all was Arthur E. Morgan, known for similar projects in the lower Mississippi Valley. Later, after bonds were sold to finance the work, nearly all of Dayton's $2 million was returned to the original donors. ■

Top: Flood waters were powerful enough to overturn trolley cars.

Middle and below: Lost lives numbered more than 300, and about 1,000 homes were destroyed.

Right: The Elder and Johnston building was under construction, completing the last part of what is now the Reibold building.

Below: An aerial view of St. Mary's College, which became the University of Dayton, showed an expanding campus with a football stadium.

Adopted...

The Commission-Manager Plan of city government, also called "The Dayton Plan," on November 4. The plan called for electing five city commissioners who set policy while a city manager ran things; the commissioner with the most votes became mayor.

The verdict

The jury pronounced NCR's John H. Patterson and Thomas Watson guilty of restraint of trade for their aggressive campaign to thwart competitors in the cash register business. Patterson and Watson were fined $5,000 and sentenced to a year in jail. Other NCR executives, including Col. E.A. Deeds, were sentenced to nine months in jail. It was quite a scandal.

Cars OK'd

Woodland Cemetery reluctantly allowed autos onto the grounds this year, but only under strict conditions:

- Hours: Between 7 and 11 a.m.
- Speed limit: 8 mph.
- Autos must stop immediately if horses become frightened.
- No passing a horse.
- No smoking or dropping of oil.
- No horn honking.

Still, things sometimes went awry: Cars were known to take off rolling downhill, knocking over gravestones along the way.

Founded...

The Metropolitan Clothing Company, at Fourth and Ludlow, by Jacob H. Margolis, who believed Dayton needed a men's clothing store.

Changed...

The name of the Dayton Chamber of Commerce, founded in 1908, to the Greater Dayton Association.

Conducted...

More hydroplane experiments by Orville Wright on the Great Miami River south of Dayton.

1914

MILESTONE

Flood control: The first step

Passed by the Ohio General Assembly and signed by Gov. James M. Cox in February was the Ohio Conservancy Law, which called for damming the rivers around Dayton. The dams would handle twice the water of the 1913 flood.

No smooth sailing

Not everyone cheered. Dam construction promised to greatly inconvenience people in the northern Miami Valley, who had less to lose in another flood. Some folks proposed their own flood-control solutions: Why not build traps under the riverbed for catching floodwaters? Or how about installing giant paddlewheels to push water back upstream? The legal battles that began this year delayed construction until 1918.

Seeking eminent domain

Also filed in February in the Montgomery County Court of Common Pleas was a petition requesting formation of the Miami Conservancy District, which would have the legal rights to buy land for the flood-control system. It took another year to legally establish the district, which remains in place today. ■

A fine leader

Dayton's first city manager under the Dayton Plan that took effect January 2 was Henry M. Waite. He ran city government like a business and was instrumental in making Dayton a model city that was eyed over the next decade by other communities. Theodore M. Vail, president and publisher of *The New York World*, wired Waite with this message: "The experiment at Dayton is being watched with great interest. Do you think city managership could be applied to a city of a million, or even NY? Reply collect...."

Any and all causes

The Greater Dayton Association's activities ran the gamut, from conducting a window flower-box campaign, to compiling a directory of

Dayton-made goods, to holding down milk freight rates. In its *Bulletin*, the association published its opinion on many issues, great and small. Opined the April 18 issue: "The extermination of the winter fly is the duty of the housewife and of everyone.... They become the parents of summer's destructive swarms.... Catch them and kill them all now before they have had a chance to lay their eggs. Now is the time.... KILL FLIES NOW."

Top left: Henry M. Waite was Dayton's first city manager.

Top right: The Steele High School lion is now on the grounds of the Dayton Art Institute.

Above: The Wright family moved into Hawthorn Hill, at 901 Harmon Ave. in Oakwood.

They stole riders

Romanced by the thought of riding to town in an automobile, many streetcar riders in July ditched the trolleys and happily paid for a ride in a new jitney. The railways, caught off-guard, lost a lot of fares to the small motor cars — which appeared about the same time folks were complaining about the nasty habits of streetcar trainmen, known for spitting and littering.

Moved...

The Wright family, to their Hawthorn Hill home, 901 Harmon Ave. in Oakwood. According to one story, the family housekeeper once complained to Orville about mopping up the kitchen floor after the ice man dripped water on his way to the icebox. Ever clever, Orville removed the outside bricks behind the icebox and built a frame that allowed the ice man to place the 100-pound block into the box without coming inside.

Arrested...

A Philadelphia man, for jaywalking, after Dayton police started a crackdown this year. (Ironically, it was reported later that one of the man's children had been killed by a wagon in a Philadelphia street.)

Formed...

The Engineer's Club, by Col. E.A. Deeds and Charles F. Kettering. The club's first home was at Second and Madison streets.

Begun...

Construction on the Miami Hotel, Dayton's newest.

Defeated...

James M. Cox, seeking re-election as Ohio governor, by Frank B. Willis.

A heck of a deal

"If you were almost barefoot and a stranger offered to pay two-thirds of the cost of a new pair of shoes for you, would you take him up?" That's how the Greater Dayton Association explained why taxpayers should be happy to pay $1 million of the $3 million bill for elevating railroad tracks in Dayton — which promised to reduce wrecks and fatalities.

Appointed...

Two policewomen, for handling female lawbreakers and social problems.

Considered...

The hiring of blacks into white-collar positions under Dayton's new government, after a formal request by prominent black resident E.T. Banks. For the most part, City Hall didn't hire blacks until the civil-rights movement of the early 1960s.

Accident prone

The top accidents in Dayton in 1914 were:
- Auto accidents.
- Streetcar accidents.
- Falls.
- Motorcycle accidents.
- Shop accidents.
- Railroad accidents.

Printed matter

Dayton had become a large printing center, publishing 51 periodicals, many of them religious in nature, with a combined circulation of more than 1 million.

An ounce of prevention

Dayton physicians began routine exams of children to find and prevent diseases early.

Above: A blizzard couldn't keep movie fans away from the Columbia Theatre. The theater manager added to the drama, however, by keeping the doors locked until an impressive line formed for this photograph.

1915

Jitneys take off

Dayton's jitney fad of 1914 led to creation of the Jitney Transportation Company, which ran 12-passenger gasoline buses. The first regular run started on February 23 between downtown and Fairview Park, and was profitable practically overnight; in a week there were 300 daily riders.

Legally established...

The Miami Conservancy District, on June 28. In the name of flood control, the agency had unprecedented legal power to survey, appraise and purchase land in the Miami Valley; deepen and straighten channels; build dams, retarding basins and flood plains; and improve levees. Funds from Col. E.A. Deeds paid for district headquarters, which opened in 1916 at the corner of Main and Jefferson, overlooking the Great Miami River.

Created...

The Dayton chapter of the National Association for the Advancement of Colored People.

Above: An advertisement for Lily Brew beer urged readers to "Blot Out Dull-Care" with the product.

Below: The Soldiers' Home was a popular picnic spot.

Retired...

Orville Wright, from the airplane business, after selling his interest in the Wright Company for more than $500,000.

Opened...

The Fashion, at 123 S. Main St., to sell women's clothing. Later, the store moved to 17 S. Main St. and was renamed Thal's.

Dayton world leaders

The world knew Dayton for the airplane, the cash register and the bicycle. But other Dayton-based companies were world leaders in as many as 27 other industries. Among them:

■ Airless auto tires: The Dayton Rubber Manufacturing Company.

■ Automatic toys: Dayton Friction Toy Works.

■ Cast-iron vases: The Kramer Brothers Foundry Company.

■ Clothing (white duck): The Roehm-Richards Company.

■ Computing scales: The Computing Scale Company.

■ Fare-recording registers: The Ohmer Fare Register Company.

■ Golf clubs: The Crawford, McGregor & Canby Company.

■ Paper-trimming knives: The A.A. Simonds & Son Company.

■ Sealing wax for fruit jars: The Dicks-Pontius Company.

■ U.S. stamped envelopes: The Mercantile Corporation.

■ U.S. stamped envelope paper: The Aetna Paper Company.

Above: Coast-to-coast travelers stopped in Dayton and posed in front of the Johnson-Shelton store and the police station/market house.

Right: St. Mary's College would become the University of Dayton five years later.

Here one minute, gone the next

The city's new police cruiser looked great, but it was just a day old on August 22 when a reckless thief hopped in and stole the Ford from its parking spot right in front of City Hall. Nearby towns were on the lookout, but if the car was ever recovered, there's no record of it today.

Down and out

The Speedwell Motor Car Company folded this year, a late flood casualty. Other Dayton auto companies, however, introduced new models this year: the Darling Motor Car Company rolled out the Darling; the Apple Automobile Company made the Apple; and the Custer Specialty Company produced the electric Custer.

Torn down...

The fence around the Kossuth Colony. Parts of it had been used for rafts to save flood refugees.

Stopped...

Legal prostitution in Dayton.

1916

A big-bucks operation

The United States paid $1.5 million a year to run the Soldiers' Home, where 3,430 veterans lived. Among the benefits they enjoyed: 152 newspapers and 20 periodicals from across the country, and fresh milk from 75 cows kept on the grounds.

We even had pro football, for a while

The Dayton Triangles, formed this year, in 1920 became charter members of the nation's first professional football league — the American Professional Football Association. The Triangles relied on manager Carl "Scummy" Storck and quarterback Al Mahrt.

A historic closure

The Wright School of Aviation, where 119 civilian and military pilots had gotten their wings, closed after being sold by Orville Wright. Also this year: Orville moved into his new lab at 15 N. Broadway.

Above: The Dayton State Hospital baseball team.

Left: The Miami Paper exhibit in the Dayton Industrial Expo.

Below: Looking north on Main Street from Third Street.

Above: The last two fire horses in the city were Hans Wagner and Ty Cobb. They were replaced the next year by motorized fire engines.

Below: The Dayton State Hospital nurse graduating class of 1916 was proudly photographed in crisp, white uniforms.

Adopted...

An official building code, by Dayton City Commission.

Elected, again...

James M. Cox returned to Columbus as Ohio's governor, after having been beaten in 1915. He served two more terms, from 1917 to 1921.

Opened...

St. Ann's Maternity Hospital, with 20 beds.

Sold...

Delco, by the barn gang, to United Motors Corporation, which later joined General Motors.

Merged...

Miami Commercial College and Jacobs College.

Formed...

The Business and Professional Woman's Club, in the spring.

Purchased...

The former home of Robert Steele, 225 N. Wilkinson St., by the Dayton Woman's Club, which used it as headquarters. It's thought to be the oldest residential structure left downtown.

Founded...

The Danis Company.

SLICE OF LIFE

Dayton stats:

- Population: 140,000.
- Factory output: $143 million.
- Factory employees: 36,000.
- Manufacturers: 600.
- Retailers: 3,000.
- Churches: 133.
- Steam-railroad passengers: 1,364,144.
- Interurban passengers: 3,660,445.
- Street railways: 11 lines operating 115 miles of track.
- Streets: 280 miles (95 miles paved).
- Motion-picture theaters: 40.

An offer you couldn't refuse

To promote sales of electric irons, stores gave away a folding ironing board with each iron purchased.

1917

America joins the war to end all wars

The United States entered World War I on April 6. Some 1,500 Daytonians volunteered, black and white alike, and 5,000 more were drafted. Draft-dodging was common, however; public places were often raided to nab men without registration cards.

Dayton Wright Airplane Company

If airplanes could help win the war, America had to figure out how. The Dayton Wright Airplane Company — organized on April 9 for aeronautical research and development by Col. E.A. Deeds, Charles F. Kettering, H.E. Talbott and H.E. Talbott Jr. — was important to the war effort. By August the Moraine-based company was gearing up to produce 500 training machines and 5,000 Liberty engine DeHavilland-4 warplanes for U.S. pilots.

McCook Field

Col. Deeds took the job of military aircraft procurement in August. The Army Signal Corps engineering and procurement divisions were based at McCook Field, built in October on 254 acres in northeast Dayton, site of today's Kettering Athletic Field. McCook was the nation's first center for military aviation tests and engineering research. Named after the Civil War's famous "Fighting McCooks" from northeast Ohio, the field grew to 69 buildings — hangars, shops, laboratories, offices, a wind tunnel and a hospital — and employed 56 officers, 322 enlisted men and 1,096 civilians.

Wilbur Wright Field

What they built at McCook was tested at Wilbur Wright Field, created in May when Deeds leased 2,075 acres — including Huffman Prairie — to the Signal Corps. The Army put a flying school and test field at the same place where the Wrights had their own flying school from 1910 to 1916.

Above: A DeHavilland-4 reconnaissance airplane at McCook Field.

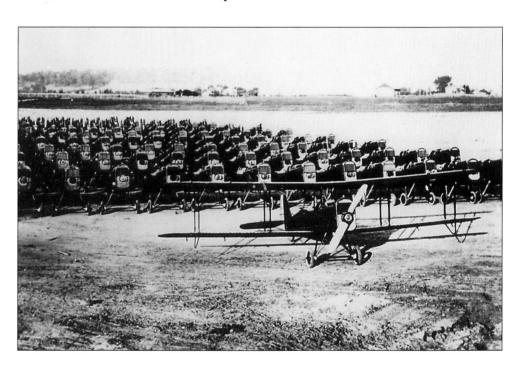

What they made for the war

- The Duririon Company: Equipment to make nitric acid for explosives.
- NCR: Precision airplane instruments and other products.
- Platt Iron Works: Munitions.
- Seven kinds of aerial bombs were made here, too. ■

Above: The Dayton Wright Airplane Company was building its inventory and speeding production.

The district did it all

Rather than hiring contractors, the Miami Conservancy District tackled the entire flood-control project itself — buying equipment; building barges, shops and warehouses; laying railroad track; assembling vehicle fleets; and hiring workers. The district even built workers' homes near the dam sites.

Sold...

More than $24 million in bonds to pay for the project, with $10 million more sold later.

Twice burned

Turner's Opera House, which had burned in 1869, suffered another fire this year.

Subscribed...

15,198 residents to the Dayton Bell Telephone Exchange.

Long may she wave

Dayton adopted its official flag on August 15. Designed by Mabel Hyer Griep, it featured a Wright airship and primarily three colors: orange, for agricultural bounty; blue, signifying citizen loyalty; and white, for civic righteousness. Griep's flag-designing career, however, was almost cut short when she was accused of being a German spy by some folks who grew suspicious while watching her sketch an airplane on display at a Delco electrical exposition.

Formed...

The Dayton branch of the Altrusa Club, on August 17, for administrative and executive women.

Began...

Construction of the Miller's Ford Station power plant, in October, by Dayton Power and Light. It became known as Tait Station.

Accepted...

The first woman lawyer into the Dayton Bar Association: Bessie D. Moore.

Retired...

Ty Cobb and Hans Wagner, Dayton's last two fire horses, who were replaced by motorized fire vehicles.

SLICE OF LIFE

Running on empty

The popularity of the interurban peaked this year — its days numbered, thanks to the ever-more-popular automobile.

Below: Some 1,600 Dayton-area men enlisted to "fight the Kaiser."

1918

The war grinds on, and so does the relief work

Back home, far from the horror of the trenches, there were garments to knit and nursing classes to teach. There were planes, tank parts and ammo to be produced in local factories. More people were employed than ever. At Pratt Iron Works alone, employment grew from 450 to 2,500 by war's end.

In memoriam

Lt. Frank Stuart Patterson was killed in a DeHavilland-4 airplane crash in Dayton on June 19, while flight-testing the plane's machine gun and propeller synchronization. Patterson Field was later named after him. The flier was a cousin to Frederick B. Patterson, son of John H. Patterson.

Ready, aim, fire!

Charles F. Kettering tested the first guided missile October 2. The government was so impressed that it ordered 2,000 "Kettering Aerial Torpedoes" — which, as it turned out, were never used. The war ended the next month.

Armistice signed

It was 2 a.m. on November 11 when the whistles started to blow: The war was over! Church bells rang at dawn, and by midmorning people jammed the streets — hollering, waving flags, throwing confetti and carrying placards that read, "We Put the I Can in American" and "For Sale — One Misused Throne." The next Sunday, 15,000-plus marched in Dayton's official victory parade.

Killed in action

Of the thousands who served from Montgomery County, more than 50 young soldiers never came home.

Left: With the Armistice signed, Dayton celebrated the Allied victory.

Below: Troops came home to a warm welcome.

After the war: McCook Field

Research and development continued at McCook Field, where engineers made great strides in aviation. The controllable and reversible-pitch propeller is credited to McCook's Propeller Lab; aerial-photography improvements were made by McCook's Equipment Section; and weather forecasting was improved by McCook's Meteorological Branch. McCook grew to become today's Aeronautical Systems Division (ASD), Air Force Logistics Command (AFLC) and Air Force Institute of Technology (AFIT).

After the war: Wilbur Wright Field

War surplus was stored temporarily at Wilbur Wright Field; all flight training ceased.

The post-war Dayton Wright Airplane Company

Nearly 400 Curtiss JN-4's were built by the Dayton Wright Airplane Company in Moraine after World War I. During World War II, the famous "Jenny" planes became the primary trainer for the Royal Air Force and the American Expeditionary Force.

Above: Building the dams involved the construction of massive retaining walls. Here, Lockington Dam, near Piqua on Loramie Creek, was in progress.

MILESTONE
Raising the dams

Despite the war, the Miami Conservancy District got started on Dayton's flood-control project on January 1, finishing in 1922. Total cost: $31 million. At the project's height, it employed some 2,000 workers who improved levees and channels in Piqua, Troy, Tipp City, Dayton, West Carrollton, Miamisburg, Franklin, Middletown and Hamilton, and who moved 13 million cubic yards of dirt to build five large earthen dams:

■ Germantown Dam, on Twin Creek south of Dayton.

■ Huffman Dam, on the Mad River near Dayton.

■ Englewood Dam, on the Stillwater River.

■ Taylorsville Dam, on the Great Miami near Vandalia.

■ Lockington Dam, on Loramie Creek north of Piqua.

Of the five, Englewood Dam was the largest — nine-tenths of a mile long and 415 feet thick at the base.

Pomp and circumstance? No time for that

Dam work began with no celebrations, no ceremonial turning of the first spadeful of earth, none of the customary formalities.

■ Arthur E. Morgan, who planned and designed the system, selected the best 50 of the 3,000 engineers who applied for jobs.

■ Construction equipment from across the nation was collected, disassembled, moved here and then reassembled in the District's machine shop. By February, the District had 29 locomotives, 200 dump cars, 80 trucks and autos, 15 miles of railroad track and 73 miles of high-voltage electric transmission lines ready to go.

■ Workers lived in makeshift villages adjacent to the dam sites, each complete with homes; sewer, water and electric service; and a mess hall, store and school.

■ Besides moving earth, District engineers also had to move tracks for the Erie and New York Central railroads and the Ohio Electric Railway, which would have been blocked by construction. ■

Like gold, if you really need the stuff

A winter coal shortage in Dayton forced some people to steal the fuel wherever they could find it. In fact, Dayton led the state in the number of reported coal thefts.

A pilot no more

While Orville Wright retired from piloting this year, he kept up aeronautics research. He later developed an automatic pilot system and the split-flap airfoil.

Opened...

Dayton's first day-care center for black children, the West Side Nursery. It later became the Melissa Bess Day Care Center, in honor of its founder.

Moved...

Winters National Bank, to 40 N. Main St., and the Engineer's Club, to the southeast corner of Monument and St. Clair.

Reopened and renamed...

■ Turner's Opera House, after the 1917 fire. Its new name: Victory Theatre.
■ Also renamed this year: the Greater Dayton Association, to the Dayton Chamber of Commerce.

Established...

An occupational therapy school in Dayton, one of the nation's first. The Barney Community House, which trained women to serve in military hospitals, later became Children's Medical Center.

Elected...

Democrat James M. Cox, to his third term as Ohio governor.

Donated...

The Hills and Dales area, by John H. Patterson, to the city of Dayton for a park.

Sold...

The Algonquin Hotel, to Michael J. Gibbons, who renamed it The Gibbons Hotel.

Joined...

United Motors, to General Motors.

Above: The canal had become an eyesore, and John H. Patterson began gathering support to have it cleaned up and filled in.

Below: Seen from Third Street to Monument Avenue, the canal was a dumping ground. It spoiled the view of many buildings, including the library (far left). The canal's path through downtown Dayton is now followed by Patterson Boulevard.

Above: Young Dayton athletes posed for this unmarked photograph.

Right: John H. Patterson's campaign to clean up the canal included full-page ads in the *Journal*.

Below: Baseball fans got their World Series news from a giant scoreboard the *Dayton Daily News* hung on the side of its building. The game shown was part of the scandalous 1919 World Series between the Cincinnati Reds and the Chicago White Sox. It was later learned that the "Black Sox" threw the series. In the bottom of the fifth inning, Chicago's "Shoeless" Joe Jackson was leading his team with two hits.

Abandon the Canal

These pictures show the improvement made by abandoning the Hydraulic

This improvement could be made by abandoning the Canal

We don't want the filthy canal running through the Heart of Dayton

Anti-Canal Association
Dayton, Ohio

Falling from the sky
Outfitted with a backpack parachute, Leslie Irving jumped from a DeHavilland-9 on April 28 — the first such jump. Soon after Floyd Smith invented the first practical parachute at Wilbur Wright Field, pilots were required to carry them.

Don't even think about it not working
Later, in July, Englishwoman Sylvia Boyden tested parachutes at McCook Field. Bypassing platform tests, she routinely gave chutes their initial test by leaping from airplanes.

'Paper! Get yer paper here!'
Dayton's Lakeside Park invited local newsboys, carriers and corner hustlers to visit for free on July 17. The kids enjoyed the Derby Racer, Old Mill, Merry-Go-Round, the Whip, Circle Swing and Hilarity Hall. And then it was back to work.

Created and tested...
The Wright Whirlwind, the first air-cooled radial engine, at McCook Field. Radial engines were used on World War II bombers.

Merged...
Wilbur Wright Field, with the Fairfield Aviation General Supply Depot, to become Wilbur Wright Air Service Depot. From the 1920s until the '40s, it was known as the Fairfield Air Immediate Depot, a major Air Corps center.

Added...
Five more stories, to the five-story Callahan Bank Building. A clock cupola topped it.

Born...
Mitchell "Booty" Wood, who would become a jazz great, playing with Duke Ellington and Count Basie.

Appointed...
William E. Stokes and his wife Hazel, to run the Montgomery County Children's Home.

Incorporated...
The Dayton Art Association, as the Dayton Museum of Arts. Its mission: teach locals about visual arts and let them enjoy masterpieces.

Acquired...
Frigidaire, by General Motors.

1920

MILESTONE

Newspaper publisher for President

Nominated as the Democratic candidate for President of the United States on July 6 was Dayton's own newspaperman and three-time Ohio governor, James M. Cox. His campaign kickoff was August 7 at the Montgomery County Fairgrounds, where he accepted the nomination before some 100,000 onlookers.

FDR for VP

Cox chose Franklin Delano Roosevelt as his running mate without even meeting him. Cox believed FDR's New York background would balance the ticket.

The campaign

Cox campaigned aggressively, promoting a progressive platform. His Republican opponent, Warren G. Harding, quietly campaigned from his front porch in Marion, Ohio, promoting simply a return to "normalcy" after the war. Harding, incidentally, was also a newspaper publisher — he owned the *Marion Star*.

The defeat

Harding won in November. Cox, satisfied that the nomination had been the culmination of his political career, left public office and returned to publishing, buying papers in Florida and Atlanta. Later, he founded radio and TV stations, including WHIO-AM, WHIO-FM and WHIO-TV. ■

Days of temperance

Overnight, the Miami Valley went from wet to dry when Prohibition began at midnight on January 16. At first, dry days and nights seemed to reduce minor crimes. From June through October, only 283 people were sent to Dayton's workhouse — about half the number from the year before. But Prohibition wasn't good for everyone: Long-time brewer and respected Daytonian Adam Schantz had to close his brewery. While his "Lily Water," a local purified water, did well, Schantz couldn't survive without selling spirits.

Above: Democratic presidential candidate James M. Cox (left) and his then-healthy running mate Franklin Delano Roosevelt (right) appeared at the Montgomery County Fairgrounds during their campaign. FDR was diagnosed with polio the following year.

Left: Military testing at McCook Field included studies of impact on aircraft.

SLICE OF LIFE

'The Icicle King'

At 33,114 feet on February 27, Maj. Rudolph "Shorty" Schroeder, a McCook Field pilot, had flown his supercharged, open-cockpit Packard-LePere LUSAC-11 biplane into the stratosphere — a world altitude record. The temperature up there: minus 45 degrees.

Lifting his goggles to read instruments, Shorty's vision went black as his eyes froze, blinding him temporarily. The plane started to dive. Schroeder was just a few thousand feet above ground when he came to and struggled to find Wilbur Wright Field. Miraculously, he landed safely. Afterward, McCook engineers went to work on protective flight clothing and better equipment — leading eventually to closed cockpits, heated cabins and, much later, pressurized cabins.

Schroeder, undaunted, made many more high-altitude flights at Wright. He was one of many pilots here willing to risk their lives to fly higher, faster, farther.

A potential 'den of decadence'

City Manager J.E. Barlow was worried. What had the Island Park Dance Pavilion become? The music was slow and sensual, the dancers' movements suggestive. What, pray tell, was next? Correct the music, Barlow ordered in July. Make the tempo faster. Barlow sent five chaperones, his own dance-floor police, to enforce the rules.

Formed...

The local chapter of the League of Women Voters, the most powerful of all women's clubs, and an outgrowth of the National Woman's Suffrage Association.

SLICE OF LIFE

A woman scorned

Katharine Louise Kennedy was elated: The Montgomery County Republican Party had just nominated her to chair its executive committee. But elation turned to insult when she lost the honor because she was a woman. An offended Kennedy promptly rounded up the county's Republican women and formed a vote-conscious group to represent women throughout Ohio.

Renamed...

St. Mary's College, to the University of Dayton, after it received university ranking.

A permanent site for art

Julia Shaw Patterson Carnell opened Dayton's first art museum after private citizens bought a home at St. Clair and Monument for housing artwork. The new museum had three permanent exhibits.

Increased...

The black population in Dayton, from 4,824 in 1910 to 9,025 in 1920, as blacks left the rural South for the industrial North.

Left: Katharine Louise Kennedy

Below: Powerful water jets were used to sluice material into the site as construction continued on the five dams.

Closed, finally...

The venerable Barney & Smith Car Company, which had struggled since the 1913 flood.

Introduced and sold...

Business and accounting machines, by NCR.

The city's first black pharmacist

It was Dr. LeRoy Cox who opened the Cox Drug Store at 842 W. Fifth St.

Arrived...

Arthur Beerman, in Dayton, after serving a retail apprenticeship. His first jobs here were at several department stores.

Organized...

The Westminster Choir, during the 1920s in Dayton. The group's concerts earned it national fame.

Reorganized and renamed...

The Fischman Orchestra, to the Dayton Orchestral Club. Later, the club was joined with the Dayton Civic Orchestra.

1921

Same faces, new place

It was the Greene County village of Osborn that experienced the greatest upheaval in the flood-control project. Located in a flood plain, as many as 400 buildings in the tiny village (population 200) had to be moved to a new site two miles away so they wouldn't be submerged behind Huffman Dam. After the Miami Conservancy District bought the village, the Osborn Removal Company went to work, moving building after building, home after home. It took 90 minutes to move a structure just one mile. By 1925, all of Osborn had been moved. Its new neighbor: the village of Fairfield.

Now hear this

Cities as far away as Dallas and Denver heard news and music on Dayton's first radio station in May. R. Stanley Copp started WFO (Wireless From Ohio), a 250-watt station, from the seventh floor of Rike's downtown. Dayton's first commercial radio station, WING, was founded May 24.

Burying a giant

Machinery was auctioned at the now-defunct Barney & Smith Car Company. The grounds, too, were divided and sold. Most Hungarian Kossuth Colony dwellers either found new jobs here or went to work for a Columbus car works.

Jitneys targeted

The onslaught of jitneys had taken Dayton by storm. By now, city commissioners were fed up. It was time for some rules. A new ordinance required license fees, indemnity bonds, set fares and provisions for the comfort and safety of passengers. Apparently, this was all too much: With profits plummeting, jitney owners eventually disappeared from city streets.

Manufactured en masse...

Electric refrigerators by W.C. Durant of Frigidaire, who had bought the fledgling company from former Daytonian Al Mellowes, who had invented an air-cooled refrigerator.

Above: Bathers at Island Park

Left: A farmers' market at Library Park on East Third Street.

Below: Dam construction involved temporary railroads for hauling materials.

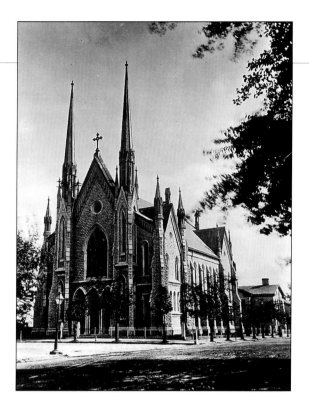

Right: Grace United Methodist Church occupied the southeast corner of Fourth and Ludlow streets before it burned and moved to Salem Avenue.

Below: After leaving work, NCR workers lined up outside the main office building for the trolley.

Charity prevailed

John H. Patterson and family established an endowment for charitable, educational and benevolent needs in Montgomery County. The Dayton Foundation's original endowment: $137,000 from Patterson and $110,000 from his sister-in-law Julia Carnell and his nephew, Robert Patterson.

Passing the torch

NCR's presidency went from John H. Patterson to his son Frederick, who began running the company's daily operations this year. The elder Patterson remained as chairman of the board. This year, NCR recorded $29 million in sales and profits of $2.8 million.

Founded...

Leland Electrical Company, by noted Dayton inventor George H. Leland. Today Leland Electrosystems Inc. supplies aerospace electrical power systems.

Opened...

Loew's Theater, and a new supermarket chain, Liberal, by Abe Schear.

Sold...

Dayton's Davis Sewing Machine Company, to Eastern interests. The company soon went bankrupt.

Moved...

The Natural History Museum, from the second floor of the public library, to the Steely Building at Second and Ludlow. Later, it was renamed the Dayton Museum of Natural History.

Married...

Future Republican politician Katharine Louise Kennedy, to Kleon Thaw Brown, treasurer of the Dayton Yellow Cab Company.

Constructed...

Grace United Methodist Church, for $376,000.

Applied...

Radium, by Dr. Franklin I. Shroyer for the first time in Dayton, to treat cancer.

Manufactured...

The Spencer auto, by Research Engineering Company.

SLICE OF LIFE

Connected by wire

Daytonians used their 20,415 telephones as many as 5,000 times an hour, 24 hours a day, for an average of 120,000 calls daily. The most popular time to call? At the opening of most businesses, from 9 to 10 a.m., and from 6 to 8 p.m., when most social chats took place.

Inflation

Dayton families felt the squeeze of post-war inflation. Some typical prices:
■ Pork chops: 22 cents per pound.
■ Bacon: 24 cents per pound.
■ Chuck roast: 10 cents per pound.
■ Coffee: 25 cents per pound.
■ Rent for a five-room house in Dayton View: $25 per month.

1922

The place to go out to the old ball game

Honus Wagner, Babe Ruth and Lou Gehrig were just a few of the 30 or so baseball legends who played at Dayton's North Side Field, which opened near Leo and Troy streets. The semi-pro Dayton Shroyers, plus Dayton's two most popular minor-league teams, the Aviators and the Ducks, played at the field until 1934.

Black baseball greats

Negro League Exhibition games were popular throughout the '20s and '30s. Some of the players fans saw at North Side Field went on to earn Hall of Fame honors: outfielder James "Cool Papa" Bell, who played with the Detroit Stars and Pittsburgh Crawfords; pitcher Satchel Paige, another Pittsburgh Crawfords player; and first baseman Ray Dandridge of the Hartford Giants.

White vs. black

Dayton baseball fans saw either two all-white teams, or an all-white and an all-black team, play at North Side Field. Integrated teams were unthinkable at the time. A rivalry soon developed between The Marcos, Dayton's best black semi-pro team, and the all-white Shroyers. The C.M.I.A.s (Colored Men's Improvement Association) was another popular black Dayton team. ∎

Completed...

All five new dams — just in time to perform perfectly on April 11, when a severe storm drenched the Miami Valley.

Red light, green light, yellow light, stop

Skittish Dayton officials wouldn't pay for a centralized traffic-light system downtown but agreed to let the Dayton Auto Club install one, if it financed the experiment. The club did so willingly, building a central-control signal tower at Third and Main and installing seven signals along Main, Third, Jefferson and Ludlow. Dayton's first traffic lights were turned on July 14.

Left: Officers shut down 192 stills in 1,165 Prohibition raids.

Below: By April, Huffman Dam was taking shape.

Wanted: A home for military aviation research

As Congress debated how much to spend for aeronautical R&D, John H. Patterson was drawing up a plan to convince the government that Dayton was the best choice for a research station. Thirty other cities were vying.

Patterson died before seeing the realization of his plan, which called for giving the feds nearly 5,000 acres for military aviation research. His son Frederick took up the cause, forming the Dayton Air Service Committee of prominent citizens to raise money for the land.

In two days, they got more than $400,000 — enough to buy 4,520 acres east of Dayton, including Wilbur Wright Field and Huffman Prairie. In 1924, Dayton's gift would be accepted by President Calvin Coolidge.

Grape crush

Lt. Harold R. Harris landed in a north Dayton grape arbor on October 20 after parachuting from his disabled plane at 2,500 feet. It was the first emergency parachute jump.

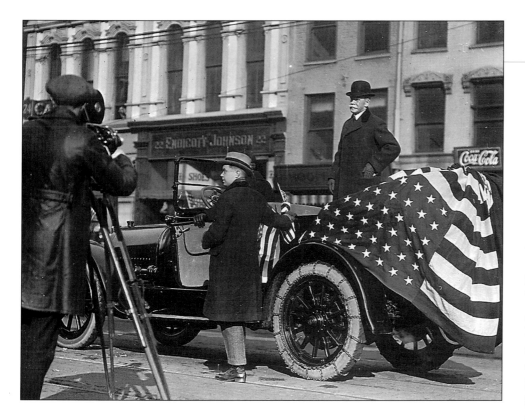

Above: John H. Patterson (standing in car) posed for this photograph four years before his death.

Right: The top three floors of the building at Second and Ludlow were occupied by Miami Jacobs Business College. The Red Cross headquarters is on the left.

SLICE OF LIFE

Step right up, ladies, and have a peek at the future

Women of all ages scrambled for an up-front look at Dayton's first all-electric house at Otterbein Avenue and Catalpa Drive. Housework, they were told, would never be the same.

Died...

Dayton's beloved John H. Patterson, civic leader and founder of NCR, on May 7. His son Frederick became chairman of the board.

Strength in numbers

Frederick Rike and Fred Lazarus formed the Ohio Council of Retail Merchants, one of the first associations of its kind. The two believed united retailers could solve community problems and help business at the same time.

He fought injustice

West Virginia Collegiate Institute graduate Joseph Peters, promised a job as a contractor in Dayton, was anxious to get to the Gem City — only to have his dreams shattered when his would-be employer saw that Peters was black. Peters, angry and bitter, became an independent contractor and worked to fight employment discrimination.

Continued...

The Dayton Triangles, as a pro team, even after being excluded from the new National Football League.

Established...

General Motors' Inland Manufacturing Division, which became the world's largest maker of wooden steering wheels.

Built...

Keith's Theater, a grand place at Fourth and Ludlow that seated more than 2,700 and hosted movies and stage shows featuring Fred Allen, Jack Benny, Ben Bernie, Will Rogers and Bing Crosby.

Hired...

Dora Burton Rice, the city's first black woman police officer.

1923

Above: Dayton was thriving, and several of the city's landmark buildings had been constructed. This photograph looked north along Main Street.

Right: This mobile library service proclaimed that "The man who succeeds is the man who reads," but the patrons pictured here were all women.

Below: The Barling Bomber, the world's largest airplane, was in Dayton for testing.

Spoke...

American Socialist leader Eugene V. Debs, at Memorial Hall on June 20.

Daytonians sign up for KKK

As the Ku Klux Klan gained national prominence, people here joined the secret organization in great numbers; Dayton became one of the nation's white-hood capitals. Statewide, KKK membership was estimated at 300,000. Some 7,000 Klansmen marched down Main Street.

Welcome, Roosevelt

The largest high school east of the Mississippi, and one that quickly became a prestigious Midwestern institution, opened in Dayton this year. Roosevelt High School — which rose four stories and covered two city blocks — had more than 400 rooms, a 1,500-seat theater, two swimming pools, two gyms, an indoor track and terrazzo-and-marble entrances. The school was integrated; the pools were segregated.

A GM town

General Motors' Moraine Products Division was established. Besides Delco Moraine, GM divisions here now included Delco Products, Frigidaire and Inland Manufacturing.

Died...

Famed Dayton madam Lib Hedges, at age 82. She ran a prominent prostitution operation beginning in 1876. Her Woodland Cemetery monument is said to have inspired Thomas Wolfe's first novel, *Look Homeward, Angel*, in 1929.

Moving on...

■ Union Biblical Seminary, to 35 acres in Upper Dayton View.
■ McCall's Corporation's printing operation, to Dayton.

It revolutionized the auto

A Dayton motorist made history February 2 by purchasing the first tank of ethyl gasoline ever sold. The new motor fuel — an anti-knock mixture that eliminated costly engine overhauls from fuel detonation and deposit build-ups — was sold by Refiners Oil Company at Sixth and Main. Thomas Midgley Jr. and Charles F. Kettering developed ethyl gas at GM's labs. The first company to adopt the new gas for its fleet was Dayton Power and Light, which changed over on June 1.

Completed...

100 percent of the Miami Conservancy District's flood-control project, on April 17.

From New York to LA

Flying a Fokker T-2 transport modified here, two McCook Field pilots made the first U.S. nonstop transcontinental flight on May 2.

Rike's parades toys

It took almost a year to plan, assemble and rehearse the Rike-Kumler Company's first Annual Toy Parade, held on Thanksgiving morning. The 10 a.m. event featured floats, balloons and toys, culminating with Santa climbing a ladder to a chimney atop the Men's Store. More than 1,000 Rike's employees participated.

1924

They went 'round the world

Commercial aviation companies preparing for the first circumnavigational flight had to work with McCook Field engineers, who evaluated and monitored designs and production. Air Service pilots flew Douglas World Cruisers in that historical flight, April 6 to September 28.

Passing muster

A June 8 storm forced the Stillwater River's rapid rise — and everyone was relieved to see the new Englewood Dam hold the high waters.

Patterson would have been proud

It was a steal — 4,520 acres for a buck. The U.S. Army accepted Dayton's gift, made possible by the Dayton Air Service Committee, which had raised more than $400,000 to buy land east of town in the government's name. Dayton's only reward: the promise that military aviation research would remain centered here. In 1925, the land was renamed Wright Field.

Above, right and below: Wilbur Wright Field and Fairfield Air Intermediate Depot hosted the International Air Races October 2-4. The event — which attracted military and civilian pilots and 100,000 spectators — featured races, balloon flights, formation flying and exhibits.

Created...
A new City Plan Board, charged with finding ways to improve the quality of urban life and control growth in Dayton.

Founded...
An airfield north of town, which evolved into the James M. Cox Dayton International Airport.

Hired...
Miriam Rosenthal, by James M. Cox, as a reporter and columnist for the lovelorn.

Manufactured...
145,000 cash registers at NCR's Dayton plant.

Established...
Donenfeld's Inc., a women's apparel shop at 35 N. Main St., by Jack A. Donenfeld.

SLICE OF LIFE

Local KKK members: 1 in 10

Prominent Daytonians — including a Montgomery County sheriff's official, a police officer and a county commissioner — were among the 15,000 local members of the Ku Klux Klan. The group was having its greatest surge of national popularity, which didn't last much longer.

Above: The Refiners Oil Company service station at the corner of Salem and Grand featured a tile roof, painted curbs and plenty of service.

Below: The Victory Theatre had businesses on the first floor and painted advertisements on the side of the building.

Swindled...
The Soldiers' Home, in March, after entertaining a con man disguised as a U.S. inspector.

Making the city grow
Extend the city's boundaries — that was the conclusion from the Technical Advisory Corporation, a New York engineering and city-planning firm hired to develop a comprehensive plan for Dayton. But what did that mean? Annex Oakwood? Well, actually, yes — and so the talks began.

Seed sown for Shawen Acres
Montgomery County voters allowed the sale of $400,000 in bonds to build a new children's home. The vision: cottages for raising 200 kids in a homey, neighborhood setting. Prominent Dayton physician Dr. Charles E. Shawen donated 22 acres north of downtown.

1925

McCook: A competitor no more
It came down from on high: McCook's Engineering Division, said the U.S. Army Air Service, would acquire and evaluate aircraft designs from commercial aviation companies, rather than competing with them. The goal: to create a more efficient Air Service.

A hot operation
After selling its sewing machine business, the Davis Sewing Machine Company changed its name to the Huffman Manufacturing Company, which began making blowtorches and plumbers' furnaces. Later, it became the bicycle-making Huffy Corporation.

A political vanguard for women
Katharine Louise Kennedy Brown returned to politics after the death of husband Kleon Thaw Brown. Mrs. Brown, who served on the Montgomery County Republican Committee and the Republican State Committee, rose to become one of the nation's most prominent Republican women.

Sold...
Properties of the Barney & Smith Car Company, for $452,761.61.

Born...
Future funnyman Jonathan Winters, on November 11.

Joined...
The Dayton Gas Company, to Dayton Power and Light, which now offered four utility services: gas, electric, steam and water.

SLICE OF LIFE

Smart spouses
Wives of NCR workers got the opportunity to expand their horizons after John H. Patterson's niece, Edith McClure Patterson, opened a company-sponsored adult education school especially for employees' wives.

Cashing in
NCR made a whopping 17 percent profit this year — $7.8 million on sales of $45 million.

Above: The building that housed the Miami Hotel, at Second and Ludlow, is now known as the Lazarus building.

Above: Raising the railroad tracks at Sixth and Main allowed traffic to flow more freely.

Below: This aerial view showed Union Station, complete with an arched entrance and a tower.

Set...

A world altitude record by pilot John Macready at McCook Field on January 29. Lt. James H. Doolittle (who went on to WWII flying fame) replaced Macready, who resigned in April.

Nipped in the bud

A reluctant handful of Oakwood leaders met with Dayton officials on February 16 to hear the city's annexation invitation. The Daytonians shared charts and data illustrating how one government would benefit both communities. At meeting's end, Oakwood Mayor Oscar C. Olt agreed to bring Oakwood residents and Dayton officials together to discuss the idea again. Oakwood's distaste for annexation, though, was apparent: The second meeting was never held.

Held...

A groundbreaking for Wright Field, by the U.S. Army Air Service, on April 16. Today it's Area B at Wright-Patterson Air Force Base.

Razed...

The Phillips Hotel, in May.

Honored...

Wilbur Wright, on August 21, with the naming of Wilbur Wright Elementary Junior High School on Huffman Avenue. Today it's Wilbur Wright Middle School.

They were all wet to begin with, anyway

Drenched by a cold rain, 1,500 Ku Klux Klan members rallied at the Montgomery County Fairgrounds on September 25. Despite the crowd of 25,000 spectators, fairgrounds officials felt obliged to give the KKK a rebate because of the weather. The Klan's popularity, already on the wane, soon worsened after word of scandals and poor money management.

Sweet success

She started by selling fudge from her Fauver Avenue home and became a Dayton legend. Esther Price — Dayton's most beloved candy maker — sold Esther Price Candies Corporation for $2 million in 1976.

Opened...

Grandview Hospital, by two osteopathic physicians.

SLICE OF LIFE

Read all about it

The two-wheeled stand at Fifth and Main meant one thing to downtown shoppers: Joe Horvath was selling newspapers. Horvath was a downtown fixture until he was slain during a robbery in 1981.

Stocks for sale

Dayton made history again with NCR's 1926 stock offer of $55 million in shares — the largest public stock offering at that time.

Constructed...

The ornamental Veterans Memorial Bridge, over Wolf Creek, to honor those who served. It's still standing.

Flyer to flyer

Charles A. Lindbergh stayed overnight at Hawthorn Hill while visiting Orville Wright shortly after Lindbergh's historic May 20-21 transatlantic solo flight from New York to Paris. The young hero also paid his respects to Wilbur on August 5, placing a wreath on his Woodland Cemetery grave.

Dream realized

McCook Field operations moved to the newly completed 4,500-acre Wright Field, dedicated and presented to the government on October 12. Orville Wright led the ceremonies.

Helping hands

Dayton folk, familiar with the pain of natural disaster, in May donated more than $20,000 for flood relief in Mississippi.

One king-size bonfire

Thomas Conway Jr., new owner of the Cincinnati, Hamilton & Dayton Railway, was revamping tracks and buying new cars in hopes of reviving the foundering interurban. He was looking for a gimmick, too. Conway decided to fire up public enthusiasm by ceremonially burning seven of his oldest interurban cars on June 22. A huge crowd helped itself to popcorn and ice cream, courtesy of Conway.

A theater of their own

Duke Ellington, Ella Fitzgerald, the Mills Brothers and other entertainers performed at the Classic Theater, established for black theater-goers at 815 W. Fifth St. Blacks opened the Classic on August 25 after being repeatedly excluded from Dayton's white theaters.

Killed...

Polo ponies, after a $100,000 fire at the Dayton Country Club in September.

Died...

Frederick Ohmer, founder of the Ohmer Fare Register Company, on October 1.

Top: Charles Lindbergh (right) visited Orville Wright and Dayton soon after his historic flight across the Atlantic.

Above: Josephine and Hermene Schwarz founded the dance school that later evolved into the Dayton Ballet.

Right: Baptisms were performed in the Mad River.

Below: A fire at the Beckel Hotel drew hundreds of onlookers — almost all of them men — to the scene.

Right: Vandalia had become the permanent home of the Amateur Trapshooting Association's Grand American Tournament in 1926.

For art's sake

Construction of the Dayton Art Institute got under way on land purchased by Julia Shaw Carnell at Forest and Riverdale avenues. The building was modeled after a 15th-century Italian Renaissance palace, a five-sided villa 40 miles north of Rome. Before Carnell cinched the deal, the land was slated for apartments.

Back home again

The Dayton Public Library Museum moved from the Steely Building at Second and Ludlow back to the second floor of the new library annex.

Established...

A 250-bed hospital, which later became Good Samaritan Hospital and Health Center, by Cincinnati's Sisters of Charity. Dayton folk donated more than $1 million, and Dr. D.W. Beatty gave land.

Donations, donations, donations

■ Charles F. Kettering, ever generous, gave $3 million to Antioch College in Yellow Springs. He liked Antioch's cooperative work/study educational system.
■ Also founded this year was the Charles F. Kettering Foundation for research in medicine and natural sciences.
■ Kettering and Alfred P. Sloan founded the Sloan-Kettering Institute for cancer research in New York City.

Born...

Erma Fiste — who later became Mrs. Erma Bombeck — in Dayton. Bombeck went on to national fame as an author and humor columnist, focusing on the lives and daily frustrations of American housewives.

Organized...

■ The English Club, with 118 teachers as members.
■ The Nomad Club, for men interested in travel.

Toe dancing

The Schwarz School of Dance was founded by sisters Josephine and Hermene Schwarz. It evolved into the Dayton Ballet.

1928

Full house

Twenty to 30 children at a time were cared for by surrogate parents in the brand-new cottages of Shawen Acres, which replaced the Montgomery County Children's Home. Shawen Acres administrators felt the cottage setup would provide a home atmosphere, rather than an institutional setting, for orphaned children.

Masonic masterpiece

The Masonic Temple on Riverview Avenue was occupied. It boasted 250 rooms, including a 1,900-seat cathedral, 2,000-seat dining room and 3,500-volume library. One of the temple's seven pipe organs had as many as 4,375 pipes. The magnificent six-story structure took 450 workmen almost three years to build.

Left: The North Main streetcar track ended in a loop, allowing streetcars to turn around.

Below: The Masonic Temple was under construction. The site now occupied by the Dayton Art Institute is on the right. The Canby house, on the upper right, was torn down in 1988.

Above: Photographer William Mayfield sometimes worked from the bed of a *Dayton Daily News* delivery truck.

Reminiscing

West-side residents who had watched the Wright brothers work their magic were special guests at a Rotary Club banquet hosted by George D. Antrim in Orville's honor. Antrim related a story often told by Charlie Webbert, one of the Wrights' mechanics, who had gotten discouraged one day by their machine's failure to fly. But then it happened: "And by God, the damn thing flew. Round and round and round that field it went for 31 minutes. Some of the time he must have been a hundred feet up and every time he passed over us we all threw our hats in the air and yelled our damn heads off."

1929

Wealthy enough, until the crash

By 1929, Dayton was a prosperous, up-and-coming manufacturing center. Its per-capita building-and-loan investment was the nation's highest. Its factories numbered 521 and employed an impressive 50,446 people. But no place escaped the fallout from the devastating October 24 stock-market crash. At NCR, stock plummeted from $154 a share to a mere $6.87. Freight movement on Dayton's railroads ground to a virtual halt. Relief kitchens opened for those who were suddenly jobless.

Pride cometh before the fall

Despite the crash, the Biltmore Hotel opened as planned on November 16. The opulence — elegant lobbies and ballroom, marble stairs, meeting and music rooms, an indoor parking garage — was a stark contrast to the Depression-era hardships that would soon plague Dayton. Soon enough, however, the Biltmore became yet another victim of the times: By 1930, it was in receivership.

They're out!

The Dayton Triangles lost their pro-football status after enduring a miserable 0-6 record.

Welcomed...

David L. Rike, son of Frederick Rike, to the Rike-Kumler Company. Said his dad: "The best resource this company has is my son."

Occupied...

The new $1.325 million YMCA building on Monument Avenue, about a month before the stock-market crash.

Continued...

Construction of downtown's elevated railroad tracks, despite the stock-market crash. They were finished in 1931.

Completed...

Construction of the Dayton Art Institute.

Manufactured...

The first electric gasoline pump, by the Dayton Pump and Manufacturing Company.

Left: Federal agents raided a bootlegging operation in the back of a service station.

Below left: Evidence was confiscated in the raid.

Below right: Auto racing was held at the fairgrounds.

Above: Gen. John Pershing, commander of the American forces in World War I, visited Dayton.

Goodbye, canal ... hello, highway

Plenty of people were overjoyed to learn that at long last, the Miami and Erie Canal would be closed. The once-vital waterway had been a decaying, disease-ridden, garbage-filled eyesore since its unofficial abandonment in the early 1900s. Now it would be filled in and turned into a superhighway for motor cars.

The rededication ceremony took place in Middletown on November 2 at the very site where Ohio Gov. Jeremiah Morrow and New York Gov. DeWitt Clinton shoveled the first spadeful of canal dirt in 1825. But this time, it was Ohio Gov. Myers Y. Cooper and New York Gov. Franklin D. Roosevelt who broke ground. In Dayton, the canal bed became Patterson Boulevard.

Still some life left in the canal

Construction of the highway didn't happen overnight. In fact, even after the rededication, superintendents were hired to watch the canal. Their duties included fishing timbers and dead animals from the water, along with shooing away the muskrats that tore up the banks and ruined farmers' fields. Supers also collected rent from squatters who lived inside the old locks, evicting those who couldn't pay. Superintendent John R. Wood was responsible for the 134-mile stretch from Ft. Loramie to Cincinnati. ■

Top: The Dayton Art Institute was completed, and dedicated the next year.

Above: The Cincinnati & Lake Erie electric railway transported travelers in luxury.

MILESTONE

Shattered economy, depressed people

■ Dayton wasted no time signing up for the Federal Surplus Commodity Food Stamp Plan, becoming the second U.S. city to enroll.

■ Charity was the order of the day. Moviegoers paid for tickets with canned goods for the poor; proceeds from college football games and wrestling and boxing matches went to the needy.

■ City employees accepted scrip, a local currency redeemable in the future, as their weekly wage.

■ NCR Women's Club members not only ran relief kitchens in the former Dayton City Club, but also made sure clothes and shoes were available at great discounts to those in need.

■ A half-mill property tax levy for poor relief passed 2-to-1 in November. Revenue let the city hire 150 men for $3.60 per day — payable in food tickets.

■ By the end of 1930, Dayton's private relief agencies had given away 700 percent more aid than in 1929.

There were still a few bright spots

Once the Works Project Administration was established, people helped improve parks and repair bridges and streets. In Dayton, WPA workers built the Island Park band shell. Federal funds allowed construction at Wright Field to continue during the Depression. ■

SLICE OF LIFE

Population:

200,982 — up from 85,333 in 1900.

Self-made man

"There is not a man living who doesn't look better in a hat — provided that it is carefully selected." So went the philosophy of Walter Uhrig, 40, Dayton's soon-to-be favorite haberdasher, who opened a shop in the Gibbons Hotel. A former London Hat House employee, Uhrig kept at it until 1962.

Left: Al Shartle shined the shoes of many VIPs — including four U.S. presidents.

Below: At this downtown market, heads of lettuce and oranges were priced at 5 cents each.

Right: This photograph of a famous race between an airplane and an interurban car was retouched by photographer William Mayfield to make the airplane appear lower than it actually was.

Below: The newsstand at the southeast corner of Third and Main sold customers the *Dayton Daily News*, the *Journal* and most national papers.

Dedication of a Dayton landmark

"I feel as if I were giving into your hands a child of my own. Be good to it." Those were the words of Julia Shaw Carnell as she presented the new Dayton Art Institute to the city on January 7. She financed the entire land purchase and building construction — a total of $2 million.

Faster, of course, is better

On July 7, a downtown theater newsreel showed an interurban car racing an airplane. The famed race, from Dorothy Lane to West Carrollton, was to promote the Red Devil interurban cars adopted by the Cincinnati & Lake Erie Railway (reorganized from the old CH&D). The C&LE's Red Devils, said to be the finest cars ever, ran the 277 miles from Cincinnati to Detroit three times a day until 1932. (And the winner of the big race? The interurban, of course.)

Surprise, surprise

Prohibition was 10 years old, but booze was still plentiful. In 1930, more than 2,500 people were jailed here for drunkenness and transporting liquor.

No meant no

Oakwood continued to staunchly oppose Dayton's annexation push. By 1930, village leaders drew the line: A charter establishing Oakwood as a city was obtained. No more problem.

Died...

Al Shartle, Dayton's beloved shoe-shiner, who had polished the shoes of four U.S. presidents (Hayes, Garfield, McKinley and Harding) and many other VIPs traveling through Dayton over the years.

Incorporated...

Mead, as the Mead Corporation. By this time, the company employed 1,000 people in four states. George H. Mead was president.

1931

They closed their doors

Dayton banks — including The Dayton Savings and Trust and The Mutual Building and Loan Company — closed because of the Depression. Union Trust, Dayton's largest bank, failed on Halloween.

Accepted...

The chairmanship of NCR, by Col. E.A. Deeds. Frederick Patterson believed Deeds could restore stockholder confidence in the company, which was struggling like most others in the throes of the Depression.

Renamed...

Land, east of Huffman Dam within Wright Field, as Patterson Field — in honor of pilot Lt. Frank Stuart Patterson, killed there in a 1918 airplane crash. Before 1925, this piece of land was called Wilbur Wright Field.

Quack, quack

The Dayton Ducks, a baseball team, was organized.

Invited...

Nationally known black baseball teams, to Dayton, by local baseball promoter John Shroyer. The teams played at North Side Field.

The going wasn't always easy for black teams on the road in the South and Midwest, where a night's stay in smaller cities — which had few or no accommodations for blacks — sometimes meant bedding down in shabby quarters. Black teams stopping in Dayton were a little luckier; they often lodged at the West Side YMCA, in rooming houses or at private homes.

SLICE OF LIFE

A remarkable newspaper woman

A household name was Penelope Perrill, 71, who wrote book and music reviews and a column titled "From the Window" for the *Dayton Daily News*. This "tapper of the keys," as she called herself, spent time at *The Columbus Dispatch*, London *Daily Mail* and a London news syndicate. In 1931 she was Ohio's oldest newspaper woman. Perrill was also the first American woman to fly in a hydroplane.

Above: Union Station was in its heyday.

Left and below: The Miller Brothers 101 Ranch Wild West Show was held at the fairgrounds.

Above: Dayton's Hulman Building was influenced by New York's Empire State Building.

Right: Local fans missed baseball until the Dayton Ducks' season opener. Here, a Duck fielder missed the ball.

SLICE OF LIFE

They pined for *Frankenstein*

The manager of the RKO Keith's Theater had to get a second copy of *Frankenstein* to show at the Colonial Theater around the corner after patrons blocked the sidewalks lining up to see the Boris Karloff horror film.

Depression notebook

■ Formed: The Dayton Vigilance Committee, charged with protecting banks from rumors.
■ Ran: Free classified ads, by the *Dayton Daily News*, for job seekers.
■ Applied: 42,292 at the city-state employment service, for only 4,084 jobs.
■ Given away: Groceries, by the city to those who volunteered to provide services such as park maintenance.
■ Removed: 600 bulbs and globes, from Dayton's street lights, to save money.
■ Failed: Tax levies, one after the next. A few bond issues passed, which (barely) kept city government going.
■ Spent: $672,416.63 by the city, on relief efforts this year.

A moneymaker

Over the next 30 years, "Miriam Rosenthal" and "fund-raising" became synonymous. Working from her own public relations firm, she rallied support for the Memorial Hall renovation, Sinclair College building fund, the new Montgomery County Library building and expansions at the University of Dayton. UD's Miriam Hall is named for her.

Play ball!

Baseball returned to Dayton on May 4 with the opening home game of the Dayton Ducks. The club's fearless leader was Howard E. "Ducky" Holmes, a manager who hated umpires and wasn't afraid to show it. His temper got him thrown out of two games and fined by May 26. On August 7, after he punched an umpire, Holmes was suspended for 10 days and ordered to leave the park — so he climbed a nearby telephone pole and managed his team with exaggerated hand signals. (Ducky earned his nickname after being given two ducks before the home opener. The ducks watched the Ducks from their pen behind the grandstands.)

Many Dayton Ducks moonlighted at the Biltmore Hotel as on-call security guards for quieting nighttime disturbances.
Their pay: a room, for just $1 a night.

Dedicated...

Good Samaritan Hospital, on May 12, at 1225 W. Fairview Ave. It cared for 1,614 patients its first year.

Fire!

Sixteen streetcars and two buses burned in the August 24 car-barn fire at the Dayton Street Railway Company at Lorain and Pritz avenues. With its oil-soaked floors and wooden roof beams, the barn went up fast. The blaze devastated Dayton's streetcar business, which was already reeling from strikes, rising expenses, and of course, the automobile.

Liquor? Where?

Catching Prohibition violators was becoming less of a police priority. Evidence: Only 10 alleged liquor violators were turned over to federal court here during an eight-month period in 1931 and 1932.

Built...

Dayton's first skyscraper, the art-deco Hulman Building, inspired by the Empire State Building.

Established...

A department store at Main and Sixth, by Sears Roebuck & Company.

1933

MILESTONE
Music to their ears

It was a sultry day on June 1 when 500 people paid 25 cents each to hear the first concert of the Chamber Orchestra. Paul Katz conducted 25 players in the Dayton Art Institute auditorium, and later resolved to build a permanent, professional orchestra that would enrich the lives of all Daytonians — not just the elite.

An orchestra is born

By June 30, the Chamber Orchestra was incorporated and started business with nothing more than a rented phone, a filing cabinet and $100 in cash ($50 from Katz and $50 from Albert Epstein, the business manager). Musicians got $5 per performance and Katz got $90 for the first season, which consisted of eight pairs of concerts from October to April 1934. In 1934, the Chamber Orchestra became the Dayton Philharmonic Orchestra.

Just a few sour notes, though

The infant orchestra had more than just tight-budget problems. While members were loyal and enthusiasm ran high, launching the venture in the midst of the Depression was risky. When members wanted Sunday-morning rehearsals, they were promptly condemned by several ministers, who claimed the musicians' rightful place was in church. And when the orchestra logged a $90 deficit in one of its early seasons, it had to run a paper drive to get the money. ■

Opened...

The city's first all-black high school, Dunbar High, at 215 S. Summit St.

Trackless trolleys

The Dayton Street Railway Company, down and out from the 1932 car-barn fire, converted to trolley buses on April 23. They were an immediate hit.

Overdue!

Dayton collected only $2.3 million in taxes this year. Delinquent taxes exceeded $3.1 million.

Above: Good Samaritan Hospital cared for more than 1,600 patients during its first year.

Below: The bus depot stood at Fourth and Wilkinson, where the *Dayton Daily News* parking lot is now.

A change of direction

After NCR employment fell to 3,500 in 1933 from 8,500 in 1930, the company developed new products, cultivated new markets and acquired companies in Europe and Asia.

Served...

James M. Cox, as vice chairman of the American delegation to the World Economic Conference in London.

SLICE OF LIFE

Fans galore

Dayton Ducks manager Howard E. "Ducky" Holmes didn't hesitate moving his fledgling team to the Middle Atlantic League after the Central League folded before the 1933 baseball season. The Ducks routinely played for standing-room-only crowds that topped 3,500.

Tavern under glass

How do you protect a historic landmark? Simple — just seal it up in glass! That suggestion came from a Dayton Historical Society board member who worried about the deterioration of Newcom Tavern. (The idea was, happily, rejected.)

On their own

Plenty of folks dreamed of homesteading. The federal government awarded $500,000 in funds and lots of advice to a Dayton homesteading committee, which vowed to convert the 160-acre farm of Dr. Walter Shaw, on Dayton-Liberty Road south of U.S. 35, into a self-sufficient community. The community — expected to become a pilot project for hundreds of U.S. homestead units — never materialized.

Top: Barnstorming stunt pilot Roscoe Turner appeared in Dayton with the Zeigfield Follies dancers. Turner was the holder of several world air speed records.

Right: Hills and Dales Park

Below: Baseball fans flocked to the field for Dayton Ducks home games.

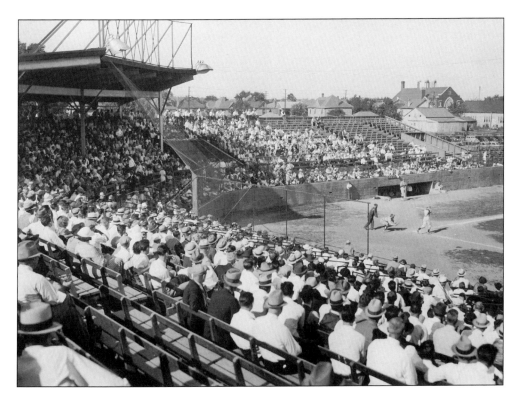

Good samaritans

Three bachelors who shared an apartment but drew single relief during the Depression accumulated 542 extra cans of donated food, which they returned to the city of Dayton for redistribution among the needy.

Showered...

Howard E. "Ducky" Holmes, with birthday presents on July 8, by his beloved Dayton Ducks. It was the manager's 51st birthday.

Opened...

Citizens Federal, a savings and loan association, on East Third Street on August 6.

Blind ambition

Eleanor Gertrude Brown — who earned a Ph.D. from Columbia University — became the nation's first blind person to earn a doctorate. Brown, born on Dayton's outskirts, was a Dayton schoolteacher for 40 years.

Tennis, anyone?

Tennis fans for a long time associated Dayton with the sport after Virginia Hollinger's respectable showing at the Women's National Indoor Tennis Tournament.

A permanent solution

The tents of NCR's Sugar Camp were replaced with permanent buildings for employee training, thanks to Col. E.A. Deeds.

Built...

Facilities at Wright Field, for studying the effects of high-performance flight on humans.

Changed...

The name of the Lyric Theater, to The Mayfair. It became the city's top burlesque theater.

Founded...

The Dayton Civic Band, by Don Bassett.

Closed...

Dayton's North Side Field, a site for baseball and other sports events since 1922.

1935

Founded...

WHIO radio, by James M. Cox, on February 9.

TRAP frees artists for work

Another Depression-era project: 19 Dayton artists created fountains, pools, wood carvings, lithographs, paintings, maps and murals for local schools while participating in the federal Treasury Relief Art Program. TRAP paid unskilled workers $55 a week; professional artists got $94. While artists had to provide their own materials, they had free use of Dayton Art Institute studios.

Relief gardens

Lots of down-on-their-luck Daytonians were fed thanks to city-sponsored relief gardens, worth an estimated $51,525 when this year's harvest yielded 200,000 pounds of green beans, 250,000 pounds of tomatoes and 95,000 pounds of turnips.

Logged...

More than $8.7 million in delinquent taxes, by the city of Dayton.

Given...

Weekly radio talks on nature by Selma Hermann of the Dayton Public Library Museum. Also this year: Works Project Administration crews cleaned and mounted specimens and helped develop the museum's card catalog.

Left: Bathing ensembles included footwear at Island Park.

Below: A lone artist worked in one of the Dayton Art Institute's studios. Local artists were paid by the government for work on area schools.

Top: Paul Laurence Dunbar's house was dedicated as a state memorial.

Above: Trolleys had given way to electric buses.

Right: Henry Ford (right) and Orville Wright inspected the Wright brothers' Hawthorn Street home before the building was moved to Dearborn, Michigan.

SLICE OF LIFE

Campus changes

Women began attending classes with men at the University of Dayton, making UD the nation's first coeducational Catholic university.

Strategic success

NCR's expansion plan was paying off. By 1936, it employed 16,000 people worldwide, more than 6,900 of them in Dayton.

Moved...

The Wright brothers' last bicycle shop, from 1127 W. Third St., to Greenfield Village in Dearborn, Michigan. Henry Ford moved the building after buying it on July 2 from landlord Charles Webbert for $13,000. Ford also took the Wright family home from its foundation at 7 Hawthorn St.

Wedding bells, balls and bats

Dayton Ducks second baseman Joe Paiement married his sweetheart at home plate on July 15. After the customary "I do's," the Ducks promptly took up their bats against Canton.

Dedicated...

The North Main Street bridge, on October 12, after 19 months of construction and a cost of $1.08 million.

Purchased...

Land, used by the former Dayton Airport Corporation, by the city of Dayton. The city used the land to establish the Dayton Municipal Airport on December 17, the 33rd anniversary of powered flight. The same day, TWA began offering the first transcontinental air service into Dayton.

Converted...

The Oakwood Street Railway, to trackless trolley buses, three years after the Dayton Street Railway Company made the switch.

Dedicated...

Paul Laurence Dunbar's home, by the Ohio General Assembly, as a state memorial — the first honoring a black American. The Dunbar House State Memorial is located at 219 N. Summit St. off West Third Street. Summit Street is now Paul Laurence Dunbar Street.

Slow recovery

Although some Dayton businesses had resumed five-day work weeks and new positions were opening up, more than 13,000 people still needed work, and the housing market remained depressed.

Epidemic!

Polio struck 47 Daytonians, killing 12 and paralyzing 20.

1937

A dam success

Heavy rains forced the Great Miami River to its highest level since the 1913 flood — but the Miami Conservancy District's dams held the rising waters nicely (with as much as 85 percent storage capacity remaining, in fact).

Things just weren't ducky anymore

After financial problems struck the Dayton Ducks, its board of trustees made manager Howard E. "Ducky" Holmes hand over his stock in the baseball club (he'd owned nearly all of it). The board gave Holmes operating funds as needed. By season's end, the deficit was $5,000.

On the road with Mrs. McCormick

Oakwood resident Anne O'Hare McCormick became the first woman to win a Pulitzer Prize for foreign correspondence. McCormick's career took shape while she traveled abroad on business trips with her husband, a Dayton manufacturer. The award-winning journalist also wrote editorials and freelance stories for *The New York Times*.

All work and no play
(is something to be avoided)

Olmsted Brothers, the famous American landscape architecture firm, designed Old River Park, a 104-acre recreation center for NCR employees, families and friends.

Failed...

The Hamilton, the last of the Cincinnati & Lake Erie Railroad's interurbans. The interurban, finally, proved no match for the Depression — or the automobile.

Won...

The 1937 Collier Trophy, by a modified Lockheed Model 10E Electra XC-35, for advancements in cabin pressurization made at Wright Field. Cabin pressurization was later incorporated onto both bomber and transport aircraft.

Sold...

Printing equipment used by the Wrights, to Henry Ford for his Greenfield Village exhibit in Dearborn, Michigan. Stevens & Stevens, which bought the brothers' printing business in 1899, made the sale.

Above: Football fans filled the stadium for this University of Dayton home game.

Below: Streetlights cast an eerie glow on the NCR complex along Main Street.

Established...

The Experimental Group for Young Dancers — renowned nationally for training dancers who went on to the American and Joffrey ballets — by Josephine and Hermene Schwarz. Performances were held throughout Dayton, from living rooms and schools to the Dayton Art Institute and Memorial Hall.

Turning points

Although some 10,500 Daytonians were still on relief, signs were everywhere that the city was easing out of the Depression. Gone were the bread lines. Men were no longer picking coal from railroad tracks. Parties were touted on the newspaper's society pages. The Dayton Country Club's dining room reopened. And employment at General Motors rose to 22,500.

Top and right: A huge number of spectators turned out to watch the Rike's Children's Christmas Parade.

Below: The expansion of Rike's was heralded throughout the store with commemorative medallions.

Risky business

Could Rike's become bigger and better, even during a depression? The Rike-Kumler Company thought so, embarking on a massive expansion of its downtown store that included a new floor, an eight-story service building, new air-conditioning, four high-speed elevators, an auditorium and two new restaurants. "We're building your greater Rike's" went the campaign, which culminated with the grand opening of the new addition on May 12. Rike's expansion taught Dayton an important lesson: hope, in a time when dreams and greatness seemed light years away.

Ducks downhill

The Ducks' deficit went from $5,000 in 1937 to $7,500 by mid-July. By December, the Dayton baseball team was in receivership.

Graduated...

Jessie Hathcock, the first black woman to receive her degree from the University of Dayton. She went on to teach at Dunbar High School.

1939

Stretched beyond the limit

Despite signs of recovery, Dayton's relief expenditures topped total city-government operating costs for the first time. The community's dedication to its needy was never more apparent than this year, when the safety director, legal aid attorney, city engineer and building director positions were eliminated to free up extra dollars for relief.

Wings replace Ducks

The Ducky Holmes baseball era ended after the Brooklyn Dodgers and Dayton businessmen became the main financial backers of the Dayton Ducks — who then became the Wings.

Gone, but not forgotten

Old traction cars lay abandoned in the countryside in the late '30s and '40s, rusting in the weeds and reminding folks of the interurban's sad failure.

He helped them get around

World War I veterans had Daytonian Luzern Custer to thank for inventing an electric three-wheeled "invalid chair." The Custer chairs were also a hit at the 1939 New York World's Fair, where 110 of them were rented.

Early computing

Vacuum tubes? Electronic counting? NCR sowed the seeds for high-speed computing in the late '30s with the development of an electronic adding machine.

Not for men only

Earning distinction as the first woman member of Dayton's Engineers Club was aeronautical engineer Maude Elsa Gardner, who worked at Wright Field from 1936 to 1941.

Completed...

The first units in the DeSoto Bass Complex, one of the nation's first public housing projects.

Above: An afternoon at the Dayton Canoe Club was just one of the many ways in which people enjoyed the city's rivers.

One of the world's oldest forms of musical expression

Construction began on a magnificent shaft of granite, steel and limestone that would house "a chandelier of bells" to pay homage to the finer things in life. The Deeds Carillon was built thanks to Mrs. Edward A. Deeds, who bought the property, paid for the structure and established an endowment for its maintenance and operation. Ultimately, she said, the carillon would be a memorial to her husband.

'Absolutely unique'

■ In 1940, only six carillon towers existed in the United States. The Deeds Carillon became the first with exposed bells, which produced the purest tones and allowed the music to travel farther.

■ The architects who designed the Rockefeller Center also designed the Deeds Carillon.

■ The carillon's steel work was designed by James L. Edwards, who completed the same for such landmarks as the Empire State Building.

■ The "king" bell had a diameter of 6 feet and weighed 7,000 pounds; the smallest bell had a diameter of 20 inches and weighed 150 pounds.

■ The 32-bell ensemble (there are 50 today) is played via an elaborate electrical system operated by a musician touching keys at a console.

Right: The Deeds Carillon

Dedicated...

The Wright Brothers Memorial, on August 19 (National Aviation Day and Orville Wright's 69th birthday). Today, the monument overlooks Huffman Prairie. Ironically, the monument is made of 35 tons of marble — from North Carolina, of all places.

Hail to the chief

President Roosevelt visited Dayton on October 16. Orville Wright and James M. Cox accompanied FDR on a parade and city tour.

Death of a salesman

"If our clothes don't make good — we will." That was the motto for Jacob H. Margolis, founder of The Metropolitan clothing store, who greeted customers at the door and made sure they left satisfied. To Margolis, quality was the ultimate concern; customers, he said, would always remember quality before they remembered price. Margolis died October 19.

Pigskin: The final game

With Steele High School preparing to close, the last big game between archrivals Steele and Stivers would be the biggest ever. Victory was sweet for the soon-to-be-closed school (Steele won 13-0), and Stivers fans missed out, sadly, on that last excuse to paint the Steele lion statue with their own black and orange tiger stripes. Steele, built mostly of wood, was closed after being condemned for safety reasons. Its majestic lion mascot, cast in bronze and imported from Italy after student donations paid its way, now overlooks downtown from the grounds of the Dayton Art Institute.

Named...

Stanley C. Allyn, as NCR's president. He joined NCR soon after his 1913 college graduation.

Dayton stats

■ Population: 210,718.

■ Industrial payrolls: More than $100 million.

■ Factories: 432.

■ Products produced: 750 (many war-related).

The Great Migration

The number of blacks migrating from the rural South had increased Dayton's black population to 20,273 — up from 17,045 in 1930.

1940

Right: Leisure time brought people to Island Park, where they could rent boats, canoes and bicycles.

Below: Dayton's skyline, as seen from the Dayton Art Institute.

Above: Taken shortly before the attack on Pearl Harbor, this photo showed a crowd of downtown shoppers oblivious to the changes that were about to affect their lives.

A safe, if temporary, place to forget the woes of war

It was the evening of December 7, just hours after Pearl Harbor, and the horror of it all was still sinking in: Our nation was now at war. Thousands of service men and women would soon be passing through Dayton, and they would have many needs. Patterson Field's commander, Lt. Col. Merrick G. Estabrook Jr., made the phone call to Mrs. Viola Mansur: Would she organize a soldiers' club? Mrs. Mansur agreed, raising money and business support. Volunteers painted, hammered and nailed away to convert the Dayton Municipal Building's annex into the Soldiers Service Club, a lively activity center complete with library, hobby room, game room, chapel and kitchen. Charming junior hostesses (all single) broke the ice by leading groups in games, music, roller skating, art classes and big-band dances.

Over the next four years, a million service men and women (more than 17,000 a month) visited the Dayton Soldiers Service Club — and many of them, one would hope, were able to forget their troubles for a while.

Marked...

The 100th anniversary of Woodland Cemetery, on February 18.

Ran...

The last interurban traction car, from Third and Kenton in Dayton to Moraine, on September 27.

Moved...

The Dayton Public Library Museum, from the library building's annex to the Roberts Building at Second and Patterson.

SLICE OF LIFE

They're back!

After two years and no profit, the Brooklyn Dodgers threw in the towel on the Dayton Wings (the former Ducks). And who was waiting around for it to happen? Why, Howard E. "Ducky" Holmes, of course, the founder and former manager of Dayton's original ball club. The Dodgers leased the ball park to Ducky, who promptly renamed it Duck Field, and reorganized the Wings as — what else? — the Dayton Ducks.

Celebrated...

Dayton's centennial, June 15-22, with what the city deemed "fascinating, entertaining and educational activity." (Dayton officially became a city on May 3, 1841.) Highlights included Religious Day, Governors' Day, Youth of America Day, Defense Day, Homecoming Day, Aviation Day, Miami Valley Day, Ohio Day, dancing, exhibits, a midway and a historical outdoor program dubbed "Frontiers of Freedom," in which a 2,500-member cast dramatized Dayton's achievements.

1942

MILESTONE

The changeover to war

Almost overnight, Dayton-area industries turned themselves into war materiel plants — producing airplanes, gun carriages, bullets and bombs instead of refrigerators, washing machines, cash registers, car parts and percolators. The city's specialty: aircraft development and parts.

Many Dayton companies had been turning out war materiel for the Allies even before the United States got into the war.

'E' Flags

NCR, which just before the war had rolled out prototype machines with high-order computing functions, became the first Dayton company to win the Navy "E" flag for excellence in wartime materiel production; Frigidaire and Delco Products got their "E" flags soon after. All three produced munitions and precision war instruments.

For sale: War bonds

Folks at home were the "army behind the army," and their sacrifices were many — higher taxes, for one. Every dollar and dime a family could spare bought defense bonds and stamps. (Who could resist a pitch by stars such as Ilona Massey, Fred Astaire, Hugh Hubert, Bob Hope and Tony Pastor?)

On the ready

With all the defense facilities based here, enemy air raids seemed possible. Dayton appointed an air-raid warden and chief fire watcher; sirens cost the city $15,000. People learned how to prepare meals in prototype shelters — just in case.

Top: A war bonds drive included a flag-raising ceremony in front of the Old Court House.

Above: Bombers destined for action overseas were repaired in Dayton.

Donating money, saving scrap

War fund-raising efforts were streamlined into a War Chest, which combined campaigns into a single lobby. Blood drives and scrap drives were common; in 1942 alone, Daytonians collected a whopping 95,000 tons of salvage. Other items saved: paper, cooking fat, toothpaste tubes and tin foil.

Rosie the riveter

As the soldiers marched off, the Miami Valley's work force took on a new look: For the first time, women were working alongside men on the production lines. This meant a few changes were necessary. Who would care for children, for instance? NCR chief Stanley C. Allyn set up day nurseries for working moms and made sure defense-training programs were in place for women new to the factories. ■

SLICE OF LIFE

Shortages galore

Wartime life was simply not as sweet: By May, 246,000 Montgomery Countians had registered for sugar-ration books (7,000 suspected sugar hoarders were turned away). At first, people got 8 ounces weekly; later, they got 12. Soon coffee, cigarettes, soap and butter were rare sights in stores; even newsprint was in short supply.

Scarcest of all, perhaps, was natural rubber, since Japan had seized most of Asia's supply. To save on tires, gas was rationed via stickers. Salesmen, delivery people, emergency-vehicle drivers, clergy, reporters and photographers had nearly unlimited gas-up privileges; commuters were limited based on their driving distance. Those unlucky souls with "A" stickers, pleasure drivers, got a mere 5 gallons a week. But gas rationing worked better in principle than it did in practice. A black market for stamps flourished, and service-station attendants were known to take bribes for fill-ups.

With so many raw materials in short supply, substitutes had to be developed and produced en masse. Synthetic rubber replaced natural; metal alloys replaced tin; plastic aircraft canopies replaced glass. Nylon replaced silk for parachutes, tire cord and glider tow rope; wood and magnesium were used instead of aluminum on light cargo planes, gliders and some trainer aircraft. Research on materials substitutes was performed at Wright Field.

Top: Women worked assembling bomb fuses at NCR.

Above: Buses were a popular means of mass transportation, as this crowd at the Cincinnati & Lake Erie line attested.

Right: Women filled the void left by men in local factories. Here, aircraft engines were being assembled.

1942

Dream realized

The bells of the just-completed Deeds Carillon Tower rang loud and proud on Easter during the first concert. Who played? Mrs. E.A. Deeds, of course.

Paved...

Grass runways at Wright Field, so that large aircraft could be tested.

A lot of hard questions, bravely answered

Wright Field became a center for expanded aviation medicine research and flight-stress studies, pioneered by Capt. Harry G. Armstrong. He and other researchers became willing guinea pigs in the lab's cold-altitude, all-weather and decompression chambers, seeking answers to such questions as: What happens to the body during high-speed, high-altitude flights? How fast and how high can a pilot go? When is oxygen needed?

Joined...

Delco Moraine, with Delco Brake.

The music lived

The Dayton Philharmonic Orchestra hung on tenuously as player after player went to war. Conductor Paul Katz was determined to keep playing, and snagged some Wright Field personnel to round out his corps in the interim.

The Ducks' end

"Ducky" Holmes, who had again taken over Dayton baseball in 1941, continued being expelled and suspended from games throughout 1942 (as was his habit). After the Ducks were eliminated from the Middle Atlantic League championship, Ducky suffered a mild heart attack and finally called it quits on his baseball career.

Top: Rallies during the war years drew large crowds to the steps of the Old Court House.

Above: City services — including trash collection — continued during the war.

Left: After a controversial career and health problems, "Ducky" Holmes left baseball.

MILESTONE

War work

Working around the clock to "keep 'em flying" during the war were the tens of thousands of civilian and military employees at Wright and Patterson fields — 37,789 civilians and 13,545 military personnel in 1943.

Ultimately, it was the aircraft that were designed, tested, improved and repaired at Wright and Patterson that assured an Allied victory. The logistical support by these men and women sustained 243 combat groups, 80,000 planes and 2.4 million troops.

Labor: In short supply?

The U.S. War Manpower Commission announced that Dayton was a No. 1 "critical labor area" — meaning it had a genuine labor shortage. Because skilled labor was in great demand, companies had set up training programs to make new employees as productive as possible as quickly as possible. The labor shortage, insisted Dayton's industrial leaders, was at Wright and Patterson fields. Business leaders worried the commission's designation would give the industrial community a black eye, potentially resulting in canceled or fewer government contracts, which could hurt the local economy.

Not quite life as they knew it

In Montgomery County, 30,000 had marched off to war; at home, people were doing the jobs needed to help defend the country. But as always in wartime, there were problems: The Dayton area was grossly unprepared for the influx of workers in its factories and at Wright and Patterson fields. With 75,000 to 125,000 new people in the area, traffic was terrible, and the housing shortage was acute.

BOMBE

Top: Military repair work continued around the clock at the Dayton Municipal Airport.

Middle: With its high-speed computing technology, NCR turned its efforts toward the war, building a code-breaking machine.

Right: Citizens Federal's war bonds sign was bigger than the White Tower diner that held it.

Without bounty

Canned, fresh or frozen — food cost more, and was rationed; ceilings were set to prevent price-gouging. People received a canned-food allotment of 48 points per month, which wasn't much. Gone were the days when housewives opened three to five cans of food for a single meal. In February, folks were urged to plant vegetable gardens to maintain balanced family diets (unhealthy workers, after all, could lead to factory absenteeism, which would hurt the war effort). By July, gardens were thriving. Some families even grew milkweed, used to stuff life jackets.

Full steam ahead

Employment was up 124 percent from 1933, and Dayton was producing 750 different products — many for war — in its 432 factories.

Begun...

Linden Center Service Men's Club, for the 700 black servicemen from Patterson Field.

War secrets: The 'Dayton Project'

Scientists at the Monsanto Chemical Company began work in Dayton on a secret project that would not only end the war — but also change the world forever. Inside an old warehouse on West First Street, built in 1879 to house Bonebrake Theological Seminary, scientists studied polonium, vital to building the atomic bomb. By 1946, a permanent polonium-production facility was needed. Miamisburg's Mound Laboratory, which became the first facility of the Atomic Energy Commission, opened in 1948. ■

SLICE OF LIFE

Sheepish among tombstones

At Woodland Cemetery, keeping the grass mowed was tough, with so many men away. When someone suggested using sheep as natural mowers, it seemed like a good idea. In April, 100 sheep were trucked in and turned loose on the cemetery's lawn. As it turned out, they preferred chomping on Woodland's exotic trees and plants — which made some sick, others crazy. By July, exasperated administrators had given the critters their walking papers.

Above: Daytonians reported to the local Internal Revenue Service office where they paid their taxes under a sign that advised, "You can prepare your income tax return in only 5 minutes."

Left: David Rike (center) waved to the crowd during the Christmas parade.

Below: Patrons of the arts filled the lobby of Memorial Hall.

MILESTONE
War grinds on

Dayton's war role included housing several hundred Italian prisoners of war in the old Gentile Air Station, later known as the Defense Electronics Supply Center. At Wright Field, several hundred Axis prisoners were housed at barracks on Fifth Street.

Wartime women stayed busy

Between 1940 and 1944, manufacturing employment among women in the Dayton-Springfield area more than doubled, to 50 percent of the work force. Most worked in Army Air installations; many others made artillery shells. Code-breaking machines that later cracked German secrets were assembled by 600 Navy women at NCR's Sugar Camp.

At the fields: Hustle and bustle

Wright and Patterson fields hummed with activity 24 hours a day toward the goal of building the world's strongest air force. Long vacations were forgotten as a 48-hour work week became common; many people worked even longer hours in the labs or at home.

■ Wright Field concentrated on aircraft design, development and flight testing; it wasn't unusual for 40 or more aircraft programs to be under way simultaneously. Specifications for new aircraft were developed; technical problems reported by pilots were investigated and resolved. R&D focused on everything from pressurized cabins and deicing systems to fuel-tank technology and controllable bombs.

■ Patterson Field focused on supply, maintenance and repair. Warehouses were built to handle overseas materiel needing repair and to store supplies from Fairfield Air Depot. The amount of materiel coming and going was staggering: In September alone, 6,165 tons of domestic shipments and 2,350 tons of overseas shipments were made — enough to fill 460 freight cars. That same month, warehouse personnel accepted 17,622 tons of incoming supplies and equipment — enough to fill 630 more freight cars. ■

Above: On May 31, a flagpole donated by Mr. and Mrs. Joe Guy was dedicated in a ceremony at Valley and Keowee streets. The Wright Field Firing Squad did the honors.

How could anyone turn her down?

None other than Shirley Temple, who was a teen-ager now, arrived in Dayton to sell war bonds at Roger's Jewelry store on Main Street. She also appeared September 13 at Rike's to drum up support for the war.

Music that inspired

The Dayton Philharmonic Orchestra received a distinguished service citation from the Music War Council of America. Since January 1942, the orchestra had given pops concerts to help folks escape, at least briefly, from the worries of war. The council recognized its "patriotic and inspiring use of music to aid the war effort."

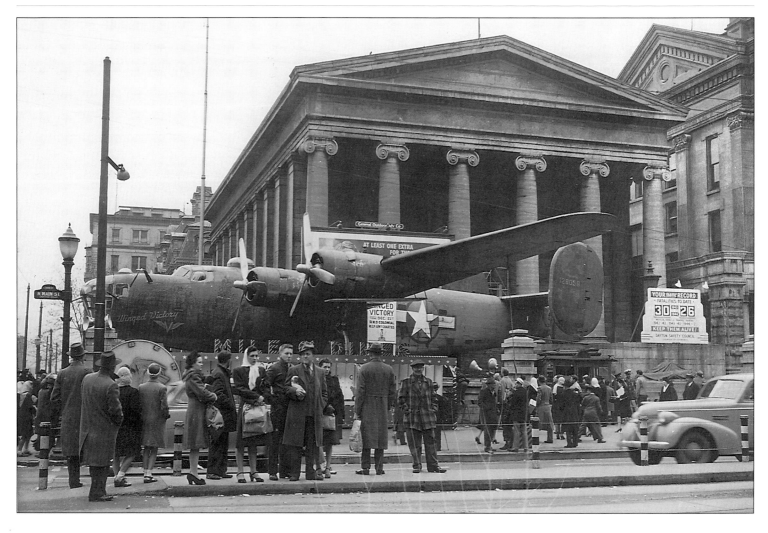

Above: Fund-raising in support of the U.S. war effort included the display of a full-size bomber on the front lawn of the Old Court House. Money was donated through the "Mile O' Dimes."

Right: Navy WAVES worked at NCR's Sugar Camp on code-breaking projects.

Above: The B-29 Superfortress, developed in Dayton at Wright Field, helped speed the end of the war with its large payload of bombs and its field-tested durability.

Below: In March 1944, war bonds paid for a $31 million cruiser in Dayton's name. The U.S.S. Dayton not only shielded aircraft carriers from attack in the Pacific, but also helped bombard Japanese shore installations.

Fox trot

WHIO radio organized an unlikely New Year's Day event: a fox hunt. Gathering southeast of Centerville were 3,000 men, women and children, all armed with clubs and bats and ready to do battle with eight foxes that somehow had gotten blamed for damaging local farmers' crops. Despite the odds, the foxes won: Six of the eight got away.

Necropolis

The old City Lot at Woodland Cemetery was closed to any future burials, on September 21. Nearly 3,000 were buried here.

Entertainment at its best

The war didn't stop Dayton's night life. People still enjoyed big bands; dancing at the Biltmore, Van Cleve, Gibbons and the Miami; stage shows; movies at Loew's, Keith's and the Colonial; and Red Skelton, Eddie Fisher and Stepin Fetchit at Lantz's Merry-Go-Round on Main Street.

Back in the saddle again

Passenger Orville Wright took the controls briefly on the Army's C-69 Lockheed Constellation — his first piloting in 26 years — during a demonstration flight over Dayton. After this, back trouble kept him out of the planes he'd pioneered.

Flown...

A jet aircraft, by an American woman for the first time. Anne Baumgartner flew the XP-59A at Wright Field for 30 minutes.

Served...

Dayton's Katharine Louise Kennedy Brown, as vice chairwoman of the Republican National Committee from Ohio, until 1952.

Died...

Julia Shaw Patterson Carnell, founder and benefactor of the Dayton Art Institute.

Moved...

Mead's headquarters offices, from Chillicothe to Dayton.

Increased...

Dayton's black population, by nearly 50 percent, since 1940.

SLICE OF LIFE

Built...

■ 1,075 housing units in Dayton, by the Federal Public Housing Agency.
■ 334 family units (whites only), by private builders.
■ 30 units (blacks only), by private builders.

Groceries: What they cost

■ Bacon (1 pound): 35 cents.
■ Smoked ham (1 pound): 33 cents.
■ Hamburger (1 pound): 25 cents.
■ Broccoli (two bunches): 25 cents.
■ Carrots (two bunches): 15 cents.
■ Flour (25-pound bag): $1.25.
■ Potatoes (100-pound bag): $2.98.

1945

MILESTONE
Hard at work

The total payroll at Wright and Patterson fields this year reached $131.5 million — one-third of Dayton's total industrial payroll.

Building a better warplane
One of Wright Field's longest wartime projects was development of the B-29 Superfortress. Near war's end, B-29s were dropping 1,200 tons of bombs daily. The B-29 dropped the atomic bombs on Hiroshima and Nagasaki, ending the war. ("Bock's Car," the plane that dropped the second bomb, lives today at the U.S. Air Force Museum.)

GM's reliable M-30
The Inland Division of General Motors, which before the war had made running boards, steering wheels and small molded parts, produced America's standard ground weapon: the M-30 carbine, a five-pound rifle later judged the nation's best ordnance effort of the war. By 1945, Inland had produced 2.6 million carbines.

Purchased...
More than $314 million in war bonds, by patriotic Dayton-area folks.

Skyrocketed...
Employment at NCR, from 8,000 just before the war to 20,000 this year.

The aftermath
In all, Dayton's war contracts topped $1.645 billion. By 1945, a Dayton Chamber of Commerce survey predicted that war prosperity — which had fattened the pocketbooks of most Dayton companies — would help produce an $80 million postwar expansion program of public improvements as well as private investments in new construction, machinery, equipment, fixtures and remodeling.

The end of the war
Germany surrendered on May 7. After Japan surrendered on August 14, the streets of downtown Dayton were filled with joyous people who caroused, kissed, cheered and hugged and could hardly believe the wonderful

Above: The Classic Theater, with black ownership and management, was still thriving. It had opened in 1927, when blacks were denied admission to many white-owned theaters.

Left: A crowd gathered as a fire damaged the upper story of the Kuhns Building (now the Chemineer Building) downtown.

news. It was a new world again; anything seemed possible. Service people returned home to pursue the American dream, flooding the University of Dayton, Miami University, Miami-Jacobs Business College and Sinclair College, thanks to the GI Bill. ■

Died...
Howard E. "Ducky" Holmes, former manager of the Dayton Ducks, in September.

Resigned...
Frank M. Tait, from the Dayton Power and Light Company on December 31, to become chairman of the board.

Expanded...
McCall's Corporation's printing plant, on McCall Street, to the tune of $11 million.

Resumed...
Research by NCR, for applying electronics to business machines, after the war's end.

This page and next page: News of the Allied victory reached Dayton, where the sounds of celebration filled the night.

Right: The shield from the U.S.S. Dayton was returned here after the war. It had accompanied the ship across much of the Pacific, including the scene of the Japanese surrender. E.V. Stoecklein, Dayton's city welfare director, held the flag for the photograph.

Below: In its heyday, the Dayton Arcade offered the city's largest selection of food.

Taking control

Oversight of Shawen Acres, the children's home, was assumed by the Child Welfare Board on January 1.

Better late than never

In a typewriter case, of all places! After 30 years, Orville Wright on December 9 found the historic wind-tunnel balance instrument that he and Wilbur used in the early 1900s to collect data about air-pressure forces on wing surfaces. Apparently, brother Lorin had packed the instrument inside the typewriter case before Orville's move from the 1127 W. Third St. bicycle shop to his laboratory on 15 N. Broadway in 1916.

Renamed...

The Miller's Ford Station power plant, on the Great Miami River south of downtown Dayton, to the Frank M. Tait Station. Tait, elected Dayton Power and Light's first president in 1934, served in that capacity for 34 years.

Rode...

More than 66.4 million people, on the city's transit system of trackless trolleys and motor coaches.

Hired...

John W. Berry, son of Loren M. Berry of the successful Yellow Pages sales company, to an entry-level post in the family business.

Used...

An ejection seat, for the first time, by Sgt. Larry Lambert — who ejected from a P-61 at almost 8,000 feet.

In service again

The highest-ranking black female officer in the Women's Army Corps — Lt. Col. Charity Earley — retired this year, joining many Dayton civic groups.

They wanted more, more, more

Annexation was again the talk in Dayton as city officials presented an aggressive plan for taking over 31.1 square miles of territory in all directions of the 25-square-mile metropolitan area. Oakwood and Van Buren Township, which a few years later became Kettering, were among the areas targeted.

Park plans

Seemed like a good idea: Salute the Miami Valley's role in the development of industry and transportation in a grand and permanent way. Col. E.A. Deeds thought a park would be quite a fitting commemoration. Today's Carillon Historical Park is the result of his vision.

To be (or not to be)

They married in record numbers — and divorced in record numbers, too. Montgomery County recorded 5,229 marriages and almost as many splits (4,075).

End of an era

Cars 712 and 702, joined in a two-car train, made Dayton's last streetcar run down the tracks of the Third Street line at 1:30 a.m. on September 28. While some of the retired streetcars were sold in South America, most were burned and the steel cut into scrap. Last to feed the flames: No. 72, "Old Barney," of the Barney & Smith Car Company.

Rebirth of a legend

Restoration began on the original 1905 Wright III Flyer, which would be displayed at the new historical park planned by Col. E.A. Deeds. Aircraft parts stored in an out-of-state museum were returned to Dayton and combined with other parts from Orville's Dayton lab. Orville painstakingly supervised the work by aircraft mechanic Harvey Geyer, who had worked with the Wrights from 1910 to 1912. Approximately 60 percent of the restored Wright Flyer III is original.

A new outlet for shoppers

Dayton got its first shopping mall after Arthur Beerman built McCook's on Keowee Street. He soon followed suit with three other malls: Northtown, Eastown and Westown.

Licensed...

TV2, by the Federal Communications Commission. This was Dayton's first FCC-licensed television station, though another station, WHIO, beat it onto the airwaves.

Merged...

The Dayton Historical Society, with the Montgomery County Historical and Archaeological Society.

Purchased...

The traction lines' bus operation, by Greyhound.

And the first sonic boom, too

The world's first supersonic flight happened in the California desert on October 14, with Capt. Charles E. "Chuck" Yeager at the controls. Much of the theory and testing for the flight had been worked out back in the Miami Valley at Wright Field, where Yeager had been a test pilot.

Above: Dayton was known for traffic safety.

Below: The waiting room at Dayton Municipal Airport.

Boom town

■ Dayton had the most automobiles per capita of any Ohio city.

■ Dayton Municipal Airport, with 1,700 acres, was Ohio's largest city-owned airport.

■ General Motors employed 40,000; NCR, which employed 14,500, got busy filling $100 million in backlogged orders.

■ Sales were up 25 percent at Reynolds and Reynolds and Standard Register.

■ Employees at Wright and Patterson fields pumped $2 million into the Dayton economy — every two weeks.

Out of this world?

Wright Field became involved in the investigation of a mysterious crash in Roswell, New Mexico. Officials said the downed object was a weather balloon, but stories persisted that it was a flying saucer. Some even claimed that alien bodies had been recovered and transported here for further study. That investigation and others involving UFOs fell under Project Blue Book, headquartered at Wright Field.

Named...

Stanley C. Allyn of NCR, by *Forbes* magazine, as one of the nation's 50 most influential business leaders.

Established...

The Sunshine Biscuit Company, from a merger between Dayton's Green & Green Company with the Loose-Wiles Biscuit Company. (During World War I, Green & Green manufactured hard bread for the army; by 1926, the company had become the largest biscuit bakery in Ohio.)

Died...

Frederick H. Rike, leader of Rike's department store since 1907 and a builder of modern Dayton. His son David L. Rike became president of the Rike-Kumler Company.

Right: The Pvt. Fair statue and Civil War monument were dismantled and moved to Riverview Park. They were returned to Main Street in 1993.

Below: Downtown Christmas shoppers bought paper bags from entrepreneurial youths who "worked" the sidewalks.

1948

Consolidated...
Wright and Patterson fields, which were renamed Wright-Patterson Air Force Base on January 13 after the government created an independent Air Force in 1947. The southern part of Patterson Field was called Area A, Wright Field became Area B, and the northern portion of Patterson Field became Area C.

Died...
Orville Wright, at age 76, on January 30 in Miami Valley Hospital, after a heart attack. He never got to see his Wright Flyer III restored, nor the original Wright Flyer installed at the Smithsonian Institution. Thousands of mourners lined the streets for his February 2 funeral. The value of his estate: nearly $1.024 million.

Retiring a workhorse
NCR replaced its old Corliss steam engine with the more efficient, less expensive modern steam turbine. This new 44-ton, 200-square-foot turbo generator produced more than 25 times the power of the Corliss per square foot of floor space. Col. E.A. Deeds had the honor of shutting down the venerable Corliss on March 13.

No room for a soldier
Traffic jams became a problem in post-war Dayton, especially where the Soldier's Monument created a bottleneck on Main Street. The solution? Pvt. Fair had to be moved. Riverview Park was chosen as the monument's new home. The city's best-known Civil War veteran was removed April 14, and then cleaned and rededicated before a crowd of 10,000 on September 2. The bill: $37,061.71.

Called in...
1,200 National Guardsmen, to keep order in late July after striking workers at the Univis Lens Company fought 150 police officers near the Leo Street plant.

Purchased...
Hawthorn Hill, for $75,000, by NCR on November 11. The company redecorated the home for its guests, and left Orville's library intact.

Night shopping

His customers wanted it, but would his employees go for it? David L. Rike gambled and left his store open in the evening, Mondays only. Another gamble, thought his fellow retailers: Rike's decision to build a nine-story store addition on the site of the old Miami Hotel.

He stayed at the Biltmore

Gene Autry — with his white hat, colorful shirt and a horse named Champion — was America's favorite singing cowboy. He appeared at Memorial Hall this year.

Distinguished guests

Dayton was visited by Harold Stassen and Robert A. Taft, who were seeking the Republican nomination for President. They were defeated by Thomas Dewey, who ran against Harry S. Truman and lost.

Appointed...

John W. Berry, as general sales manager at the L.M. Berry Company.

Purchasing the competition

The Dayton *Journal* and the *Herald* were bought by *Dayton Daily News* publisher James M. Cox.

Resigned...

George H. Mead, as chairman of the board at the paper company.

Movie-going masses

Dayton's three RKO theaters — Loew's, Keith's and the Colonial — brought in $2.324 million in revenue this year.

It makes you proud, doesn't it?

The original Wright Flyer, installed at the Smithsonian Institution December 17, bears this description:

The original Wright Brothers aeroplane

The world's first power-driven, heavier-than-air machine in which man made free, controlled, and sustained flight

Invented and built by Wilbur and Orville Wright

Flown by them at Kitty Hawk, North Carolina, December 17, 1903

By original scientific research the Wright brothers discovered the principles of human flight

As inventors, builders, and flyers they further developed the aeroplane, taught man to fly, and opened the era of aviation

Above: Wright-Patterson Air Force Base was growing, both in size and importance.

Above: Lakeside Park was a popular picnic spot.

Right: The Irwin, Jewell & Vinson Company on East Third Street catered to painters.

On the air

TV2 got its license before anyone else, but it wasn't first on the air. The first television station to sign on in Dayton was WHIO, on January 26. WLW-D, TV2, also made its first broadcast this year with Milton Berle hosting the premier of *Texaco Star Theater*. In 1976, WLW-D became WDTN.

Besides watching "Uncle Milty," families tuned in to see Jackie Gleason, Lucille Ball, Groucho Marx and Howdy Doody. Miami Valley viewers also enjoyed such local TV personalities as Uncle Al, Ruth Lyons and Paul "Baby" Dixon.

Free and clear, finally

Paid off this year was the $34 million debt for the five dams in Dayton's flood-control project. After this point, taxes collected by the Miami Conservancy District were slated for system maintenance.

Completed...

A high school stadium in the Carillon neighborhood — later renamed Welcome Stadium after P.B. Welcome, the Dayton schools' director of athletics — only nine months after the fund drive was launched. Today the stadium is jointly owned by the city and the University of Dayton.

Dedicated...

Beth Abraham Synagogue, at Salem and Cornell.

Born...

Mike Schmidt, in Dayton, on September 27. He graduated from Fairview High School, became a major league baseball star as a third baseman with the Philadelphia Phillies, and joined the Baseball Hall of Fame in 1995.

1950

Merged...

Osborn (incorporated 1876) and Fairfield (incorporated 1834) to form the town of Fairborn on January 1. The Greene County communities were forced together several decades before, when Osborn had to be moved to make way for Huffman Dam.

A grand opening

People flocked to see the opening exhibitions at Carillon Historical Park, the 1946 brainchild of Col. E.A. Deeds. The featured exhibit at the 65-acre park: The restored 1905 Wright Flyer III, the world's first practical airplane, displayed for the first time inside Wright Hall in June. Today the park features 20 museum buildings, including Newcom Tavern and other historical structures from around the Miami Valley.

Began...

The Korean War, on June 25.

Begging to pay taxes, believe it or not

Dayton citizens, concerned about the city's financial crisis, were steamed when the Ohio Supreme Court ruled that City Council's passage of a half-percent city income tax was invalid. So they hit the pavement, collected signatures and had the measure placed on the ballot. Voters passed the tax with an overwhelming 75 percent majority, making Dayton the nation's first city to restore a tax formerly declared illegal. Later, the city income tax was increased to 0.75 percent.

Opened...

Town and Country Shopping Center, in what would become Kettering.

Born...

Cathy Lee, who would become Cathy Guisewite, in Dayton. She became a famous cartoonist and creator of the popular cartoon strip *Cathy*, which was syndicated in 1977.

Moved...

Esther Price's candy business, from the Prices' Fauver Avenue home to its present location on Wayne Avenue.

Dayton stats:

- Size: 25.91 square miles.
- Population: 258,000.

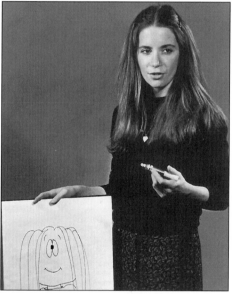

Above: A savage blizzard hit the area, paralyzing traffic and nearly every other outdoor activity. It was talked about for years.

Left: Cathy Guisewite

Below: Carillon Historical Park preserved several of Dayton's significant buildings.

See for free

Families on a budget didn't have to go far to find entertainment in the 1950s. Movies were shown for free in the NCR Auditorium on weekends. Children got a special treat: free candy after the show.

Won...
The Central League title, by the 4-year-old Dayton Indians, a Class-A baseball team. The Indians' winning season, however, turned out to be its last year in baseball.

Traveled...
The University of Dayton's basketball team, to the National Invitational Tournament. UD lost to LaSalle in the finals.

Recorded...
Sales of more than $200 million, by NCR. Of these, one-third were international.

Born...
Ronnie and Donnie Galyon, Dayton's own Siamese twins, on October 28. Doctors decided against separating the two, who were joined at the abdomen and spent some of their youth touring with a circus before settling down here.

Above left: Tom Blackburn coached the University of Dayton basketball team.

Above right: Christmas carolers entertained patrons in the Miami Hotel.

Above: The National Cash Register complex sprawled across much of South Main Street.

1952

Hurray for Harry

President Harry S. Truman was treated to a downtown procession in an open convertible. The crowd cheered wildly, as office workers dumped confetti from Main Street buildings.

Company acquired

NCR took a giant step into the computer age when it bought a California-based computer company this year.

Printed...

More than three million magazines, by the McCall's Corporation's Dayton printing plant.

Founded...

Chemineer Inc., for making mixers and agitators.

Kids saved the museum

The museum part of the Public Library and Museum of Dayton, incorporated this year as the Dayton Society of Natural History, started a fund drive after learning it had to vacate the Roberts Building at Second and Patterson by the end of 1954. The campaign was jump-started by Dayton schoolchildren, who raised a whopping $25,000. The museum's new building on Ridge Avenue finally opened in 1958. And what was slated to replace the Roberts building? A parking lot, of course.

Renamed...

Dayton Municipal Airport, to the James M. Cox Dayton Municipal Airport.

Coping with cars

■ With automobiles gaining ever more popularity, some wags predicted that passenger trains were doomed. Nonetheless, lots of folks came out to see the "Train of Tomorrow," on display at Union Station downtown. What they saw stunned them: upholstered chairs, sun decks, reading rooms, modern kitchens and plush sleeping quarters and restrooms.
■ Cars had already stolen lots of riders from the city's transit lines, which carried 47 million passengers this year — down significantly from 1946, when the city's trackless trolleys and motor coaches carried 66.4 million riders.

Above: President Harry S. Truman, who campaigned in Dayton in 1948, returned in 1952 for another visit.

A grand centennial celebration

Rike-Kumler Company employees gave up their free time to act in a musical telling the company's 100-year story. If you couldn't make it to the NCR Auditorium to watch, you could listen to David Rike tell the tale on WHIO and WING radio. Both events were part of the department store's centennial celebration, which kicked off February 2. Shoppers enjoyed cake, souvenir matchbooks and specially designed shopping bags and wrapping paper. Rike-Kumler's sales were $41 million in 1953, a per-capita volume that ranked it among the top five U.S. retailers that year.

On December 17, an armed robber hit the Rike's cashier's office for $32,597. The bandit, later captured, said he was unemployed and had stolen the money to help support his family. David Rike quietly saw to it that the man and his family had a nice Christmas.

Ended...

The Korean War, in July. With the peace, though, came the fear of an atomic superpower conflict — and the Dayton area's heavy concentration of military might made folks even more worried that the Cold War could heat up in their back yards. Bomb shelters and Civil Defense drills were serious concerns.

Needed: Rain, and lots of it

Rural families across the Miami Valley roasted and suffered as a drought parched the Midwest.

Arrived...

The National Air Show, in Dayton, for the 50th anniversary of flight.

Purchased...

Moraine Farm, Col. E.A. Deeds' former 50-room estate, by NCR. The company used it as a guest house for customers and prospective clients.

Dedicated...

The Temple Israel synagogue, at Salem and Emerson avenues.

Celebrated...

Sesquicentennials, by Xenia, Greene County, Montgomery County and the state of Ohio.

Above: July Fourth celebrations were held at the Diehl Band Shell at Island Park.

Urban renewal: To save Dayton, tear it down

The Safety Building at Third and Perry streets, completed this year, was one of Dayton's first urban-renewal projects designed to combat city blight. Another demolition project financed by the city's first urban-renewal bond issue: eliminating an area once known for Lib Hedges' prominent prostitution operation of the late 1800s.

1954

Robbed...

The Farmers and Citizens Bank in Trotwood, on September 23, by two crooks who got away with $80,000.

A new and better dog food

Believe it or not, minks were what inspired Paul Iams, a self-taught animal nutritionist, to create what he called the first nutritionally complete dog food. Visiting a mink ranch, Iams noticed the glossy coats and vitality of some dogs there. When he learned the pooches were eating the same food as the minks, he went to work — eventually developing a premium dog food and founding the Dayton-based Iams Company.

Getting away

The car was giving Daytonians their ticket out of town, and things looked bleak for downtown — which recorded a retail sales increase of only 6.1 percent from 1948 to 1954, compared to 56.3 percent in the suburbs. Theater owners were suffering, too. Dayton's three RKO theaters had revenues in 1948 of $2.324 million — which fell to $1.828 million in 1954. Why? Television, suburban drive-ins and neighborhood theaters.

Renewed...

Dayton's half-percent income tax.

Completed...

St. Elizabeth Hospital's first new building, which faced Miami Boulevard.

Formed...

The United Theological Seminary in Dayton, from the merging of Bonebrake Seminary and the Evangelical School of Theology in Reading, Pennsylvania. The seminary's roots date back to 1871, with the old Union Biblical Seminary on Home Avenue. Bonebrake, a later incarnation of the school, moved to its present Harvard Boulevard campus in 1923.

Opened...

Eastown Shopping Center.

Reopened...

The U.S. Air Force Museum, which had closed during World War II. It first opened at McCook Field in 1923.

Above: In the burgeoning auto age, drive-in movies drew late-night customers, who often saw frontier-style justice in action on the outdoor screen.

Left: A Civil Defense training center featured "Rescue Street," where emergency crews could prepare for the worst.

**Above:
Edwin C. Moses**

**Right: Edna
Goodpasture stood atop
her family's bomb
shelter on Maeder
Avenue in Drexel.**

Dedicated...
Orville Wright Elementary School, on
February 9.

Needed: Schools for the baby boomers
The Dayton District Development Committee
passed a $20 million bond issue for building
new schools. It was Ohio's largest bond issue for
school construction.

A new look
Upholstered seats for 2,500 guests, better
acoustics, air-conditioning and an orchestra pit
were some of the improvements slated for
Memorial Hall. Restoration began this year.

American athlete
Born this year was Edwin Corley Moses, the son
of two Dayton teachers. Moses became a
two-time Olympic gold medal winner in
hurdling (1976 and 1984) and captured the
bronze at the 1988 Olympics in Seoul,
South Korea.

Above: The gutted stage of Memorial Hall became like a scene for street theater during the building's renovation.

1955

A gem of a deal

Dayton's old Callahan Bank Building got a new name — the Gem City Savings Building — after being bought by Gem City, which soon changed its name to Gem Savings. In the 1980s, Gem Plaza was built at this site. The clock atop the Callahan Building was later moved to crown a Reynolds and Reynolds office building.

Incorporated...

Kettering, as a city, from what had been Van Buren Township. The new suburb's core: Town and Country Shopping Center.

Printed...

52 national publications, all at the McCall's Corporation's Dayton printing plant.

Opened...

The Antioch Shrine Temple, for Dayton's Masonic organizations, at the northeast corner of First and Jefferson streets.

Invented...

Carbonless copy paper, by NCR.

Top: Looking north along Main Street, the Callahan Bank Building was in the center, topped by its clock.

Above: The Main Street bridge was getting its first major overhaul since its construction.

Right: Roy Rogers was in town for the Grand American trapshooting tournament.

Below: American Airlines flew the Flagship Dayton.

It happened on April 24
Fire tore through the two upper floors of Thal's downtown store.

Dedicated...
The $1.08 million North Main Street bridge, on October 12, after 19 months of construction.

System maintenance
The Miami Conservancy District began a 20-year series of improvements to the Valley's flood-control system. Levees were raised, bridges and deflecting walls constructed, pumping stations built, channels widened and gravel deposits removed. The price tag: $4 million.

Going south
JC Penney left downtown in favor of a spot in Kettering's Town and Country Shopping Center.

Not foreign to Rike's
Rike's patrons enjoyed espresso in the main dining room, sampled international entrees and watched ladies model clothing from other countries in the Foreign Bazaar of 1956. Rike's bazaars were popular well into the 1960s.

Completed...
Memorial Hall renovations, for $865,000. Civic booster Miriam Rosenthal spearheaded the effort.

Renamed (but only a little bit)
The Dayton Chamber of Commerce became the Dayton Area Chamber of Commerce to reflect its mission of serving the entire metropolitan area.

Opened...
Westown Shopping Center, by Arthur Beerman.

SLICE OF LIFE

Stop and go
By this year, Dayton's traffic lights numbered 8,262.

No news was bad news

The *Dayton Daily News* and *The Journal Herald* were forced to stop publication December 20 after a crippling strike by the local mailers' union. During the 23-day strike, reporters and photographers sent news to local TV and radio stations; stories and photographs were prepared and stored in file drawers until publication of the *Daily News* resumed January 12, 1958, and *The Journal Herald* on January 13. When they hit the streets again, both papers recapped top stories from the strike weeks. The shutdown hurt advertisers, too, since it hit during the Christmas season.

During the strike, popular Daily News *sports editor Si Burick attended the Rose Bowl — but got to report none of it for his readers.*

Moved...

The *Dayton Daily News* and *The Journal Herald*, into the same plant at Fourth and Ludlow streets. Dayton's two dailies began sharing mechanical facilities, but kept separate news staffs. ■

Died...

Newspaper publisher, former governor and presidential hopeful James M. Cox, on July 15, at the ripe old age of 87.

Founded...

Philips Industries, in October, by Jesse Philips, who believed there was lots of money to be made in the manufactured-housing industry. The company's first product: aluminum windows for mobile homes.

Spiraling sales

NCR's sales in 1957 were $380 million — nearly three times the 1947 sales figure of $138 million. Sales were also healthy for the Reynolds and Reynolds Company, which surpassed the $12 million mark for the first time.

Above: Mayor's was a prime downtown shopping spot for jewelry, watches, and later, records. Located at Third and Main, the store was on the site where the One Dayton Centre building is now.

Left: The latest home appliances were displayed inside the Gas & Electric building.

Below left: Si Burick followed Ohio State home games from the stadium press box.

Bye-bye buses?

People began showing a preference for cars over public transportation. Dayton-area trackless trolleys and motor coaches carried half the number of passengers in 1957 that they had a decade before. Ridership this year: down to 33.5 million.

Computers: In their infancy

The middle of the decade saw NCR develop its first all solid-state computer for business use.

Live!

Daytonians enjoyed live summer theater at the newly renovated Memorial Hall. John Kenley brought the stars to Dayton.

Retired...

Col. E.A. Deeds, who had been NCR's chairman for 26 years.

Dayton stats

■ Population of the Dayton standard metropolitan area, which included Greene and Montgomery counties, was 612,000 — up about 12,000 from 1956.

■ Dayton-area payrolls topped $995 million a year; of this, $160 million came from Wright-Patterson Air Force Base and Gentile Air Force Depot.

Burned...

Ray's furniture store, at Fourth and Main streets, in June.

Planning ahead

Metropolitan Studies Inc. began a survey to determine how the Dayton area could cope with the problems of growth. Specific needs, according to the *Dayton Daily News*:

■ Metropolitan cooperation to solve area-wide problems.

■ Expressway construction to relieve traffic congestion.

■ Downtown revitalization based on careful appraisal of needs.

■ A new airport terminal.

■ A capital-improvement package to meet multiple county building needs.

■ Urban renewal through slum clearance and rehabilitation.

■ Water conservation measures to perpetuate natural resources.

■ Development of a medical center.

Where once there were cornfields

Was it possible that Dayton and Cincinnati might someday become the north and south poles of a giant metroplex? Unprecedented growth in Montgomery, Greene, Butler, Warren and Hamilton counties led visionaries to predict the merging of the Dayton-Cincinnati areas by 1975, which would produce "one gigantic linear metropolis."

No room at the dorm

A housing shortage at the University of Dayton encouraged school officials to transform part of the downtown Gibbons Hotel into a dormitory for 350 freshmen.

Above: A driver's training car maneuvers through busy traffic at the corner of Main and Monument. The Dayton Fire Department headquarters was — and still is — located on the corner.

1958

And they built it in Kettering, of course

In pondering how best to memorialize Charles F. Kettering, his son and daughter-in-law, Eugene and Virginia, decided nothing could be better than a hospital. The couple, who became two of the Dayton area's leading philanthropists, began the drive to build Kettering Medical Center.

No welcome mat

It wasn't uncommon for restaurants to shun black patrons. One Dayton restaurant owner stopped black convention-goers from eating at his establishment by placing "reserved" placards on dining tables.

Opened and dedicated...

The new Dayton Society of Natural History museum building, at 2629 Ridge Ave., on city-donated land.

The pilferer

A 57-year-old clerk from Piqua embezzled $375,000 from Troy's Hobart Manufacturing Company — and used it to buy antiques. Lots of them, apparently.

Dayton stats

■ The plane, not the train: For the first time, more people traveled from Dayton via airplanes than railroads.
■ Safer roads: Dayton recorded only 24 auto deaths this year, an apparent benefit of the city's installation of 145 new traffic lights.
■ High earners: Industrial workers earned more than their counterparts in other large Ohio cities. Weekly wages for the average Daytonian: $101.21; Columbus and Cincinnati workers earned $83.21 to $85.18 weekly.
■ Shoppers' bonanza: From 1950 to 1958, 10 shopping centers were built in Dayton's suburbs, with 150-plus stores.

Above and below: *23 Paces to Baker Street* **played at the RKO Colonial (above) at Fifth and Ludlow, while** *Take the High Ground* **was at Loew's (below), across Main Street from the old Victory Theater.**

Top: The NCR 304 was the company's first solid-state computer for business use.

Above: Summer shoppers had the sidewalk almost to themselves at the corner of Fourth and Main streets.

Died...

Eight Beavercreek Girl Scouts and two of their mothers, after their station wagon collided with a train in March. Citizens groups formed immediately to demand safer railroad crossings.

In Lincoln's memory

The Young Republican Club of Montgomery County placed a new placard at the Old Court House on September 17. It reads: *"Abraham Lincoln appeared on these Court House steps on the afternoon of September 17, 1859, and spoke denying the assertion of the Hon. Stephen A. Douglas, senator from Illinois, that human slavery was protected by the Constitution."*

Crashed...

An Air Force Starfighter jet, into a home at the northwest corner of Grange Hall and Indian Ripple roads in Greene County on November 2. The wreck killed two children and their mother.

Weaknesses — and strengths

Dayton and its suburbs in Montgomery County began recognizing their problems as a major metropolitan area:

■ Uncontrolled growth and slums.

■ Downtown business decline and shabby commercial development at the city's outskirts.

■ Factories and shops in residential areas.

■ Hemmed-in industries that could not expand logically.

■ Jammed highways and ailing public transportation.

■ Disorganized local governments suffering severe budget crunches.

Despite the problems, 1959 saw some progress:

■ Montgomery County began its "fight against blight."

■ Partial segments of new expressways were completed.

■ A separate city aviation department was formed.

■ Delta Air Lines began north-south service from Dayton, and United Air Lines started east-west service.

1959

Abroad they went

The Dayton Area Chamber of Commerce sponsored its first-ever European tour for Dayton businessmen, who visited a dozen countries.

New owners

Without a male heir, worried David Rike, what would happen to Dayton's famed department store? Instead of dissolving the corporation, Rike agreed to allow the Rike-Kumler Company to become a division of Federated Department Stores, a national conglomerate, after an exchange of common stock.

Incorporated...

■ Heidelberg Distributing Company.
■ Sinclair College.

Opened...

■ The city's first intensive-care unit, at Miami Valley Hospital.
■ The first multi-level parking garage, at Main and Monument, for Rike's customers.

Toward more Catholic schools

After an archbishop's appeal for funding new high schools, 19,000 Dayton-area Catholics reached into their pockets and came up with a grand $5 million. The result: Carroll High School in East Dayton and Alter High School in Kettering; expanded were Chaminade, Julienne, and St. Joseph Commercial high schools.

Announced...

Plans by Monsanto Chemical Company to build a special metallurgical facility in Miamisburg. The purpose: to produce neutron sources for starting atomic reactors.

Retired...

Joe Keller, 76, as Rike's downtown Santa Claus. Taking over the red suit was Emery Conrad, who played the jolly old elf through 1985.

Broadcast...

A daily half-hour news program on WHIO-TV, by Phil Donahue.

SLICE OF LIFE

Playing at the movies

Brigitte Bardot in *Crazy For Love*; Gary Cooper in *Wreck of the Mary Deare*; Fabian in *Hound Dog Man*; and Victor Mature in *The Big Circus*.

Below: Third and Main streets, seen from the steps of the Old Court House.

1960

Top: John F. Kennedy was received warmly in Dayton.

Above: Lucinda Adams (right) coached Dayton runners after bringing home an Olympic gold medal.

Right: Sam Hall earned a silver medal during the same Olympic games.

Dayton-area Olympians

■ Dayton teacher Lucinda Adams took a break from class to win the gold medal in the 400-meter relay at the summer Olympics in Rome. Later, Adams supervised health, physical and driver education in the Dayton City Schools.

■ Kettering diver Sam Hall, son of future Dayton Mayor Dave Hall and brother of future Congressman Tony Hall, brought home a silver medal in diving in August.

'New Frontier'

Both John F. Kennedy, the Democratic presidential nominee, and Richard M. Nixon, the Republican nominee, campaigned from the steps of the Old Court House. A *Dayton Daily News* editorial said of Kennedy:

"He is a vigorous man, this composite thinker-doer on the new frontier — youngish, committed to the philosophy that public problems can be solved and the American creed reborn as the greatest revolutionary doctrine of all time.

"Is he naive? Will Congress block him? Or will the people catch his vision? At least he promises action, forward motion, for 1961."

Both Kennedy, who appeared on October 17, and Nixon, who spoke on October 26, reportedly drew crowds of 25,000.

189

1960

Won...
The state AA basketball title, by the Roosevelt High School Teddies, on March 26.

Died...
Dayton industrialist and former NCR board chairman Col. E.A. Deeds, on July 1. He was 83.

Mourning for loved ones
Five Daytonians were among the 125 people killed when a TWA Super Constellation that had left the James M. Cox Dayton Municipal Airport collided with a United Air Lines DC-8 over New York City on December 15.

Hints of cooperation
A regional planning commission seemed possible after an effort initiated by 22 chambers of commerce in nine counties: Butler, Clark, Clinton, Darke, Greene, Miami, Montgomery, Preble and Warren.

Completed...
The northern leg of the U.S. 25 expressway through Dayton, from Neff Road to North Main Street, and the highway south of the city to Cincinnati, both later called Interstate 75. U.S. 35 also began to take shape. After much debate, city, state and federal officials finally agreed that the rest of the new expressway should be aligned east of the Great Miami River.

Continued...
Urban-renewal projects in East Dayton.

Opened...
A Montgomery County family court center.

Discriminated against...
Blacks, in Dayton's housing market.

Ranked...
Huffman Manufacturing Company, as the nation's third-largest bike manufacturer.

Converted...
Brown Hospital, of Dayton's Veterans Administration facility, into a men's dorm for University of Dayton students.

Above: The Montgomery County sheriff's office planned to provide communications for Civil Defense operations in potential emergencies. Manning the phones were Sgt. Mel Casey (right) and Sgt. Paul Whalen.

Left: Workmen placed the stairway to a fallout shelter being built in Washington Township.

Above: Dayton's Main Street, mapped "four poles wide" by Daniel Cooper in 1801, still gave drivers plenty of room to maneuver in the 1960s.

Dayton stats

■ Population: 262,332, only a slight increase from the 1950 population of 258,000. Dayton suburbs, on the other hand, were growing fast: By 1960, for example, Kettering's population was 55,000.

■ A new economy: Manufacturing employment declined by about 500 employees this year, when the monthly average was only about 90,150. Ohio Gov. Michael DiSalle announced that a committee would study how to handle the consequences of machines replacing workers, and how to help those considered "chronically unemployable."

■ Good news and bad news: More retail and service businesses in suburban shopping centers helped push total employment in the Dayton Standard Metropolitan Area to 246,500, up from 237,000 in 1959. Nevertheless, unemployment climbed to 3.9 percent — up from 1959's rate of 2.3 percent.

No more status quo

Life as Dayton knew it was changing. A *Dayton Daily News* editorial summarized: "Businesses and services are reaching out to serve wider areas. Factories are reaching out farther to attract employees. People are going greater distances for boating, shopping, hunting and fishing. Colleges and universities are reaching out with branches and adult programs to meet new demands for education."

1961

Elected...
Dayton's first black city commissioner, Don L. Crawford.

Reaping what you sow
It was bound to happen, eventually, in a city that was so deeply segregated and where blacks had been excluded for decades from theaters, many neighborhoods and businesses. The Rev. W.S. McIntosh led local blacks in a march down West Third Street, ushering in Dayton's Civil Rights era.

Yet another blowup
An explosion occurred for the 14th time in 26 years at United Fireworks in January. Between 1934 and 1959, 12 men died in 13 accidental blasts here.

Turned pro...
Tennis player Barry MacKay, of Oakwood. He played professionally until 1966.

Things hopping at Rike's
■ Rike-Kumler Company announced a major expansion of the downtown Rike's store, on the old Miami Hotel site, on March 3.
■ In October, the company opened its first suburban store, in Kettering.

Sold...
The Dayton Tire and Rubber division of Dayco Corporation, to Firestone, on April 1.

1+1=1
Dayton's two smallest banks — Merchants National Bank and Trust, and Peoples Bank and Trust, a state bank — merged on June 5. They formed the National Bank of Dayton, with assets of more than $80 million. Dayton's other two home-based banks: Winters, with $250 million in assets, and Third, with $105 million.

Leaving town
Daytonians were alarmed to learn on July 27 that Master Electric, with its 1,600 jobs and $9.5 million payroll, would move to Columbus and Madison, Indiana.

Keeping 'em cool
Frigidaire, meanwhile, was enjoying growth in its auto air-conditioning business.

Above left: City Commissioner Don L. Crawford

Above right: Barry MacKay

Below: The downtown Rike's store (shown here) was expanded, and the company's first suburban store opened in Kettering.

Even higher education
■ Ohio State and Miami universities announced plans on August 8 to operate a state university division near Wright-Patterson Air Force Base. Folks wondered: Could it someday turn into a full-fledged university?

■ About the same time, the University of Dayton announced plans for $3 million in new construction. A $6 million capital-fund drive was launched, with half the money slated for UD's projects and half for the new OSU-Miami branch university.

Right: The old library could be seen through the framework of the new library during construction.

Opened...
The James M. Cox Dayton Municipal Airport's modern terminal, replacing a rickety tower and shed.

Completed...
Ohio 4, to its junction with U.S. 25, later known as Interstate 75. Construction of U.S. 35 forged ahead.

Announced...
$15 million in new construction, by the Dayton Power and Light Company, mostly for electric transmission and distribution.

Planned...
A Montgomery-Greene County regional study committee, to find ways to save open spaces.

Seeing stars
A planetarium was added to the Dayton Museum of Natural History, thanks to the Junior League of Dayton.

Changing of the guard
Stanley C. Allyn retired this year from NCR, which by now had annual sales exceeding $500 million — 45 percent from overseas customers. Robert S. Oelman became the new chairman of the board.

Expanding
GM's Inland Manufacturing Division announced in September that the former Aeroproducts plant in Vandalia would house some of its expanded manufacturing operations.

'Blue law' battles
The owner of Woody's Market in West Carrollton got a 10-day jail sentence on October 13 for violations of the "blue laws" that prevented businesses from opening on Sundays. The conviction was overturned a year later.

Saboteurs under every bush, back then
The Air Force Logistics Command headquarters annex at Wright-Patterson Air Force Base burned to the ground on November 22, causing a $2 million loss. Just three days later, three more buildings on base went up in flames — a $1 million loss. Base officials suspected sabotage.

Let the rivalry begin
By November, real-estate developer Arthur Beerman had bought enough stock to control the Elder & Johnston Company — and the "feud" began between Rike's and what eventually became the Elder-Beerman Stores Corporation. Beerman, owner of the downtown and suburban Beerman Stores, became board chairman of Elder's.

The bus stopped here
Shoppers wanting to take the bus downtown to finish Christmas shopping had to shop elsewhere, thanks to a 32-day strike against City Transit. Downtown retailers suffered because of the strike, which was finally settled the week before Christmas.

Golf, anyone?
Feeling the need to expand its recreational facilities, the city approved spending for a new public golf course, which opened at the Miami River Well Field in 1965. Today the Kitty Hawk Golf Course, which includes two championship 18-hole courses and an 18-hole, par 3 course, hosts an average of 100,000 golfers annually and has been the site of many major tournaments.

SLICE OF LIFE

The times, they are a-changin'
Dayton, its suburbs and all of southwest Ohio saw more changes in 1961. Said a *Dayton Daily News* editorial:
"Bends in the roads became villages, towns and villages headed for city status, and cities, like hungry magpies, pecked away at unincorporated land through annexations. With more people and more land serving them, problems mounted for Southwest Ohio. Classrooms swelled with students, zoning and land use problems rose, highways and airports took on additional traffic, recreational lands became crowded and sparse, water conservation suffered."

High hopes for the computer
Dayton-area experts predicted many scientific advancements for the coming years. Said Brother Leonard A. Mann, dean of UD's College of Arts and Sciences, in the *Dayton Daily News*:
"Will we finally learn how to teach (computers) to perform high level, intelligent feats, such as language translations, or the design of economic systems?
"Computers (will) be the heart of another revolution — that of relieving man of much time-consuming intellectual work, and free him to soar to the highest realms of thought and creativity."
Only time would tell, it seemed.

1962

A new public library

The old castle-like library building — in use since 1888 and memorable for its French Gothic Romanesque style featuring Dayton limestone and Marquette red sandstone trim — was demolished after library collections were moved to the new building in Cooper Park downtown. The main branch of the Dayton & Montgomery County Library is still here today.

In Tait's honor

Ground was broken in January for the Frank M. Tait auditorium at the Dayton Museum of Natural History. The new wing opened in 1963. Tait, who had been DP&L's president and chairman of the board, never saw the project completed. He died February 25 at age 88.

Merged...

Beerman Stores, with the Elder & Johnston Company, acquired in 1961 by Arthur Beerman. After the January 30 merger, Beerman began planning a new suburban store.

Closed...

Walter Uhrig's haberdashery in the downtown Gibbons Hotel, in January, after 32 years.

Pelted...

The region, by an ice storm on February 23. Dayton alone suffered $1 million in damage.

Founded...

The Dayton Human Relations Council, after debate in the midst of civil-rights concerns.

Champs!

■ The University of Dayton Flyers won the National Invitational Tournament title for the first time March 24. The Flyers were coached by Tom Blackburn.
■ That same day: Dixie High School won the state Class-A championship.

Arrived...

Pornographer-to-be Larry Flynt. The man who would go on to create *Hustler* was born in Kentucky and ended up in Columbus, but got his start in sleaze in Dayton, where he bought a string of bars and published a sexually explicit newsletter that evolved into the magazine.

Above: The old library was shouldered aside by the new building (foreground), and was soon razed.

Left and below: As the new library was finished, the tedious task of moving books from the old library started.

Converted...

The Gentile Air Depot in Kettering, to the Defense Electronics Supply Center, on May 2.

Missing commissioner

On August 2, Dayton police started searching for missing City Commissioner David Pottinger. He was found September 16 in a Knoxville, Tennessee, hospital. According to the *Dayton Daily News*, Pottinger claimed to have had "amnesia after being worked over by three men in East Dayton who were offering information on numbers rackets."

Destiny: Pro baseball

Born in Dayton on August 4 was Roger Clemens, who pitched for the Boston Red Sox starting in 1983. Clemens, a three-time Cy Young Award winner (1986, 1987 and 1991), was named the American League's Most Valuable Player in 1986.

Honoring the greats of the air

Downtown's Biltmore Hotel was the first of several homes for the Aviation Hall of Fame, founded October 5 by the Dayton Area Chamber of Commerce to honor the nation's premier aviation and aerospace legends. The first inductees were the Wright brothers. Over the years, others included Charles Lindbergh, Lt. Gen. Jimmy Doolittle and Neil Armstrong. For 26 years, famed cartoonist Milton Caniff drew inductees' official portraits.

Banned!

University of Dayton freshman basketball star Roger Brown, indicted for game-fixing in 1961, led the NCAA to place the Flyers on two-year probation. Penalty: No post-season tournament play for UD.

The voters speak

Rejected: A proposal to increase Dayton's income tax from 0.75 percent to 1 percent. The city would have collected $18 million in seven years.

The beginnings of an outer belt

The state approved an interstate highway bypass east of Dayton. Stop-and-go starts delayed the completion of Interstate 675 for 24 years.

Right: Roger Clemens

Below: Gentile Station was home of the Defense Electronics Supply Center.

1962

'Wright State'

New Ohio Gov. James A. Rhodes was working to fulfill a campaign promise to get $7 million in state money for the proposed Miami-Ohio State branch near Dayton. Meanwhile, Stanley C. Allyn, formerly of NCR, spearheaded the local effort to establish the university. He worked with NCR's Robert S. Oelman to raise the $6 million needed from the community to fund the branch and make $3 million in improvements at the University of Dayton. The branch, to be called Wright State Campus, was slated to open in 1966.

Talked about...

A regional jet airport.

Periodically speaking

More than a billion magazines — including *Newsweek*, *Reader's Digest* and *U.S. News & World Report* — were printed and bound this year by Dayton's McCall's Corporation.

Dayton: Nucleus for a 'mega-city'

"Mega-City 70-75" was the name bestowed by the Dayton Area Chamber of Commerce on the 27-county area that included the six metro areas of Lima, Richmond, Springfield, Columbus, Cincinnati and Hamilton-Middletown. The vision: making Dayton the mega-city core.

Funds get OK

Kettering citizens finally gave the city approval to fix its main roadways, long in need of repair.

Accelerated...

Home sales in the suburbs, thanks in part to a rapidly expanding freeway system.

Remodeled and opened...

The old 12-story Gibbons Hotel downtown, which became the new Dayton Inn.

Separated...

Vandalia, from Butler Township.

Paper sales

By this year, Mead had annual sales of $405 million.

Moved up...

Phil Donahue, from host to producer of *Conversation Piece*, a call-in show.

1963

MILESTONE
Rike's was surprised

It was a full-fledged sit-in, with signs and songs — and Rike's was unprepared. Thirteen members of the Dayton branch of the Congress of Racial Equity wanted to talk to store officials on July 28 about the company's minority-hiring practices. Did Rike's discriminate? Were employment practices fair?

No one from Rike's would talk. So the CORE members, refusing to leave, lay on the floor. The police were called and arrests made; in the meantime, some whites spat on the black protesters, who quietly endured the mockery.

But the incident changed Rike's, which soon afterward pledged it would give equal consideration to all job candidates, regardless of color. ■

Right: Civil-rights pickets demonstrated in front of the downtown Rike's building.

Above: Jesse Philips (right), president of Philips Industries, and executive vice president Matt Jofreda mapped customers' locations. Philips parlayed his business into a fortune. He was generous with his money, and became a major Dayton philanthropist.

SLICE OF LIFE

Dayton stats

■ Payrolls: $1.2 billion-plus (9.1 percent more than 1962's figure).
■ Number of residential units: jumped 18 percent over 1962, thanks to new apartment construction.

Annexed...
1,193 acres, by the village of Moraine, creating pockets of opposition south of town. Miami Township immediately tried to bring 1,667 acres of Moraine back into township hands.

Established...
Dayton's first microelectronics research lab, by NCR.

Founded...
Miller-Valentine, as a general contractor, by engineers Gerry Miller and Dan Valentine. Jim Walsh later became the firm's third founding partner.

Planted...
Trees, downtown, thanks to the City Beautiful commission.

Approved...
Construction of baseball diamonds at the Montgomery County Fairgrounds. The fairgrounds study committee also agreed to give Miami Valley Hospital new parking space.

Death of an executive
George H. Mead, Mead Corporation's honorary chairman of the board, died January 1. His grandfather, Daniel E. Mead, founded the business in 1846. By 1963, Mead was one of the nation's 10 leading pulp, paper and paperboard companies.

Brrrrrrrrrrr!
Temperatures plunged to an all-time low of minus 19 on January 24. A month later, on March 1, 9.1 inches of snow fell in one day; flooding came as the temperature eased up on March 3 and 4. (That same month, Dayton marked the 50th anniversary of the deadly 1913 flood.)

Defeated...
A proposal to dump Dayton's city-manager form of government and establish a strong-mayor structure, on August 8.

To be sold...
The Dayton-based Gallaher drug store chain, with 55 stores in Ohio, Kentucky and West Virginia. The announcement came November 12.

Skidding to a near halt
The U.S. 35 and Interstate 675 projects suffered temporary setbacks after receiving no state money this year.

Changing the skyline
John W. Galbreath's plan to build a skyscraping Mead tower was welcome news for downtown. Arthur Beerman won the contract in 1965.

Like father, like son
Loren Berry's move up as CEO and chairman of the board at the L.M. Berry Company allowed his son John to become president this year.

Groundbreaking
Construction began at Wright State. Planners predicted a student body of 1,000 by fall 1964 and a second building ready for students by fall 1966.

Talked about...
A home-rule charter, which would give Montgomery County independent control over local affairs.

1964

Stepped in...

Assistant UD basketball coach Don Donoher, to coach the Flyers beginning February 29, after Tom Blackburn, UD's coach for 17 years, was hospitalized for lung cancer. Blackburn died March 6.

Published...

A humor column, by Erma Bombeck, in the *Kettering-Oakwood Times*. She later wrote columns for *The Journal Herald*.

Burned...

The Beckel Hotel, at Third and Jefferson, while it was being demolished, on March 2. Also burned this year: the Plantation Country Club.

Opened...

Kettering Medical Center, on March 3.

Named...

NCR's new president, R. Stanley Laing, on April 23.

The voters speak

■ Failed: Large and small park levies, in May; and funding proposals for a new county administration building.
■ Passed: A Dayton city income-tax hike in May, from 0.75 percent to 1 percent, for operating expenses and capital improvements; and a countywide indigent sick levy, in November.

After all those years in the same place

Newcom Tavern was broken down and moved from Monument Avenue to Carillon Historical Park this summer to become a regular historical exhibit beginning in 1965. Newcom Tavern is believed to be Ohio's oldest temporary seat of justice still standing.

New school in town

Wright State opened its first building, Allyn Hall, in the fall — a full two years ahead of the scheduled opening date of 1966.

Elected...

U.S. Rep. Rodney Love, who defeated Paul E. Schenck, a 13-year incumbent, on November 4.

Above left: UD basketball coach Don Donoher

Above right: Columnist Erma Bombeck

Above: Wright State's Allyn Hall

Left: Newcom Tavern in Carillon Historical Park

Above: President Lyndon B. Johnson was greeted by an enthusiastic crowd of 35,000 in Dayton.

Campaigned...

Presidential wannabe Barry Goldwater, in Dayton, on September 30. His stay was followed by a visit from incumbent President Lyndon B. Johnson, who spoke at Third and Main on October 16.

On the horizon — regional cooperation

The formation of the Miami Valley Regional Planning Commission, representing a nine-county area, was good news for Montgomery and surrounding counties. The commission's first goal: devising a regional master plan for orderly growth.

It just got to be too much

A 69-year-old man who was tired of aircraft noise began firing at planes flying from Wright-Patterson Air Force Base on December 5. The FBI caught up with the sniper, ending his shooting free-for-all.

1964

Racial progress

Passed this year was the federal Civil Rights Act, which banned discrimination based on race, color, creed or national origin; in Dayton, blacks had more job opportunities. Also this year: the Dayton Metropolitan Housing Authority's facilities were desegregated. Not everything changed overnight, however. City Commission overwhelmingly rejected a local Fair Housing ordinance, primarily because of opposition from the Dayton Area Board of Realtors.

Urban renewal, continued

■ Folks began moving into the new Dayton Towers high-rise apartment in East Dayton.
■ Architects were drawing up plans for the new downtown post office building.
■ Planning was set to begin on the city's newest redevelopment program, Mid-Town Mart, south of Fourth Street and east of Main.

Driving here, driving there

■ Federal approval came for the Interstate 675 bypass, which promised to alleviate traffic problems around Wright-Patterson Air Force Base and the new Wright State Campus.
■ The Ohio legislature gave the nod to money for U.S. 35 construction.
■ I-75 construction continued.
■ Miami Valley residents welcomed a new leg of I-70, from Clayton to the Indiana line, eliminating the need to travel on a dangerous two-lane route.

Hockey hits town

Dayton gets its first International Hockey League team: the Dayton Gems.

Left: The Dayton Gems brought professional hockey to town.

Below and bottom: Kettering Medical Center opened on Southern Boulevard.

Right: Inventor Ermal C. Fraze with one of his creations — the pop-top can.

Below: The first beam was installed across the Great Miami for an Interstate 75 bridge.

A feather in the city's cap

Dayton's most significant land acquisition in years was the annexation of Madison Township's Hoover-Shenandoah area, with 436 acres and 2,000 residents.

Educational strides

■ Wright State broke ground for a library-classroom building and a science and engineering building, both slated for completion in 1966.

■ At UD, graduate programs were coordinated and reorganized. Completed this year: a $2 million business administration building.

Approved...

Funds for expanding Dayton's Patterson Co-operative High School.

Ohio's 197th

Moraine became a city.

Invented...

The pop-top can, by Ermal C. Fraze. He went on to establish what's now Dayton Reliable Tool & Manufacturing Company. The Fraze Pavilion in Kettering is named in his honor.

Up and running...

A new water treatment plant at the Miami River Well Field, adjacent the Kitty Hawk Golf Course.

Increased...

■ Employment at NCR, by 2,300 people.

■ Sales jumped by leaps and bounds for at least two Dayton companies: Airtemp (38 percent) and Delco Moraine (24 percent).

Holy Moses!

Montgomery County Commissioner John C. Smith in March proposed erecting a Ten Commandments tablet on the courthouse lawn. The rest of the commission responded in the negative.

Died...

Miriam Rosenthal, one of the community's best-known boosters and fund-raisers, and manager of the Dayton Philharmonic Orchestra, on April 3. She was 64.

A lifesaver who gave his own life

By shielding five wounded soldiers from enemy fire, a brave Daytonian allowed his comrades to be evacuated on August 18 in Vietnam. Marine Lance Cpl. Joe C. Paul received the Congressional Medal of Honor posthumously.

A memorable quote

"This is the greatest thing since Ex-Lax." That's how Dayton's newly elected mayor, David Hall, expressed his delight with the outcome of the November election.

The voters speak, yet again

■ Passed: An unfair housing charter amendment that essentially let whites decide housing rights for blacks; the amendment said the public would have to vote on all fair-housing legislation. Also passed: the county's incinerator program, after a delay of nearly 10 years, and a large parks levy. This year saw boating facilities at Triangle and Eastwood parks enlarged and DeWeese Park expanded through land purchases.

■ Failed: A movement to fluoridate city water, and an effort to build a new county administration building.

Out with the old, in with the new

Completed this year was the new courts and jail building. At the same time, the old stone sheriff's office and jail from 1874, on West Third Street behind the Old Court House, was abandoned. In its place: Courthouse Plaza, later to be known as Courthouse Square.

Renamed...

Sinclair College, to Sinclair Community College.

1966

MILESTONE
Strained relations

Times were tense between blacks and whites in Dayton. When would the city help its black residents with their problems? When would blacks be allowed decent housing, education and employment opportunities? When a white man allegedly shot and killed Lester Mitchell, a black man, on West Fifth Street on September 1, a riot ensued. Dayton found itself with too few police to handle the situation, which ended in the destruction of several city blocks. More than 130 people were arrested for looting, and the National Guard was called in to help patrol the streets. By September 5, after the crisis had cooled and most of the Guard had been released, President Lyndon B. Johnson spoke at the Montgomery County Fairgrounds. Prejudice and racial tension, however, remained.

During the troubles, blacks gathered at Miley O. Williamson's home for Dayton NAACP meetings. Williamson spent nearly 50 years as the organization's executive secretary.

Some small progress
Dayton's Community Affairs Committee, a task force focusing on race relations, was formed by 12 businessmen and 12 black leaders. ■

Trade park land for classrooms?
City commissioners agreed February 9 to sell Deeds Park for development by the ever-expanding Sinclair Community College. The public, however, said no way. Park lands were at a premium, so Deeds was saved. Sinclair was located on urban-renewal land west of the downtown business district. Despite the public outcry, part of Deeds Park was still sold to allow expansion at the GHR Foundry.

Won...
The state AA basketball title, by Chaminade High School, and the Class-A championship, by Dixie High School, on March 26.

Above: Police guarded a looted store on West Third Street after the riot.

Below: Bridges began to stack up at the Interstate 75-U.S. 35 interchange.

Wave as you pass by!
Interstate 75 opened through downtown Dayton.

Construction: On hold
Local building screeched to a halt as five building trade unions went on strike for 21 days, starting May 2.

Defeated...
Rodney Love, as U.S. representative, by state Rep. Charles Whalen, a UD professor, on November 8.

Right: John Kenley

Below: Arthur Beerman

Planned...

A $50 million center for advanced studies and research at the University of Dayton. Later, Kettering Laboratories became the new home for the School of Engineering and the University of Dayton Research Institute.

Struck...

Employees at Rockwell Corporation.

Happy anniversary

Reynolds and Reynolds celebrated its 100th year.

Kenley returns!

Daytonians enjoyed live summer theater again, courtesy of John Kenley. The city's last summer theater productions had been in 1963. In the meantime, plans got under way for making Memorial Hall a full-time cultural activities center.

Saving Burns-Jackson

It was an area with a lot of potential, and it caught the eye of architect Bertrand Goldberg of Chicago. His $22 million master plan for restoring the 32-acre Burns-Jackson neighborhood called for a charming community combining old and new buildings. The architect's idea led to the Oregon Historic District.

Say hello

Established this year was ITT-World Directories, a subsidiary of the Berry Company and International Telephone and Telegraph Corporation, for selling and publishing telephone directories around the world.

Goodbye, Keith's

Fittingly, *Once Before I Die* was the last movie shown on February 28 at the RKO Keith's Theater, demolished so the Miami Valley Tower (then called the Grant-Deneau Tower) could be built at Fourth and Ludlow downtown.

Mid-air disaster

A TWA DC-9 ready to land at the James M. Cox Dayton Municipal Airport collided with a private plane over Urbana on March 8. Death toll: 27.

Won...

A $3 million anti-trust suit, by Arthur Beerman, against Federated Department Stores on July 18.

1967

Finally, a fair Fair Housing law

After having rejected one in 1964, Dayton City Commission OK'd a Fair Housing ordinance this year.

Out cold

At Frigidaire, 12,200 workers were on strike September 7-18.

Awarded...

Independent state university status, to Wright State on September 15, thanks largely to efforts by Stanley C. Allyn.

Donahue, on the air, from Dayton

Phil Donahue's *Conversation Piece*, a call-in talk show, was popular enough on radio that a TV version started on WLW-D. His first broadcast was November 6; the first guest was well-known atheist Madalyn Murray O'Hair. The show, famous for Donahue's interview technique, took off. After a while, 38 cities carried *The Phil Donahue Show*, which later moved to Chicago.

Selected...

Dayton, on November 16, as one of 62 cities to take part in the federal government's Model Cities program. The Model Cities grant wasn't approved until June 11, 1969.

On strike...

Dayton's newspapers, from August 23 to October 6.

More racial disturbances

Another racial tragedy occurred September 17 when a vice squad detective killed black Social Security representative Robert Barbee, who was carrying a pipe that the officer said he mistook for a gun. Racial unrest flamed again, this time spreading to the schools; Roth students boycotted their high school for a week. The police officer was found not guilty of manslaughter the following year. His acquittal fanned tensions again, causing 500 civil-rights protesters to hit the streets downtown.

Closed...

Union Stockyards, a long-time landmark, on December 27.

Left: President-elect Brage Golding proudly pointed out Wright State's change.

Below left: Robert Barbee

Below: A silent vigil took place at the scene of Barbee's shooting.

Bottom: Dayton police controlled crowds at a protest.

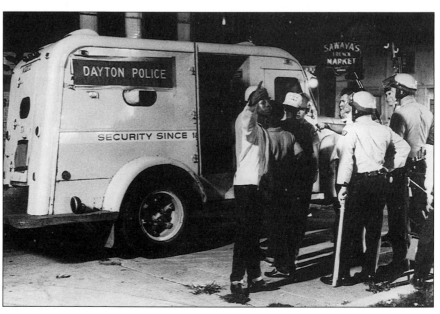

SLICE OF LIFE

Let's talk about the weather

This came from a *Dayton Daily News* 1967 recap:
"Rain or shine, cold or hot
Dayton, weatherwise, was not
Anything like Camelot.
Don't let it be forgotten
The weather here was rotten."
(Duly noted.)

Dayton teens: What was hot

Posters … miniskirts … marijuana … wild stockings … false eyelashes … the Beatles … paper dresses (and paper bikinis) … "Make Love Not War" buttons.

A Dayton's-eye view

Readers here got a better glimpse of world events after *Dayton Daily News* Editor Jim Fain brought back reports from Vietnam on the war, from Indonesia on the setback of Asian Communism, and from Detroit on the devastating race riots there.

Women's page columnist Maggie Fitzgibbons traveled to Russia to report on women's roles in the Soviet Union.

New faces on the sports scene

Women became regulars on Dayton fairways and in the bowling alleys.

Almost there

The UD Flyers got all the way to the NCAA finals — but then lost to UCLA.

Add some trees, a fountain, some bricks

A study of the central business district recommended a Courthouse Square renewal project.

Opened...

Children's Medical Center.

Top: Pickets carried strike signs outside the Frigidaire building.   **Above: Work continued on Interstate 75.**

1968

Spotless

Dayton was named America's cleanest city. Lady Bird Johnson awarded the trophy on February 20.

Black and white problems

More racial disturbances plagued the community. After Dunbar lost to Beavercreek in a March 1 high school basketball game, a skirmish followed on the court — a Beavercreek player ended up stabbed, and a fan suffered a fatal heart attack. A shooting incident on September 7 stopped a Dunbar-Roth football game at Welcome Stadium.

Marched...

Both blacks and whites, some 10,000 in all, in a tribute to the late Martin Luther King Jr. — who was shot and killed April 4.

Flooded...

The Miami Valley, on May 23, killing two people. It was the region's worst flooding since 1959.

On the trail

■ Presidential candidate George C. Wallace spoke at Hara Arena on July 6 for a fund-raiser.
■ On July 18, Nelson Rockefeller, seeking the Republican presidential nomination, campaigned in Dayton.
■ Candidate Richard M. Nixon also came to town October 22.

Died...

Rike's former Santa Claus Joe Keller, on September 9, at age 83.

Loan approval

The state announced on October 18 it would help fund construction of a sports arena at the University of Dayton.

Not here!

It could never happen at NCR — or so people thought. Nevertheless, on November 18, 15,000 NCR employees went on strike, and stayed out for a month. The local economy felt the loss of NCR's $2 million weekly payroll. It was the company's first walkout in 84 years. Despite the strike, NCR's worldwide revenues this year topped $1 billion.

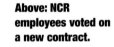

Above: NCR employees voted on a new contract.

Left: Striking NCR workers picketed at the complex's Stewart Street entrance.

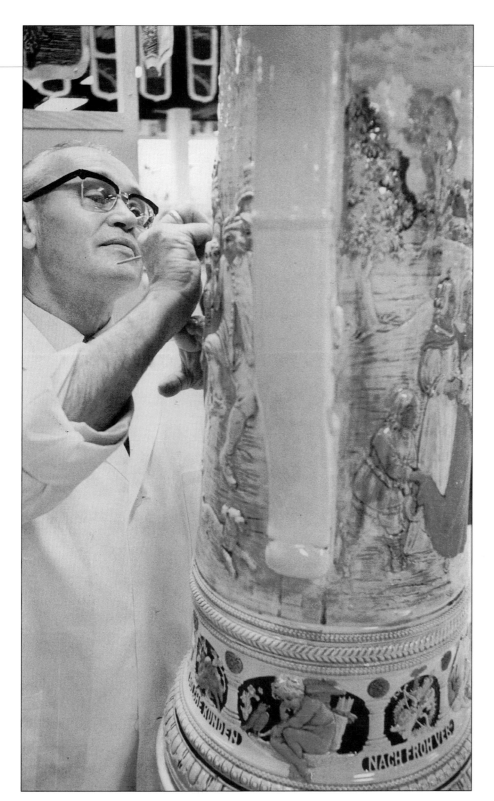

Above: Karl Lill from Germany painted a giant stein for Rike's bazaar.

Mayfair by the wayside

Skin flicks on the big screen and on stage were discontinued after November 30 at the Mayfair Theater (once a grand showplace for clean entertainment). The theater was razed. In its place: the Dayton Convention Center.

Cemetery addition

Woodland Cemetery administrators undertook one of their most ambitious projects ever: construction of the Woodland Mausoleum. Excavation began December 3.

Blockbuster buyout

In one of the biggest deals Dayton had ever seen, Pitney Bowes bought Monarch Marking for $93 million in stock.

New Hobart home

Completed was the new $2 million world headquarters building for Hobart Manufacturing Company in Troy, a maker of food machines, dishwashers and scales.

New dance troupe

The Dayton Contemporary Dance Company was created this year by Jeraldyne Blunden, who had taught ballet classes to black children.

Expansion plans

General Motors announced a two-year, $110 million capital-spending program that promised 2,000 new jobs here.

Victors!

The UD Flyers won their second NIT title in basketball.

Planned...

Construction of a $10 million, 30-story headquarters for Winters National Bank. Work on the building, which later became Winters Tower, was slated to begin on February 7, 1969.

Moved...

More blacks, into the suburbs.

Constructed...

A 500-space parking facility to serve Good Samaritan Hospital, on Philadelphia Drive.

Annexed...

The Salem Mall, into the city of Trotwood.

Acquired...

The Woodard Iron Company, by the Mead Corporation. Also this year: Allen Industries Inc. merged into the Dayco Corporation.

Accepted...

A downtown redevelopment plan, by the Center City Task Force.

A red-letter day for black Daytonians

Dayton's Fair Housing charter amendment was made moot by a U.S. Supreme Court ruling on January 20. Whites would no longer legally control fair-housing legislation in Dayton, or anywhere else.

Back to the drawing board

The UD Flyers' new 13,500-seat basketball arena got a temporary setback February 28 after much of the basic steelwork collapsed during construction. The late UD basketball coach Tom Blackburn had initiated the $4.5 million arena, which now hosts men's and women's basketball, university events and student entertainment.

Death of a philanthropist

Charles F. Kettering's son Eugene, best known for his work converting railroads to diesel-electric power and for advancing engineers and science, died April 19. His widow, Virginia, continued the Ketterings' philanthropic interests.

Mother Nature strikes

A tornado lashed Kettering on May 8 — injuring 25 people, destroying 13 homes, leaving 300 people homeless and causing $3 million in damage.

Lest we forget

Daytonian and Army Spec. Fourth Class Joseph G. LaPoint Jr. was posthumously awarded the Congressional Medal of Honor. On June 2, he tried to help two wounded men in front of an enemy bunker in Vietnam. A grenade killed all three of them.

Cremated...

The first body at Woodland Crematory, on September 25. The mausoleum was completed soon afterward.

Feeding the hungry

People with no place to go on Thanksgiving Day were invited to take advantage of Arthur Beerman's offer of a free turkey dinner. The Dayton tradition lives on through today's Arthur Beerman Foundation.

Above: Eugene Kettering donated a collection of some 600 model airplanes to the U.S. Air Force Museum, where they are still on display. His widow, Virginia (left), has become one of Dayton's most generous philanthropists.

Educational defeat

After a long history of supporting Dayton schools, voters rejected a tax levy — for the first time since the Depression — on December 9.

League leaves legacy

The Dayton Young Women's League deeded its headquarters property at 24 W. Fourth St. to Children's Medical Center, and gave the $106,000 received for the land and building to help finance expansion at the hospital. After this final act of generosity, the 200-member league — which had thrived with 6,000 members in the '20s and '30s — was dissolved.

A new gathering place for seniors

The Dayton area's elder citizens found the new Senior Citizens Center at West Fourth and Wilkinson their new home away from home.

Optimism reigns

A 1980 population of 1 million was projected for Montgomery and Greene counties, according to a 1969 regional plan. (The actual 1980 population fell a bit shy — by nearly 300,000 people.)

Died...

Marj Heyduck, *The Journal Herald's* women's page editor famous for her "Third and Main" column, and for always wearing a different hat, on September 15.

Held...

A PGA tournament, at NCR Country Club's championship course. NCR's Robert S. Oelman saw that all proceeds went toward low-income housing. Jack Nicklaus played here in the second championship tournament.

Built...

A four-story corporate headquarters for Price Brothers, as part of Dayton's urban-renewal program.

Peaked...

Worldwide employment at NCR, at 103,000 — 20,000 of these in Dayton.

Top left and right: Marj Heyduck modeled two of her many hats.

Above: Winters National Bank was at the corner of Second and Main streets. It was replaced by the Kettering Tower in 1971.

SLICE OF LIFE

The cost of keeping a roof overhead

■ Madison and Harrison townships: $14,500 for a 5-year-old home.
■ Northwest Dayton: $100 monthly rent for a five-room home.
■ Southeast Dayton: $115 monthly rent for a one-bedroom apartment; $20,000 for a three-bedroom home with 1 ½ baths and a two-car garage on a nice lot.

1970

A black leader at the helm

Dayton Mayor Dave Hall resigned for health reasons; appointed to succeed him was attorney James H. McGee, the city's first black mayor.

Completed...

Woodland Cemetery's mausoleum. It was dedicated May 1, 1971.

Died...

Arthur Beerman, one of Dayton's best-known retailers, on September 16.

Women unite!

Thirty local women organized the Dayton chapter of the National Organization for Women, which focused initially on three issues: sex discrimination in schools, potential discrimination against women and minorities by Dayton's major banks, and pornography. The local NOW chapter was founded four years after the national organization, dedicated to supporting equality for women.

Dayton company leaves town

A Canadian firm bought one of Dayton's oldest companies, Buckeye Iron and Brass, a maker of firehose nozzles and gasoline pumps. In 1900, Buckeye made tobacco cutters, hydraulic presses, and cotton- and linseed-oil extractors.

Still on the political scene

Octogenarian Katharine Louise Kennedy Brown began serving as regent of the Jonathan Dayton Chapter of the Daughters of the American Revolution. The former vice chairwoman of the Republican National Committee from Ohio (1944-52) served the DAR in this capacity until 1972.

Performed...

The region's first kidney transplant, by Miami Valley Hospital.

Left: Arthur Beerman

Below: Phil Donahue's controversial talk show included interviews with political activist Jerry Rubin and Gloria Steinem, the founder of *Ms.* magazine.

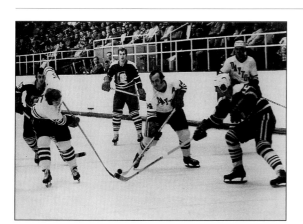

Foam rubber fueled downtown fire

Two workers from the Perl Leisure Products Company died after fire swept its Walnut Street building on March 21.

A violent year

Dayton chalked up 84 homicides, topping its previous record of 65 in 1969. One of the stranger tragedies: the June 11 accidental shooting of a 40-year-old DP&L lineman fishing in a canal at a city wellfield. The Centerville man was struck by a shot from a .22-caliber rifle wielded by a young boy upstream, who thought he was aiming at turtles.

Bankers moved in

Winters Bank employees settled in at the newly completed Winters Bank Tower at Second and Main, now known as the Kettering Tower. The 30-story tower, Dayton's tallest building, replaced the Winters Bank Building.

She became a national leader

Faye Wattleton — who in 1978 became the first black woman president of the Planned Parenthood Federation of America — began a seven-year stint in 1971 as head of Dayton's chapter. Wattleton's credits here include expanding services and doubling the office's budget.

Like grandfather, like father, like son

John W. Berry Jr. followed in the footsteps of his father and grandfather by joining the L.M. Berry Company this year.

Created...

The Miami Valley Regional Transit Authority, shortly after Dayton, Kettering and Oakwood pushed for ordinances to establish the RTA.

Formed...

A new Area Development Council, with $300,000 in funds.

Demolished...

The State Theater.

Top left: The Dayton Gems continued to draw hockey fans.

Top right: Faye Wattleton was president of the Dayton chapter of the Planned Parenthood Federation of America. She went on to become the national organization's first black woman president.

Above: The plaza area of the Sinclair Community College campus was under construction.

SLICE OF LIFE

Troubled times

The Dayton area, long known for high wages, low unemployment and years of smooth economic sailing, was plagued by a year of labor and economic problems:
■ With their high prices and wages, both Frigidaire and Airtemp began struggling.
■ Labor troubles at McCall's Dayton printing plant caused layoffs and contract losses.
■ Layoffs tormented both NCR and Armco, in Middletown.
■ Workers struck at Dayton Power and Light Company.
■ Area banks felt the squeeze with leaner commercial loan portfolios, and real-estate agents found home sales sluggish.
Nevertheless, in spite of a somewhat depressed local economy, the local consumer kept spending. By year's end, retail sales in the metropolitan area were 9 percent above 1970, topping $1.6 billion.

1972

Cracked...

A $2 million heroin ring, by Dayton police in January, who caught the crooks by pretending to accept $1,000-a-week bribes. Police were happy about the bust, but warned that at least nine similar rings remained in town.

Together (or not?)

A plan to integrate Dayton schools via busing — supported by Superintendent Wayne M. Carle — was rejected in January by a new conservative majority of the Board of Education. Carle was asked to resign in March, but refused. By April, Dayton faced a lawsuit from the National Association for the Advancement of Colored People, which asked the federal court to mandate busing in Dayton. The 1973 decision OK'd a token integration plan but barred busing and left school boundaries intact.

Pint-sized burglars

Their consciences finally got the best of them. Five children — ranging in age from 9 to 16 — confessed in March to 44 burglaries.

And someday, Muppets, too

WPTD, Channel 16, became Dayton's first public broadcasting station in April.

In the Wright brothers' honor

A national Wheelmen meet was held May 6-7 as part of a festival dedicating the Wright Cycle Shop reproduction at Carillon Historical Park. Festival-goers got to see 175 antique bikes, including many wooden models. The highlight: a parade of 81 high-wheel bikes from the park to the U.S. Air Force Museum, symbolizing the Wrights' deeds, from bicycles to airplanes.

Changes begin at NCR

William S. Anderson, appointed as NCR's new president in May, had tall orders to remake the cash register company in an industry moving quickly toward electronics and computers. Anderson's task was daunting: NCR's profits in 1971 were $2 million — down sharply from $50 million in 1969. He began by reorganizing, decentralizing engineering and manufacturing and phasing out mechanical products. By year's end, layoffs in Dayton alone totaled 2,000, and the company recorded a $60 million loss.

Left:
Tyree Broomfield

Promoted...

Tyree Broomfield, who later became Dayton's police chief, to a new major's post, in July. The job was created as part of the city's effort to move blacks into higher levels on the force.

Black vs. white

Racial tension flared in July with the injury of five Dayton blacks by a white joyrider brandishing a shotgun. In August, 100 blacks and whites attended a downtown meeting on racial harmony. But only two months later, six arrests were made after violence struck Stivers High School in a flap over an all-white Homecoming queen's court. A student committee settled the dispute by agreeing on an integrated court.

Opened...

The new campus of Sinclair Community College, on West Third Street downtown, in September. The enrollment: 6,500.

Acquired...

City Transit Company, by the Miami Valley Regional Transit Authority, in October. RTA took immediate steps to increase services and efficiency.

Rike's, Elder-Beerman: They made up

Elder-Beerman Stores Inc. accepted a $1.5 million settlement in November in exchange for dropping its anti-trust lawsuit against Federated Department Stores. Federated made the offer to settle a 10-year legal battle between the two retailers.

Defeated...

A half-percent income-tax hike, and a city charter change from the weak commission/strong-manager form of government, by Dayton voters in November. If passed, the charter change would have created a stronger city commission and new election districts.

Penalty for icing

Dayton almost got a major league hockey team this year. After the city turned down a 1971 proposal for a new 14,000-seat arena and hotel complex downtown, Dayton architect Paul Deneau withdrew his pledge to bring a hockey team to town.

Back in the saddle again

After Frigidaire realized its high wages were giving competitors the edge, the appliance maker froze wages and soon recalled some 3,000 laid-off workers.

Designated...

The Miami Conservancy District, as a National Historic Civil Engineering Landmark. It was the nation's first major regional flood-control system with retention reservoirs for controlled floodwater release.

Moved...

■ Joyce-Cridland Company, manufacturer of hydraulic lifts, from Dayton to Indiana.
■ Harris-Seybold Company, a printing machine manufacturer, to Cleveland.

Passed...

A new law allowing the sale of liquor on Sundays downtown.

Opened...

Three new suburban theaters: the Salem Mall 2, Dayton Mall 2 and the Kon Tiki 2.

Reopened...

■ The Victory Theater, renamed the Victoria Opera House.
■ Loew's theater, renamed the Palace.

Razed...

Montgomery County's "new" courthouse — the one built in 1884.

Hollywood in Dayton

Dayton-area showgoers enjoyed performances this year by stars such as Sonny and Cher, Victor Borge, Sammy Davis Jr., Bobby Goldsboro, Bob Hope, Henry Mancini, Elvis Presley, Lily Tomlin, Ike and Tina Turner, Jonathan Winters, and the "big bands" of Stan Kenton, Buddy Rich, Count Basie and Woody Herman.

New meeting place

January saw the opening of Dayton's new 77,000-square-foot Exhibition and Convention Center downtown. Not to be missed: a mural illustrating the famous "first-flight" photo of the Wright brothers. The mural, made of 163,000 mosaic tiles, depicts Orville as pilot and Wilbur running alongside the flyer.
Also this year: the Stouffer hotel chain announced it would build a 16-story hotel across from the Convention Center on East Fifth Street. The two buildings were eventually connected by a walkway over Fifth.

School super ousted

In January, the Dayton Board of Education ousted Superintendent Wayne M. Carle, refusing to renew his contract. Former Meadowdale High Principal John B. Maxwell got his job.

Above and right: A computerized print of the famous photo documenting the Wright brothers' first flight was used to guide the construction of a 62-foot tile mosaic. It was taken down and stored when the Convention Center was remodeled in the mid-'80s.

1973

The beginning of an era

An abortion clinic opened in Kettering shortly after the U.S. Supreme Court ruled in February that Ohio's law prohibiting abortion was illegal. Cost of an abortion at the Dayton Women's Health Center: $175.

Resigned...

Dayton Police Chief Robert Igleburger, considered by many to be liberal and innovative. Grover O'Connor became the new chief in August. Meanwhile, the city made good on its pledge to move blacks up the department ranks and add more black officers — much to the disappointment of whites who'd felt poised for promotions.

New faces, familiar faces

■ James H. McGee was re-elected, after having been appointed Dayton's first black mayor — and one of the nation's first in a major city.
■ After City Manager James E. Kunde resigned to take a post with the Kettering Foundation, James A. Alloway became city manager in 1973.

And a fine place to people-watch during lunch

City commissioners approved Columbus developer John Galbreath's plan to revitalize downtown's heart with two office towers and retail outlets in a third building. The result: Courthouse Plaza.

More violence

Dayton topped its homicide record again this year — from 89 in 1972 to 104 in 1973.

Ban autos downtown?

The notion was considered, but abandoned, when Montgomery County health authorities said auto pollution wasn't bad enough to call for outlawing cars downtown.

It was funk — Ohio Players' style

You couldn't help loving their brand of music. The Dayton-based rhythm-and-blues group made the big time with No. 1 hits *Fire* and *Love Rollercoaster* and platinum albums *Honey*, *Fire* and *Skin Tight*.

Headquartered...

The Montgomery County Historical Society, and a museum, in the Old Court House.

Left: James H. McGee was sworn in as mayor.

Below left: Gail Levin became Dayton's first woman commissioner, by appointment.

Above: The Ohio Players included (L-R) Chet Willis, Billy Beck, "Sugar" Bonner, "Diamond" Williams and Darwin Dortch. The group remained a force in popular music throughout the decade.

Appointed...

Gail Levin, the first woman on Dayton's City Commission. She was the only Republican, too. Her tenure was short; in 1974 Levin said she would not seek re-election the following year.

Released...

$150,000 in planning funds for a medical school at Wright State University, by the Ohio Board of Regents. But plans for the medical school were not without controversy: Another medical school being planned for northern Ohio made Gov. John J. Gilligan an outspoken opponent of the Wright State plan.

Walked out...

21 nurses at Miami Valley Hospital, claiming the emergency ward was unsafe.

Added...

The first audio-visual department, to the Dayton & Montgomery County Public Library.

Don't touch those puppies

Debark a beagle? Dayton and the nation cried foul after learning that Wright-Patterson scientists planned to snip the vocal cords of 200 beagle puppies in the name of medical experimentation. But the outcry was short-lived, and the Air Force proceeded with its debarking plans.

1974

Top: Xenia's courthouse square was devastated by a tornado, which caused damage in the hundreds of millions of dollars.

Above: After the tornado, students passed their damaged school on their way to classes.

Right: Rescuers helped this woman to safety, but the twister killed 32 people and injured many more.

A new era for the orchestra

Paul Katz, founder of the Dayton Philharmonic Orchestra, announced his retirement as music director. The 1974-75 season would be his last. Katz established the orchestra as a concert ensemble in 1933.

Sold!

A Dayton-Cincinnati-area investment group paid $1.6 million for the Biltmore Hotel and renamed it Biltmore Towers.

Struck...

Xenia, by a devastating tornado, on April 3. The twister killed 32 people, injured more than 1,000 and produced damage in the hundreds of millions of dollars.

Purchased...

The Montgomery County Airport, in January, by the city of Dayton. It was renamed Dayton General Airport South.

Formed...

The Bicentennial Commission, in March, to plan for celebrating the nation's 200th birthday in 1976.

Passed...

Two anti-handgun ordinances, by the Dayton City Commission on June 19, after a week in March that produced five homicides. One ordinance required handgun registration; the other banned "Saturday night specials."

More changes at NCR

The National Cash Register Company renamed itself NCR Corporation during William S. Anderson's restructuring. The 1970s saw NCR introduce new products, including sophisticated retail terminals, automated teller machines and computers. The company also began work on a $10 million corporate headquarters near Old River Park. By year's end, NCR's oldest building at Brown and Stewart streets — Building No. 1, built in 1888 — fell to the wrecking ball, but not before historical pieces were sold or donated. Carillon Historical Park accepted a large clock and firehose cart.

Moving out

Total enrollment in the Dayton City School District fell by nearly 2,000 students, from 49,028 in 1973 to 47,031 in 1974. Meanwhile, the percentage of black students rose to 47.5 percent, up 1.2 percent from 1973.

Growth at Sinclair

Sinclair Community College added 1,000 students this year, and hired Dr. David H. Ponitz as president. He replaced Dr. Marvin Knudson, who retired.

For women only

The Dayton Women's Center offered classes in assertiveness, sexuality and careers for women. The center also counseled rape victims and battered women. Teen mothers could finish their education at Dayton's Hawthorne School, one of the nation's first to help pregnant teens earn their diplomas.

Not to be left out

Elder-Beerman decided to build a downtown department store as part of the Courthouse Square revitalization.

Power surge

Dayton Power and Light's J.M. Stuart Station, one of the nation's largest power-generating plants, opened this year. Stuart Station was owned by DP&L, Cincinnati Gas and Electric and Columbus and Southern Ohio Electric.

They couldn't tie the knot

Two women filed a $100 million lawsuit against Montgomery County Common Pleas Judge Neal F. Zimmers after he refused to allow them to marry each other.

Passed...

A Dayton city income tax increase to 1.75 percent, from 1 percent, on the sixth try.

Opened...

The University of Dayton School of Law.

Won...

The Mark Twain Award, by Dayton's own Erma Bombeck, named the nation's top humorist. Bombeck's popular newspaper column focused on her life and times as a housewife in Bellbrook and Centerville.

Born...

Quadruplets — all girls — to Daytonians Robert and Ruth Deddens.

Slain...

The Rev. W.S. McIntosh, Dayton's civil-rights leader, when he was shot down while trying to stop robbers fleeing a downtown store.

Left: Robert and Ruth Deddens with their quadruplets.

Below left: Lou Emm

Below right: Don Wayne

Bottom: William S. Anderson took over at NCR, changing product lines extensively.

SLICE OF LIFE

Feeling the squeeze

Wallets were thinner in 1974, with inflation and recession. Food prices increased more than 20 percent, with sugar alone jumping 300 percent to $3.50 for a five-pound bag. Car prices rose 5 percent, leaving many new models in showrooms. Energy shortages and unemployment in major industries — including auto and construction — struck with a vengeance.

What they watched, listened to, and read

■ Don Wayne's WHIO Channel 7 news was the most popular local TV show.
■ Disc jockey Lou Emm's WHIO-AM morning show was the top radio program.
■ The book checked out most at the Dayton & Montgomery County Public Library: *Plain Speaking*, Harry S. Truman's oral biography, by Merle Miller.

Above: Charles Wendelken-Wilson became the director of the Dayton Philharmonic Orchestra.

Right: Pat Roach was the first woman elected to the Dayton City Commission.

Desegregation violence

On September 19, violence struck the Dayton schools' efforts to desegregate.

Dr. Charles A. Glatt, who'd been appointed by U.S. District Judge Carl B. Rubin to design a desegregation plan for the district, was shot to death in his downtown office by Neal Bradley Long, 49. The community was horrified, but Glatt's death was unable to derail desegregation in Dayton. Without him, plans prepared by Dayton school board advisers and the NAACP came to the forefront.

By 1976, Dayton's desegregation plan was approved. More than 10,000 pupils in the 40,000-student system rode buses to different schools to produce racial balance in the district.

A bicentennial kickoff

The Dayton-Montgomery County Bicentennial Commission began publishing *The Fife & Drum* in June to announce bicentennial news and activities in the Dayton area. One of the commission's first major events celebrating the nation's 200th birthday: Dayton Air Fair '75.

Rejected...

Plans to build a $10 million, joint city-county courts building, by voters in November.

Two firsts for City Commission

■ Pat Roach became the first woman elected to the Dayton City Commission.

■ Michael L. Schierloh was appointed to fill an unexpired term. At 23, he was the youngest city commissioner ever.

Music to Dayton's ears

A two-year contract was awarded to Charles Wendelken-Wilson, the Dayton Philharmonic Orchestra's new director. He succeeded founder Paul Katz.

Renamed...

James M. Cox Dayton Municipal Airport, to the James M. Cox Dayton International Airport.

SLICE OF LIFE

Economy still a worry

Concerns continued about unemployment, and the high cost of living and energy. DP&L was allowed to boost electric rates 13.5 percent, and NCR cut more jobs. By year's end, Montgomery County's jobless rate was 7 percent. A few bright spots: Food prices fell (though slightly), and many GM workers laid off in 1974 were recalled in 1975.

Everybody had one

Mood rings — which turned different colors, supposedly according to the wearer's mood — were all the rage, at least for a while. NCR was one of many producers of the encapsulated liquid crystal material inside the rings. (If you didn't have a mood ring, you might have had a "pet rock.")

1975

Bringing a little piece of history to life

Charles A. Dempsey, a Wright-Patterson Air Force Base researcher, announced he was building a full-scale replica of the Wright "B" Flyer. Dempsey, who said the Flyer would go airborne during demonstrations and community events, promised to be ready for Dayton Air Fair '76.

Flocking, flocking, flocking to Sinclair

Sinclair Community College's enrollment was 11,000 students — a new record. The college started building a 500-car parking garage, planned new classrooms and completed its $6 million physical-activities center.

A new beer and wine house

Heidelberg Distributing Company purchased the historic Centre City Building at Fourth and Main as its new corporate headquarters.

Awarded...

Provisional accreditation to the University of Dayton's new School of Law, by the American Bar Association.

Under construction...

Two medical-school buildings, at Wright State University. The medical school was slated to open in fall 1976.

Opened...

An eastern section of Interstate 675. The rest of the highway, however, remained stalled.

Finished...

The new $33 million wing at Good Samaritan Hospital.

Completed...

The downtown "river walk." Bicyclists geared up in anticipation of the completion of an eight-mile bikeway nearby.

Closed...

West Carrollton's Bergstrom Paper Company.

Above: Anticipation of the American bicentennial brought out colorful displays, including this mural.

Below: The Classic Theater on West Fifth Street had fallen into disrepair.

Above: Dayton celebrated the American bicentennial with a July Fourth parade that drew enough spectators to more than fill the Rike's parking garage.

Graduated...

The last class of Stivers High School, in the spring. Stivers became a middle school building after that.

To the finish line

Dayton track star Edwin C. Moses made his hometown proud by winning a gold medal in the 1976 Summer Olympics in Montreal. Moses set a new world record of 47.64 seconds in the 400-meter hurdles.

Flying high

Regional and national model-airplane championships were held this summer in Dayton.

The grandest of downtown openings

The much-anticipated Courthouse Plaza — which promised to breathe new life into downtown Dayton — opened in October. Two important anchors of the redevelopment: the Dayton Power and Light Company building and the Elder-Beerman department store. Courthouse Plaza, now known as Courthouse Square, is the best place for an outdoor lunch on a sunny summer day.

Also opened this year...

NCR's new world headquarters on Patterson Boulevard, and the Stouffer Hotel downtown.

SLICE OF LIFE

Bicentennial fever

Mementos of the nation's bicentennial sold here included wooden chips of Independence Hall, "Spirit of '76" socks, stars-and-stripes tank tops and bicentennial stamp albums. Besides Dayton Air Fair '76, which lured more than 80,000 people to aviation exhibits and aerial demonstrations, another big event was the July Fourth parade downtown, which drew more than 300,000 people.

An all-time entertainment low

Many Dayton-area performances by singers, actors, and comedians were canceled this year, thanks to poor ticket sales. The reason? Bad movies, bad singers, bad nightclub acts, along with unprepared stars who "didn't bother to learn their lines," according to the *Dayton Daily News*.

1976

Elected...

Paula J. MacIlwaine, the first woman Montgomery County commissioner, in November.

Changes in the ranks

As racial turmoil continued within the Dayton Police Department, 19 white officers and two black officers were promoted to sergeant. In spite of a campaign to get more blacks on the force, only eight of 188 blacks eligible to join were hired.

Welfare doesn't fare well

Trouble emerged at the Montgomery County Welfare Department. Rising costs — coupled with fund shortages — resulted in 10,000 fewer people on the welfare rolls, lower payments and some discontinued services. Allegations of fraud surfaced, too, to the tune of $6 million.

The sweet taste of success

Esther Price Candies Corporation was sold this year for $2 million. Dayton's best-loved candy maker, Esther Price, began the business by stirring and cutting fudge from her home on Fauver Avenue in 1926.

More blacks in Dayton schools

Dayton's school population was 52 percent black and 48 percent white — the first year black enrollment was greater.

Approved...

A 1.75-mill property tax increase for continuing operations of the Miami Valley Regional Transit Authority.

Named...

Charles E. Exley Jr., as NCR's new president.

Opened...

A new regional headquarters for Metropolitan Life Insurance Company, just south of the Dayton Mall. The company was known for producing the song *Great 'n Dayton*.

Above: A C-5 cargo plane provided a dramatic backdrop for the 1976 Dayton Air Fair.

Left: Sen. Barry Goldwater spoke at the dedication of the new Reception Center at the U.S. Air Force Museum.

Below: Emery Air Freight's Dayton terminal buzzed with activity as workers raced to unload and reload some 14 planes in three hours.

Above: The view east on Fifth Street in the Oregon District showed newly uncovered trolley tracks from an earlier era.

MILESTONE

A rotten, rip-snortin' winter

It was a hard, bitter winter in the Miami Valley — one that brought snow, an energy crisis and the area's nastiest cold since 1916.

Good Lord, it was cold

The worst day was January 17, when the thermometer bottomed out at minus 21 — the coldest temperature recorded here to that time. January's average temperature was 11.8 degrees — a frigid 16.3 degrees below normal.

Energy crisis!

Dayton Power and Light Company (whose workers, as luck had it, were on strike in the midst of it all) asked everyone to save natural gas by nudging thermostats down to 65. It wasn't long before schools closed en masse. New Lebanon students missed 19 days, the most in the area. Brookville, which heated its schools with fuel oil, missed the least, a mere six days.

Reduced hours, mittens on the line

Some stores and industries closed for a couple of days or shortened hours. Employees in factories that remained open had long, cold work days; at McCauley Accessory Division, for example, workers making airplane propellers kept coats and mittens on to keep warm with the factory thermostat set at 38°F. ■

Still buzzing over busing

School desegregation remained a hot topic after the U.S. Supreme Court decided to send Dayton's school desegregation case back to U.S. District Judge Carl B. Rubin in June. Dayton — the only Ohio school district that was busing for desegregation under court order — began its second busing year in the fall. After a four-day hearing in November, Judge Rubin dismissed the case, thereby allowing the Dayton Board of Education to decide whether desegregation efforts would continue. Nevertheless, after the U.S. Supreme Court was asked again in 1978 to review Dayton's desegregation and busing plan, the issue dragged on — and the buses continued to roll. Plenty of parents, unhappy with the situation, started to vote with their feet, and with "for sale" signs.

In June, Neal Bradley Long received three consecutive life sentences plus 22 to 85 more years in prison. He was the convicted murderer of desegregation planner Charles Glatt, and had also pleaded guilty to killing three people and wounding five others in West Dayton shooting sprees.

Closed...

■ Shawen Acres, for long-term residential care, by the Montgomery County Child Welfare Board on February 26.

■ The downtown Dayton Inn, on December 31, after a lack of convention business.

Mystery man

Office workers watched out for the "downtown bandit," who robbed three offices at gunpoint in March and sometimes forced victims to disrobe. The suspect, a juvenile, was arrested in April.

A chief executive visit

The 11th annual Bogie Busters benefit for multiple sclerosis welcomed former President Gerald Ford in June.

No fire protection

To the city's horror, Dayton firefighters stood idle as homes burned to the ground during a firefighters' strike in August. The strike, during which firefighters agreed to protect life, but not property, lasted 59 hours.

A fun night out that turned deadly

When the popular Beverly Hills Supper Club became a deadly inferno on May 28, nearly a third of the 164 people who died were from the Miami Valley. The nightclub, across the Ohio River from Cincinnati, was later found to have violated fire and safety standards. The huge loss of life resulted from overcrowding, inadequate exits, blocked aisles and a delay in warning some patrons that the blaze had broken out.

1977

Died...

Former Dayton Mayor Dave Hall, 71, at Miami Valley Hospital in August.

Appointed...

Doris Black, as coach of the Colonel White High School basketball team, in September. Black became the only woman in an Ohio school district to coach a traditionally male sport.

Yet another scandal

Theft, fraud and forgery — to the tune of $1.2 million — were the charges made in September against 26 people connected with the Montgomery County Welfare Department scandal.

Plunged...

Dayton employment at NCR, from a high of 20,000 in 1969 to 5,000 by this year.

A 13-mile run

Two were in wheelchairs. One was blind. In all, 1,182 runners ran in Dayton's first River Corridor Classic Mini-Marathon on October 29, which began at the Convention Center.

Syndicated...

Cathy Guisewite's comic strip *Cathy*. The native Daytonian's strip focused on a young woman struggling with feminism in the wake of traditional female roles.

New quarters

Mead Corporation employees moved into their new world headquarters building, the Mead Tower, on Courthouse Square.

Departed...

The Dayton Gems. The move left Dayton without an International Hockey League team after 13 years.

A safe landing

Emery Air Freight decided to base its operations at Dayton International Airport. At the outset, Emery made 20 daily air-freight flights to businesses within 600 miles of Dayton.

Presented...

Shoppers and other downtowners were pleased with plans for the proposed $9 million renovation of Dayton's Arcade, which would feature fashion shops, offices, entertainment centers and a farmers' market.

Above: Messer Construction installed the 45-foot-long Sinclair Community College sign along Third Street.

Above: Like the rest of the Miami Valley, Dayton's Lorain Avenue was snowed in.

MILESTONE
Blizzard!

The 15 inches of snow that fell on January 26 were "icing on the cake" in the Miami Valley: The fresh layer fell atop what was left from the two feet of snow that had blanketed the area January 20. Up to its waist in the white stuff, the Valley packed it in for the day. After all, roads were impassable, airplanes weren't flying, buses weren't running — even the mail couldn't go through. Downtown was like a ghost town. Throughout the Valley, neighbor turned to neighbor and lent a helping hand. One grocer delivered food via snowmobile; in Arcanum and Mercer County, children and elderly residents who had been evacuated from their homes after a power shortage were welcomed into the fire station, the VFW hall, churches and private homes.

The show went on (to heck with the patrons)
Even after the blizzard had virtually closed the city down, the Dayton Opera Association told the cast of *Romeo and Juliet* to go on with the performance as scheduled at Memorial Hall. Why? Guest soloists had spent the week in town rehearsing, and proceeding would help recoup costs. Understandably, the association later dealt with many perturbed patrons. ■

Smeared reputations
Scandal rocked local government at all levels after judges, county officials and police officers in the Miami Valley were accused — and many found guilty — of wrongdoing. A few of the offenders:
■ Arcanum Police Chief Charles D. "Sparky" Fitzgerald, who pleaded guilty on March 20 to planning the $34,210 robbery of the Arcanum National Bank.
■ Former Montgomery County Commissioner Oscar S. Page Jr., who pleaded guilty October 6 to one mail fraud and one federal income tax charge.
■ Former Montgomery County Engineer John D. Wysong, who was found guilty of 12 misdemeanor counts of illegally soliciting campaign contributions from his employees.

Razed...
NCR's Building No. 10, in June.

Transferred...
Ownership of the 20-acre Wright Brothers Memorial Hill, from the Miami Valley Conservancy District to the Air Force, on September 9.

Not a bad year at all
The UD Flyers went to the national Division III playoffs as the No. 2 college football team in the country, but lost 21-14 to No. 7 Carnegie Mellon of Pittsburgh. UD's final record: 9-2-1.

Opened...
Hospice of Dayton Inc., by nurse Betty Schmoll, to allow the terminally ill to die in a dignified, residential setting rather than in a hospital.

I wanna be elected
■ Former state Sen. Tony P. Hall, a Democrat from Kettering, succeeded U.S. Rep. Charles W. Whalen Jr., a Republican from Dayton.
■ E. George "Babe" Ferguson won a seat on the Montgomery County Commission. She was only the second woman to do so.

Moved...
Robbins & Myers' corporate headquarters, from Springfield to Dayton. Today the company is an international manufacturer of pumps, valves and mixers.

SLICE OF LIFE

House and home
■ The average price of an existing home in the Dayton area jumped 15 percent, from $37,103 in 1977 to $43,000 in 1978.
■ The average price for a new home rose 10.8 percent, from $46,000 in 1977 to $51,000 in 1978.

Talked about...
Resource recovery — a system of burning trash to produce steam and electricity — rather than burying trash in a landfill. Other cities around the country were trying it, with mixed success.

Goodbye, Amtrak

Miami Valley travelers who wanted to take the train had to go to Lima or Cincinnati to ride Amtrak, the national rail-passenger system, after Dayton service was dropped in October — even though ridership had been increasing.

No more Frigidaire

Dayton was stunned to learn in January that General Motors' Frigidaire Division had been sold to White Consolidated Industries Inc. and that manufacturing would move to Cleveland. Eventually replacing Frigidaire in Dayton would be Chevrolet engine and truck production.

Into the books

Entered into the National Register of Historic Places on January 4 were the gateway, chapel and the Office of Woodland at Woodland Cemetery.

Tumbling into town

The country's top gymnasts arrived for the national gymnastics championships at UD Arena in May.

They're back!

The reborn Dayton Gems resumed play in the International Hockey League in October.

You win some, you lose some

While approving construction of just a 3-mile strip of Interstate 675 (from near Wright State to U.S. 35) in November, U.S. Transportation Secretary Neil Goldschmidt in effect disapproved construction of the requested 13.5-mile segment that would have gone south of U.S. 35. After 20 years of this, people wondered whether I-675 would ever be completed.

Another Dayton landmark dies

The NCR Auditorium met the wrecking ball. For years, it had housed company training classes and meetings, high school graduations, Sunday concerts and free Saturday shows and movies for kids.

Blacks and whites

While race relations had improved, at least somewhat, by the late 1970s, community leaders warned that the economy would largely determine whether relations remained on even ground through the '80s. Unless blacks began making more than marginal economic advancements, leaders said, tensions could reach the unhappy levels of the 1960s.

School woes

The Dayton City School District was losing students. In the third year of court-ordered busing for desegregation, administrators reported an enrollment drop from 55,520 over the last decade to 34,161 this year. During the same period, the cost of educating a student doubled, to more than $2,000.

Table talk

What was in the news? And what were people here talking about?
■ Continuing inflation.
■ Rivalries between Dayton and its suburbs.
■ Declining confidence in the public schools.
■ The continued loss of manufacturing jobs — and the gradual shift to non-manufacturing jobs.
■ The decline of scheduled flights by major carriers into Dayton International Airport, thanks to airline deregulation.

Top: Sylvester Stanley waved goodbye to Dayton as his train left Union Station for the last time.

Left: Charles Eland of the Finke Construction Company helped restore the old brick streets in the Oregon District between Wayne Avenue and Patterson Boulevard.

Right: Daytonian Dorian Harewood became a successful actor, both in television and film. His portrayal of Simon Haley in the television epic *Roots* was one of his most memorable roles.

Showing off a showpiece

Local designers, landscape architects and artists joined forces to turn a local home into a handsomely refurbished showplace for the first Decorators' Show House project, sponsored by the Dayton Philharmonic Women's Association and Top Value Enterprises.

Gentlemen, start your engines

Local racing buffs cheered the reopening of the old Dayton Speedway, renamed the Greater Dayton Speedway.

Transferred...

Some 545 jobs, out of the Miami Valley, from Kettering's Defense Electronics Supply Center. Employees remaining: about 2,100.

Incorporated...

Beavercreek, on January 11.

Something from home

With one of their own in foreign captivity, Miami Valley residents were concerned. Daytonian Steven M. Lauterbach, one of the 54 U.S. diplomats who had been held hostage in Iran since November 1979, received Christmas cards from people here that arrived on January 29. The Ayatollah Khomeini finally released the American hostages in January 1981.

Art heist

A burglar stole gold and silver artifacts worth $300,000 from the Dayton Art Institute in January. Most were recovered by February.

Dedicated...

The 65-year-old former Dayton Post Office on West Third Street, as a private office building, in February.

Died...

Loren M. Berry, 91, pioneer of telephone yellow pages advertising, on February 10.

Below: Coach Rick Carter was carried off the field by his UD Flyers team after winning the Stagg Bowl.

Flyers victorious

■ UD's womens' basketball team won the Division III finals in March, led by coach Maryalyce Jeremiah. The victory was the first national championship in UD's history.

■ In December, the Flyers football team tromped Ithaca College 63-0 and captured the Division III national championship.

RTA thrives

More people opted to catch the bus rather than pay high parking rates and gas prices after the Regional Transit Authority streamlined schedules and modernized buses. Approved in April: a half-percent sales tax to fund countywide bus service.

Twist and shout

Ten people were hurt in April when tornadoes touched down north and south of Dayton.

Finally — some good news

Other state transportation projects were put on hold after Gov. James A. Rhodes announced in June that $6 million would be dedicated to help complete access roads in Moraine. The roads were needed to help GM gear up for building trucks and diesel engines at two Moraine GM plants, scheduled for full production in 1981.

Hope in town

In June, golfers enjoyed a 51-minute performance by Bob Hope at the 14th annual Bogie Busters dinner, the high point of the celebrity golf tournament held for charity.

And think of all those loans to pay off

Wright State's Medical School graduated its first class — 31 students, in June.

Last one out, turn off the lights

■ Production ceased in July at the 67-year-old Dayton Tire and Rubber Company plant, which employed 1,800, several months after parent Firestone Tire and Rubber Company announced the plant's closing.

■ Also preparing to close: Dayton Press Inc., the magazine publishing company employing 2,500. It was formerly McCall's.

Left: "Rags" spent his days and nights on Dayton's streets.

SLICE OF LIFE

We could just spruce up the place we have

Housing sales were down a severe 50 percent, thanks to record-high mortgage rates.

A beloved structure saved

It cost $14 million, but when you stepped inside, it seemed worth it. The newly renovated downtown Arcade opened May 10 and included a glass elevator, new protection for its breathtaking glass dome, stone ornamentation and a freshened Third Street facade.
Downtown office workers spent their lunch hour eating Chinese fried rice, gyros, oysters and ice cream purchased from the new Arcade eateries.

Dayton-area statistics

■ Montgomery County population: 571,697.
■ Greene County population: 129,769.
■ Dayton population: 203,371.

The death of 'Rags'

One of Dayton's best-known downtown wanderers, the gray-bearded "Rags," died May 5. The life story of Elias J. Barauskas, 60, wasn't known until after his death. Barauskas, a Connecticut native and World War II veteran, suffered from mental problems after committing to become a Roman Catholic priest but later falling in love. After spending time in at least two mental institutions, he ended up living on the streets of Dayton, people-watching and sometimes panhandling. He was buried in Dayton National Cemetery.

Above: A Dayton police officer made early Sunday rounds on a very quiet Ludlow Street.

1980

Shake and bake
It was eerie when dishes shook and windows rattled across the Miami Valley at 2:52 p.m. on July 27. What was it? A rare earthquake, with an epicenter 45 miles southeast of Cincinnati.

Died...
Elsie Talbott Mead, who led the effort to build Children's Medical Center, in August at age 86. She was the widow of businessman George Mead.

I-675: Yes or no?
People who wanted Interstate 675 to be completed were discouraged when President Jimmy Carter said during a visit to Dayton on October 1 that a lesser highway should be built instead of the planned six-lane outerbelt.

Regional cooperation
Planning for economic resurgence in the Miami Valley was the theme of a two-day meeting of 200 area leaders at the University of Dayton in November. Topics covered: tax-sharing, cooperation between labor and management, and a coordinated effort to attract new businesses.

Local boy does hometown proud
By this year, Daytonian Phil Donahue's television talk show *Donahue* was broadcast on 200 stations.

Won...
The National League's Most Valuable Player award, by native Daytonian and Philadelphia Phillies third baseman Mike Schmidt.

Opened...
A 230-unit residential living complex for the elderly and the handicapped at the Biltmore Towers, the former Biltmore Hotel.

Presented...
Sleeping Beauty, the Dayton Ballet's first full-length ballet, at the Victory Theatre.

1981

Right: Kim Seelbrede of Germantown was crowned Miss USA.

Incorporated...
Huber Heights, on January 22. The new city with 35,000 residents was Montgomery County's third largest — and proudly billed itself, without too much challenge, as "America's largest community of brick homes."

A new downtown gem
Downtowners welcomed the opening of the spacious Gem Plaza, designed by world-famous architect I.M. Pei, at Third and Main streets. Gem Savings moved in early this year.

Crowned...
Germantown's Kim Seelbrede, 20, as Miss USA in Biloxi, Mississippi.

Died...
Mrs. Viola Mansur, 86, chairwoman of the Soldiers Service Club during World War II, on April 29.

Won...
Journalism's coveted Pulitzer Prize, by *Dayton Daily News* cartoonist Mike Peters, in April.

Horrific slayings
■ Beaten to death in April was Miami Valley aviation pioneer Elbert G. Sohm, 80, and his wife, Mary, 83, in their Dayton View home.
■ Also in April: *Journal Herald* arts critic Walt W. McCaslin Jr. was stabbed to death in his Yellow Springs home by his son.

Death toll
The Valley mourned the deaths of 21 people from Wright-Patterson Air Force Base, killed on May 6 when their C-135 crashed near Walkersville, Maryland.

But I'm certain it's right here, somewhere
Memorial Hall director Fred Rose and box office manager Daniel K. Smith got their walking papers in June after a $33,849.15 shortage in box office receipts was discovered.

Guilty
That was the plea made by former Montgomery County Commissioner Ray Wolfe on June 19 to charges of bribery.

At last!
July 7 saw President Ronald Reagan's secretary of transportation, Drew Lewis, approve the long-awaited extension of I-675 from U.S. 35 to I-75 near Miamisburg. Also this year: Bids were accepted for building 2.14 miles of I-675 from North Fairfield Road to just north of U.S. 35.

The show must go on
The doors to the Victory Theatre nearly closed in August, but a last-ditch effort to save the showplace — plagued with huge debts and only a trickle of income — worked. Thanks to contributions from a small group of Miami Valley residents, performances for the 1981-82 season went on as scheduled.

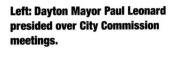

Left: Dayton Mayor Paul Leonard presided over City Commission meetings.

Below left: Freed hostage Steven M. Lauterbach (left), accompanied by *Dayton Daily News* columnist Dale Huffman, returned to Dayton.

Below right: *Dayton Daily News* Editor Arnold Rosenfeld hugged cartoonist Mike Peters, who had just won the Pulitzer Prize.

Elected mayor
Former state Rep. Paul R. Leonard was elected Dayton mayor in November, replacing James McGee, who had held the office since 1970 and did not seek re-election. Leonard was the first mayor elected without first serving on the Dayton City Commission. He became known as the fun-loving rock 'n' roll mayor.

Back home again
Two local heroes were honored in separate Arcade Square celebrations.
■ Daytonians cheered the return of Steven M. Lauterbach, one of 54 American hostages released from Iran after 444 days in captivity.
■ Folks turned out to honor Phillies third baseman, World Series hero and Fairview High School graduate Mike Schmidt, named the National League's MVP this year.

Turn of the tide
The promise of new high-tech companies and jobs kept Kettering — and the Dayton area — smiling all year. The state gave the 670 acres that once held the former Dayton Mental Health Center farm off Patterson Road to the Miami Valley Research Park Foundation. This new non-profit developer also received $150,000 from the state for park planning.

A little more good news
Erected this year was a new freight-handling terminal at Dayton International Airport by Emery Worldwide.

Jobs back
Nearly 3,000 of the 8,000 jobs lost when General Motors' Frigidaire Division closed in 1979 were regained with the opening of Chevrolet's new compact truck and diesel engine plants in Moraine.

Above: Hundreds gathered in the Arcade to honor Mike Schmidt (right, at podium) for winning the National League's Most Valuable Player award.

Something to talk about

The early '80s were hard on the Dayton area, as they were on cities throughout Ohio and the Midwest. People worried about business closings, layoffs, tax hikes, government cutbacks, crime and financial belt-tightening in the wake of constantly rising costs.

And this really hurts

Dayton-area unemployment hovered around 8 percent.

Formed...

Aviation Trail Inc., a not-for-profit corporation to preserve and promote Dayton's aviation heritage.

Opened...

The $6.2 million Dayton Career Academy, a vocational and pre-professional high school.

Merged...

The Delco Air Conditioning Division of General Motors, into the Harrison Radiator Division, in a cost-cutting move.

Created...

The Muse Machine, an arts education program, for local junior high and high school students.

A coup for Dayton

The city got a national feather in its cap after the American Symphony Orchestra League gave the Dayton Philharmonic Orchestra's 1981 Decorators' Show House its top award as "the outstanding project among all orchestra fund-raising projects in the United States." The project turned Polen Farm, a Kettering farmhouse, into a magnificent showplace. Visitors came by the thousands to see the transformation. Net proceeds for the orchestra: $90,000.

A new catchword

Area businesses and economic development leaders campaigned to make the phrase "90-minute market" synonymous with Dayton. It referred to the city's central location, relative to other major cities within easy travel distance.

Bankrupt or closing

Filing for reorganization under Chapter 11 of the U.S. Bankruptcy Act were:
■ Liberal Markets Inc., a 60-year-old company that closed its 13 stores.
■ Discount store Goldman's Inc.
■ Foreman Industries.
■ Also announced: the closing of Rink's department stores.

Sports winners

■ UD basketball coach Don Donoher not only won his 300th game this year but also took the Flyers to the post-season National Invitational Tournament.
■ Roth High School won the AAA title in basketball.

Named...

UD's Rick Carter, as college division coach of the year, by the American Football Coaches' Association.

Goodbye, Joe

Joe Horvath — the beloved seller of newspapers from a two-wheeled stand at Fifth and Main — was murdered during a robbery.

Moving a little piece of history

The 1924 Sun Oil Company service station at Brown and Warren streets, abandoned in 1963, was relocated to Carillon Historical Park.

1982

She made history

The Smithsonian Institution named retired Lt. Col. Charity Adams Earley, a 1938 Wilberforce University graduate, one of the top 110 black women in history. Earley, born in 1918, was not only the first black commissioned officer in the Women's Army Auxiliary Corps during World War II, but also commanded the only group of black women serving overseas.

After retiring from the Army in 1946, she became a prominent community-affairs advocate and volunteer for organizations such as the United Way and the Dayton Power and Light Company board of directors. ■

Killed...

Air Force Capt. Mark E. Melancon, a Thunderbird pilot and Beavercreek High graduate, when the entire aerobatic team crashed during a January flight in Nevada.

A big ribbon to cut

Construction finally began in April on the section of I-675 between I-70 and I-75.

News in the news

The city was on its way to becoming a one-newspaper town after Dayton Newspapers Inc. announced in April that it would combine the news-gathering staffs of the evening *Dayton Daily News* and the morning *Journal Herald*.

An epic outdoor drama

June saw the opening of *Blue Jacket*, a production about a white man adopted by the Shawnee Indians on the Ohio frontier 200 years ago, in a new outdoor theater east of Xenia. About 1,200 patrons — who paid $500 per seat to get the show under way — gathered for the premiere.

Top: Charity Earley with her son and daughter, Stanley III and Judy.

Right: Dr. Jerrold Petrofsky (right) and Dr. Roger Glaser experimented at Wright State with methods of electronically stimulating paralyzed muscles.

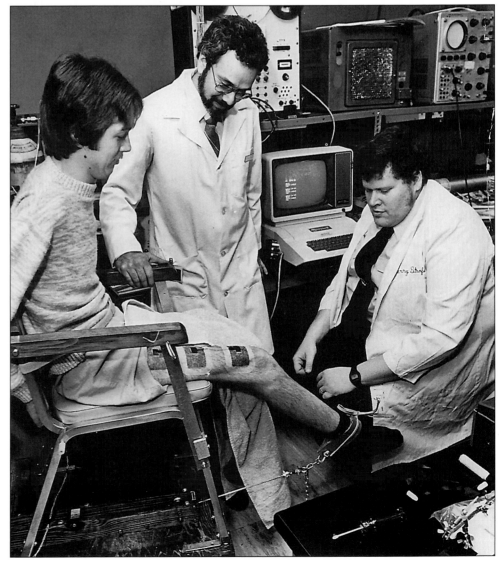

The economy: from bad to worse

Comparisons were made to the Great Depression as Ohio's unemployment rate hit 14 percent in November. The Dayton area suffered under high interest rates, weak business conditions and plunging retail sales. In the Miami Valley alone, 300 businesses failed. Government services were cut and some schools closed. The severity of the economic crisis was perhaps best illustrated in October, when 1,000 people applied for two semi-skilled street maintenance jobs in Moraine.

Getting along

Regional cooperation took a new turn under Dayton Mayor Paul Leonard's leadership. In one of the first moves toward better relations between the city and surrounding areas, the Dayton City Commission voted to sell water to the city's southern suburbs.

A pleasant place to ride

Work continued on the Miami Conservancy District's river bikeway as a section north of the Wegerzyn Garden Center was completed. By this year, the bikeway ran 25-plus miles north and south of Dayton.

Truckers enraged

A fuel surcharge? Independent truckers said no way and tried to incite a nationwide truckers' strike. Before tempers cooled, the Miami Valley saw fire-bombings and tire-slashings.

Named...

Tyree Broomfield, as Dayton's first black police chief.

Airport activity

■ Emery Worldwide completed a major expansion at Dayton International Airport.
■ Piedmont Airlines opened a passenger hub, also at Dayton International Airport.

Reopened...

Two of the Liberal Market grocery stores that had closed in 1981.

Under way...

A merged city-county jail facility.

Founded...

The city's Black Leadership Program.

Built...

Accords, at the Honda plant in Marysville. Big news, in a General Motors region.

Top: Many events and celebrations were held in the Dayton Arcade.

Left: George Naylor defended the fort against Jerome Taylor and Dan Southern in the outdoor drama *Blue Jacket*.

1983

Showing mercy

In a struggling economy, companies asked Miami Valley unions for wage concessions and reduced benefits, and the unions often had little choice but to go along.

Helping the hungry

The poorest of the poor in Dayton had a friend in Sister Dorothy Kammerer, who opened the House of Bread to feed the hungry. Later, she opened The Other Place, a daytime homeless shelter downtown, and Women Helping Women, to help low-income women find jobs.

Merged...

Winters Bank, into Bank One. The Winters Bank Tower was renamed Kettering Tower.

Named...

Charles E. Exley, as CEO of NCR Corporation.

Listed...

The Huffman Historic District, on the National Register of Historic Places.

Won...

The NCAA Division II basketball championship, by Wright State University.

SLICE OF LIFE

Hand-holding

The longest human chain? Almost. Dayton would have made *The Guinness Book of World Records* for the feat, if just 4,000 more people had shown up to clasp hands during the kickoff event for the 1983 United Way campaign. Nonetheless, the turnout was impressive — 15,620 people lined up along the River Corridor in September.

Top: Gary Jarman and Barry Graham cleaned bricks in an Oregon District renovation.

Middle: Dayton's nighttime skyline

Right: *Dayton Daily News* **sports editor Si Burick (facing camera) was inducted July 31 into the Writers Section of the National Baseball Hall of Fame in Cooperstown, New York.**

Top: Courthouse Square

Left: Daytonian Rob Lowe's film career included an appearance in *Oxford Blues*.

Above: Yvonne Walker-Taylor hugged the Rev. Edward Scott after becoming the first woman president of Wilberforce University.

Soaring popularity

Much to her surprise, 88-year-old Helen Hooven Santmyer of Xenia faced a barrage of media attention for ...*And Ladies of the Club*, her long novel about doings in a small Ohio town. It was a giant best-seller.

Lights, camera, walk

CBS planned a made-for-TV movie in January about Wright State biomedicine professor Jerrold Petrofsky, and his efforts to help paraplegic Nan Davis walk. Petrofsky became known worldwide for his computer-controlled system designed to help people with spinal-cord injuries learn to walk again.

Finally: A decision

The long-awaited fate of the controversial and expensive William H. Zimmer nuclear-power plant on the Ohio River was announced in January. The Dayton Power and Light Company and two sister utilities said the plant would be converted to burn coal.

Named...

■ Yvonne Walker-Taylor, as Wilberforce University's first female president in the school's 127-year history, on February 15.
■ Richard Hunter, as Dayton's first black school superintendent.

Higher taxes OK'd

Dayton voters agreed on March 27 to bump up their city income tax from 1.75 percent to 2.25 percent. Of course, the suburbanites who just worked in the city didn't get a say in the matter.

Another historic building bites the dust

One of the last bits of local Shaker history was destroyed April 9. Bulldozers razed the 165-year-old Center Family Dwelling on Patterson Road in the former Watervliet community of the Shaker religious sect. In its place rose the new Miami Valley Research Park.

Roll out the red carpet

For the first time since the 1960s, downtown prepared for a new family housing development. Construction on the 34-unit Cooper Place, across the street from Cooper Park, began August 1.

Died...

Long-time radio and television personality and former *Dayton Daily News* columnist Bernard Wullkotte, known as "B.W.," on August 30.

Wild blue yonder

He became the first person to cross the Atlantic by himself in a balloon, on September 21. The pioneer was Joe W. Kittinger, 56, a former Wright-Patterson Air Force Base fighter pilot.

Happy motoring

Open for traffic on October 22 was another new section of Interstate 675. Contracts were awarded on the last two phases of the highway.

New TV station in town

Miami Valley residents had a new choice on their television dial beginning September 23, when WRGT-TV, Channel 45, went on the air. It was Dayton's first non-network TV station since 1971.

Dayton Mall spinoffs

All it took was a $6 million facelift. The newly refurbished Dayton Mall began attracting record new retail growth at Ohio 725 and Ohio 741 in bustling Miami Township. The developments, some planned and others under way, promised shoppers new choices — and more traffic.

Announced in October...

The closing of the Metropolitan Clothing Company, after 71 years as a downtown retailer.

To come: More jobs

General Motors bolstered the local economy with the news that more than 1,000 jobs would be available in spring 1985 after the Moraine truck assembly plant added a second shift.

Emerging stronger than ever

Area machine-tool shops hummed with activity — busily diversifying and retooling in the wake of modern technology, new markets and techniques for making plastic instead of metal parts. By this time, the survival of the Dayton area's 150 shops seemed reasonably assured.

A marvelous comeback

In just over a year, Daytonians watched the Dayton Chrysler assembly plant more than double employment from 800 to almost 1,900.

Computers for books

Patrons of the Dayton & Montgomery County Public Library found that a computerized circulation system was up and running for checking out books and other materials.

Named...

Charles E. Exley, as NCR's chairman. By this year, NCR — with operations in 120 countries and 60,000 employees worldwide — had become a top-ranked international manufacturer of information-processing equipment.

Quite an achievement

Daytonian Julia Reichert became the first female filmmaker to be nominated twice for an Academy Award after her documentary, *Seeing Red*, was nominated for an Oscar. Reichert, along with partner Jim Klein, received a nomination in 1977 for *Union Maids*.

Renamed...

Miami Boulevard West and Sunrise Avenue, to Edwin C. Moses Boulevard, in honor of the great Dayton hurdler who won Olympic gold medals in 1976 and again this year.

Something to look forward to

A new office tower would be the crown jewel of the city's plans to renovate the Arcade Square block, announced in February. Also proposed: moving food service shops in the Arcade to the basement and retail stores to the first floor.

Running scared

Miami Valley residents with accounts at Home State Savings Bank panicked in March after hearing about the bank's dubious financial practices. Depositors here and across Ohio lined up to make withdrawals, but it was too late. Home State folded, and all state-chartered savings and loans were closed to stop the panic. By December 13, former bank owner Marvin Warner was indicted for allegedly making illegal money transfers from the bank to a Florida firm that collapsed, causing Home State's demise. Depositors were bailed out with more than $100 million of state tax money. The mess promised to continue on well through 1986.

Above: Panic ensued when the Home State Savings Bank began a financial collapse.

Trucks, trucks, everywhere trucks

After Teamsters struck and brand-new Chevrolet and GMC trucks assembled in Moraine couldn't be shipped to dealerships, the Miami Valley got used to seeing Chevrolet S-10 and GMC S-15 trucks parked wherever space could be found.

Slowly filling up

■ The Miami Valley Research Park celebrated the opening of the park's first factory by Diconix, an Eastman Kodak subsidiary, in June.
■ Also that month: BDM Corporation of Virginia committed to putting an office building at the park.

1985

Above: Police Chief Tyree Broomfield (left) and Lt. Col. James Newby, who had just been appointed assistant chief.

Right: Nan Davis had regained limited use of her legs through the use of electronic stimulators developed at Wright State.

Coming back
Dayton International Airport was relieved to hear that American Airlines and Republic Airlines would again offer flights from the Gem City.

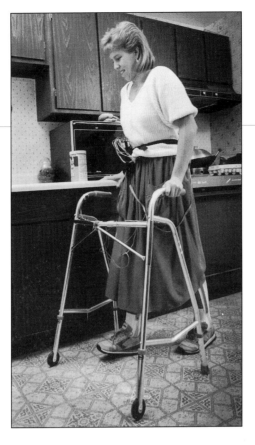

Flyers and Raiders: Tournament play
■ Once again, the UD Flyers participated in the NCAA tournament under basketball coach Don Donoher — but the Flyers lost to Villanova, 51-49, in round one.
■ At Wright State University, basketball coach Ralph Underhill took his Raiders to the NCAA Division II tournament, but the Raiders lost to Kentucky Wesleyan, 84-72, in round two.

But how do they get those planes inside?
Construction began this year on a $5.4 million, 153,600-square-foot expansion of the U.S. Air Force Museum, which would nearly double its indoor exhibit space.

Transformation of a landmark
Government money was pledged this year for refurbishing the family home of Paul Laurence Dunbar, where the famous poet spent much of his life, and died. What evolved was the Paul Laurence Dunbar Museum, now on the National Register of Historic Places. It was the first public memorial to an African-American and today is one of Dayton's national park sites.

A south-of-town expansion
The news was good at Mead Data Central, which announced a $37 million expansion that included new buildings for its Lexis and Nexis electronic data-retrieval services. Officials predicted employment would double from 850 to 1,600 in only two years.

Medical advancement
The area's first magnetic resonance imaging machine was acquired by Kettering Medical Center.

1986

Right: New Lazarus signs started springing up around town.

Rike's no more
Dayton lost a bit of history after the familiar Rike's department store, which had been a division of Federated Department Stores since 1959 and later was renamed Shillito Rike's, assumed the Lazarus name in January.

Discrimination and arson charges
Local blacks charged that Jonathan's, a nightclub in the ever-trendy Oregon District, discrimated against them by discouraging black patrons from entering. A black man who claimed he was mistreated at the club was convicted of arson after a fire there.

MILESTONE

Three disasters in a row

■ Authorities worried about the aftermath of a February 17 chemical spill into the Stillwater River after a truck ran off Interstate 70, down an embankment and overturned — dumping 1,500 gallons of a hazardous chemical.

■ On December 12, a wrecked and burning 9,200-gallon propane tanker at I-75 and Ohio 4 forced 1,200 Daytonians from their homes. Firefighters took five hours to douse the blaze, and part of northbound I-75 was closed for 24 hours so that crews could replace the burned-out asphalt.

■ But it was the July 8 derailment of a 44-car CSX Transportation freight train in Miamisburg that shook the Miami Valley worst of all. Some 30,000 people were evacuated and 100 treated in emergency rooms after one tanker car, filled with flammable white phosphorus, caught fire and an eerie, dense cloud of phosphoric acid covered the area for miles. It took five days to get the last remains of the fire — and the acid cloud — under control. Settling the lawsuits, not surprisingly, took much, much longer. ■

Verdict: The city must pay

The family of James Urseth — a 44-year-old New Carlisle man killed in a 1983 drug raid by the Dayton Organized Crime Unit — won a $3.5 million judgment in a wrongful-death lawsuit against the city of Dayton on August 4. A Community Commission on Police Policies and Procedures appointed by City Manager Richard Helwig called for improvements in the hiring and promotion of officers.

Died...

Katharine Louise Kennedy Brown, 95. She was a long-time Daytonian and Republican political force in Ohio.

Created...

The Human Race, destined to become the area's first professional theater company since the 1940s.

Top: A tanker car erupted in Miamisburg, spewing a cloud of phosphoric acid.

Above: The Rev. Jesse Jackson visited to speak at Central State University and was greeted by CSU President Dr. Arthur E. Thomas.

Left: The Kettering Tower loomed over the construction site of Cooper Place townhouses.

To trolley? Or not?

A battle began this year over whether to keep Dayton's electric trolleys — a familiar sight in the Gem City for nearly 100 years — or convert to an all-diesel fleet. The compromise: Dayton would keep part of its trolley fleet, and part of its history.

Credit cards

While it was true that many in the Valley had more money in their pockets, some of the overconfident were overloading their credit cards. By midsummer, the number of local residents filing for personal bankruptcy was up 50 percent over 1985.

Right: The Dayton Transportation Center walkway welcomed visitors.

It's Great in Dayton

ENJOY YOUR STAY

Ringing proudly

The Deeds Carillon, which played for the first time in 1942, received brand-new bells and major repairs to its electrical carillon system this year.

Arrested...

One-time Olympic diver Sam Hall, near Managua, Nicaragua, on December 12 — on charges of espionage. Folks back in the Miami Valley wondered why Hall, the brother of Congressman Tony Hall and the son of late Dayton Mayor Dave Hall, was walking around with a map of Punta Hueta air base inside his sock. The Nicaraguan government wondered, too. Hall was released after some back-and-forth diplomacy.

Opened...

The International Women's Air and Space Museum, in Centerville.

Scheduled...

Construction of the $46 million Arcade Centre complex, for March 1987. Site preparations and demolition began this year.

Died...

Dayton Daily News sports editor Si Burick, December 10, of a stroke, at age 77. He'd held the post for nearly 58 years, and was a local legend and national figure in newspaper sports writing.

Why did it take so long, is the question

Women broke new ground as they entered the Dayton Fire Department's firefighting training program for the first time.

Winning Daytonians...

■ Philadelphia Phillies third baseman Mike Schmidt won the National League's MVP award.
■ Native Daytonian Roger Clemens, pitcher for the Boston Red Sox, won both the American League MVP award and the Cy Young Award.

Announced...

Construction of a new multi-purpose activities center at Wright State University, the Ervin J. Nutter Center, in May. Estimated cost: $18 million. The Nutter Center was named after the Greene County businessman and civic leader after he made a $1.5 million gift toward the building's construction.

Changing hands

Area companies were bought and sold, and bought and sold other companies:
■ Sold to Whirlpool Corporation in January was the KitchenAid Division of Troy-based Hobart Corporation, owned by Dart & Kraft Inc. of Chicago. While some office positions were moved to Dayton, others went to St. Joseph, Michigan.
■ Sold to Armstrong Rubber Company in September were the worldwide rubber operations of Dayco Corporation, a local *Fortune* 500 company.
■ Bought by Mead was the Zellerbach Distribution Group, from James River Corporation. The $250 million purchase made Mead the nation's second-largest paper-products distributor.
■ L.M. Berry Company became a wholly owned subsidiary of BellSouth.
■ The locally based Ponderosa steakhouse chain agreed to be acquired by New York investor Asher Edelman. ■

Merged...

The Journal Herald, on September 15, with the *Dayton Daily News*. The *Journal* was a more-or-less direct descendant of Dayton's first newspaper, *The Dayton Repertory*, first published in 1808.

Rooms at the inn

The metro area geared up for more convention and visitor business as hotel construction boomed.

Leonard says goodbye

Richard F. Celeste's re-election as governor on November 4 meant his running mate — Dayton Mayor Paul Leonard — would leave for Columbus and begin his job as Ohio's lieutenant governor in January 1987. Leonard's legacy in Dayton: neighborhood revitalization, economic development and regional cooperation. Succeeding Leonard as mayor was City Commissioner Richard Clay Dixon.

1987

Gigantic fires, one after another

■ An electrical malfunction sparked the fire at West Dayton's popular Rubenstein's Department Store. The January blaze occurred as restoration was under way in the historic Paul Laurence Dunbar/Wright brothers neighborhood, where the store was located in a late-1800s building.

■ Four shops were destroyed and five others damaged in a $3 million fire at Kettering's Town & Country Shopping Center on October 3.

■ On December 22, faulty wiring was to blame for a $2 million fire at the University of Dayton's St. Joseph Hall.

■ The most fearsome conflagration, visible for miles around, was the one that destroyed the Sherwin-Williams Automotive Distribution Center off Dayton Park Drive on May 27. Since the center sat atop the Miami River Wellfield, the fire — fueled by 1.5 million gallons of paint and thinner — threatened to contaminate much of the Miami Valley's water supply.

Approved...

A construction permit, in March, allowing Dayton Power and Light to switch the Zimmer Nuclear Power Plant to a coal-fired facility. The blessing was mixed: The plant's cost was expected to hit $3.6 billion, payable by — who else? — electric customers.

Health hazard

Fishing, swimming and wading were forbidden in a 3.5-mile stretch of Wolf Creek and the Great Miami River in April after carcinogenic chemicals called polychlorinated biphenyls were found in the water. The culprits? Vandals who broke into electrical transformers at the abandoned Dayton Tire and Rubber plant, searching for copper wiring. The PCB-laden oil inside ran into the creek.

A dreadful way to die

Dr. William G. Eckman, 67, of Kettering, was mauled to death by two pit bulls on a Dayton street on April 6. Dayton toughened its vicious-dog law, and later, the state required owners of vicious animals to carry $50,000 in liability insurance. (And what about the owners of the dogs who attacked Eckman? Not guilty of involuntary manslaughter.)

Left: The Sherwin-Williams warehouse fire was visible for miles.

Below: Former Dayton Police Chief Tyree Broomfield explained his resignation at a press conference.

Sold out

Only one inter-city bus service remained in Dayton after Greyhound bought Trailways Inc. Trailways' downtown terminal was razed in August.

Celebrated...

The 40th birthday of the U.S. Air Force, in September. Host for the grand event: Wright-Patterson Air Force Base.

Broomfield out, Newby in

The turmoil and fighting within the Dayton Police Department had gone on for months. Officers in the nearly all-white force complained bitterly about Chief Tyree Broomfield, claiming he was a poor leader. Broomfield, Dayton's first black police chief, resigned December 7. New at the helm: James Newby, who took steps to hire more black officers.

Above left: Sam Hall's book

Above right: Isaiah Jackson

Top: Pieces of the Cooper Building facade awaited storage.

Glowing in the dark

It was a dangerous radioactive spill, and not well handled. Workers at Wright-Patterson Air Force Base opened an illegally stored, unmarked barrel of americium 241 in 1986 and washed off the toxic dust under a public spigot. They kept the incident from top base command for six days. More people were exposed to radioactivity when the barrel was left open for three days. The spill was made public in 1987, spurring a drive to make sure the Air Force complied with federal regulations on handling radioactive materials. The building that had contained the stuff was dismantled and carted to a radioactive waste dump.

Paying up

U.S. District Judge Walter Rice said Anomi Urseth, the New Carlisle widow whose husband, James Urseth, was shot to death by Dayton police, should get $1.65 million — not the $3.5 million awarded by a federal jury. In 1989, the city gave Mrs. Urseth another $930,000 to end the case.

Free at last

Dayton-area native Sam Hall, freed from a Nicaraguan jail cell, put pen to paper and wrote *Counter Terrorist*, about his experiences as a suspected spy in the Central American country. Hall claimed in the book that he'd been a "soldier of democracy," advising contra rebels.

Tearing down

Saving facades was the battle cry of preservationists as 19th-century commercial buildings in the Second Street Historic District were torn down to make way for the 20-story Citizens Federal Centre tower. The Cooper Building facade, at Main and Second streets, was boxed up and saved after a $100,000 donation by the city of Dayton; Beerman Realty Company saved the 1880s Lafee Building facade on East Third Street.

Demolished...

Buildings on the Arcade Square block, to make way for the new Arcade Centre, another 20-story office and retail complex.

Talked about...

- Building a performing-arts center downtown.
- Baby boomers going back to church.
- Denim, denim, denim — jeans and jean jackets, skirts and dresses (stonewashed, acid-washed, frosted).
- Shorter skirts.
- Rap music.
- Cicadas, out in force this summer.
- Shop-at-home TV programs.
- DINKS (couples with double incomes and no kids).
- "Cocooning."
- Crack cocaine.
- AIDS.
- The $500 billion stock-market tumble of October 19.

Named...

Isaiah Jackson, as the Dayton Philharmonic's third music director. Jackson succeeded Charles Wendelken-Wilson.

Broken...

Ground, by Honda, on a $450 million expansion of its Anna engine plant.

Won...

An Emmy, by Daytonian Cathy Guisewite for the animated *Cathy*, based on her newspaper strip.

1988

Died...

Comic-strip artist Milton Arthur Caniff, 81, who grew up in Dayton. Caniff, who died April 3, was popular for *Terry and the Pirates* and *Steve Canyon.*

Dedicated...

■ The restored Wright brothers bicycle shop at 22 S. Williams St. on June 25. Cost: more than $135,000.
■ A new set of bells at the Deeds Carillon. People heard them for the first time at the October 23 dedication recital.

Building, building, building

It was a year for bricks and mortar, asphalt and steel girders. Under construction this year:
■ Two 20-story downtown towers, the Arcade Centre and Citizens Federal Centre.
■ The new county courts building addition.
■ Building 11 of the ever-expanding Sinclair Community College.
■ The $18 million rehabilitation of the Victory Theatre, which got under way in June.
■ U.S. 35 West, the long-planned highway that promised development for West Dayton.
■ Commercial and office buildings along the I-75 and I-675 corridors.

Gimme shelter

Residents of the downtown YMCA, all 130 of them, had to move by June 30, when workers began an $18 million conversion of the 13-story tower into upscale apartments.

Rain, rain, where are you?

All heat and no rain made the Miami Valley a dry and dusty place this summer, as the Midwest's worst drought since the 1930s made everybody miserable. Hardest-hit were farmers, whose corn and soybeans withered beyond hope.

Died...

Noted Dayton politician and state Rep. C.J. McLin Jr., 67, on December 27, from cancer. An influential black Democrat, McLin had just been sworn in to his 12th term as a state representative on December 8.

Above: C.J. McLin Jr.

Left: Virginia Kettering Kampf helped kick off the 16th annual Holiday Festival.

Below: The Victory Theatre was renovated both in building and in name as it became the Victoria.

Yet another razing

The year before, the Canby House was a showpiece, a 26-room English Tudor mansion in Grafton Hill that was spruced up as the Dayton Philharmonic's Designer Show House. This year, its owner, the Greek Orthodox Church, said the historic 1915 house would be demolished — to make room for a parking lot.

Tortured and killed...

Antonio "Pooh" Cooley of Dayton, 12, by two 15-year-old friends who were angry that Cooley wouldn't allow them into his father's apartment.

Above: Chevrolet trucks continued to roll out of the Moraine GM plant, and grew in popularity.

No saving Shere

Plenty of readers had something to say about the firing of *Dayton Daily News* Publisher Dennis Shere, who lost his job after he said his Christian principles wouldn't let him publish classifieds publicizing health lectures sponsored by local gays and lesbians. Hundreds of Shere's supporters demonstrated in front of the *Daily News* building. Editor Brad Tillson was named publisher.

The Daily News *made headlines again after an employee, Theodore Sinks, was charged with killing his wife, Judy, 44, and hiding her body at the newspaper building. Mrs. Sinks, also a newspaper employee, had been missing five months when she was found sealed inside fresh concrete on the top floor of the building.*

Elected...

Dr. Sarah Harris, as county treasurer. She was Montgomery County's first black female administrative official.

No more electric trolleys

That was the decision made by the RTA this year. (Later, trustees would change their minds.)

Love surgery

Several Miami Valley women complained to the Ohio State Medical Board that Dayton-area gynecologist Dr. James Burt had hurt them by performing experimental vaginal reconstruction surgery without their consent. They complained of irreversible damage, infection and painful complications. Burt stopped doing "love surgery," as he called it, and the case gained national attention — not to mention lawsuits.

Air-freight troubles

Emery Worldwide wallowed in debt, struggling with service problems and financial losses. People worried about the company's 1,600 jobs here.

Retired...

Anchorman Don Wayne, after a 40-year career at WHIO-TV and radio.

SLICE OF LIFE

Moving on up

More people were hired in wholesale and retail trade, service industries and government this year. Meanwhile, economic boosters tried to promote high-tech job growth by touting the Miami Valley's accessibility, land availability, labor force, technology base and energy supply.

Crack cocaine

The proliferation of crack cocaine in Dayton — estimated at $400 million worth of business this year — took its toll on families, neighborhoods and the police, who struggled to tackle the problem.

Talked about...

■ The "Greenhouse effect."
■ Space shuttle Discovery, back in space after the 1986 Challenger explosion.
■ Radon scares.
■ Air safety.
■ *Glasnost* and *perestroika* in the Soviet Union.

Began...

■ A $10 million, two-year renovation of the empty Forest Park Shopping Center on North Main Street.
■ Demolition of what was left of Dayton's historic Union Station, by Conrail.

Introduced...

Cycolor color copier paper, by Mead Imaging.

Sold...

The Ponderosa steak house chain, to Metromedia, by Asher Edelman.

Merged...

Piedmont Airlines, with USAir. Piedmont had kept a hub at Dayton International Airport.

Closed...

Unity Bank, the area's only minority-owned bank.

Opened...

An expanded, beautified Dayton Convention Center.

A costly habit

TV news viewers were surprised when WHIO weatherman Bruce Asbury went on the 6 p.m. news on January 30 and admitted he had used cocaine. By March 14, after a leave of absence and a short time back on the air, Asbury was fired.

Foul weather

■ This spring saw a deluge of rain (all that the Valley missed in '88, it seemed). Fields and basements flooded. Several people drowned in the Great Miami River. Farmers had to delay spring planting.

■ In October, an early snowfall weighed down the leaves still hanging from the trees, snapping limbs by the thousands.

Re-elected...

Richard Clay Dixon, as mayor of Dayton.

Fired!

After a quarter-century as basketball coach of the UD Flyers, Don Donoher was ousted and replaced by assistant New York Knicks coach Jim O'Brien. Donoher's record in 1988-89: 12-17.

Just like the Mounties, except no red coats

Dayton's police force put officers on horseback downtown. The mounted police became a familiar sight to downtowners.

Completed...

■ A three-year renovation of Dayton International Airport.

■ Construction of the Citizens Federal Centre and Arcade Centre towers.

Left town...

United Color Press. Dayton remembered the days when the city had been a publishing center.

Above: Seen from the east side of Main Street, at Third, the Arcade Centre was taking shape. The building would offer 335,000 square feet of space at the corner of Third and Main.

Above: At the Dayton police horse stable, Scott Stimmel (left) led "Scrap Iron," and Kenny Soward led "Doc" out of the barn. "Rex" leaned out of his stall to keep an eye on activity in the barn.

1990

MILESTONE

More than just rumors

The region watched nervously as communications giant AT&T started a bid to take over NCR, which had just launched a new product line and was positioning itself to grow in the computer business.

AT&T was relentless, making two friendly offers that NCR directors promptly rejected. AT&T came back with a third bid — a $90-per-share tender offer on December 6 — but NCR Chairman Charles Exley still said no.

The battle went on until 1991, when AT&T won NCR for $110 per share, and Dayton lost one of its oldest, most distinguished companies. ■

Blazing trails

The production lines were humming in January at GM's Moraine Assembly plant as four-door Chevy Blazers were produced en masse. By April, there was more good news: Moraine Assembly employees learned the plant would produce Chevrolet's next generation of the popular sport utility vehicles and small pickups.

Break out the champagne

It was a gala reopening — a week's worth of events in mid-January reminiscent of the grand balls and festivities Daytonians enjoyed long ago. The 124-year-old Victory Theatre, refurbished and renovated, was reborn as the Victoria. One featured event: Metropolitan Opera singers and others from opera houses throughout America and Europe.

Died...

Nine people, when dozens of cars piled up on I-75 near Tipp City during a February white-out.

Opened...

■ The Ervin J. Nutter Center, Wright State University's multipurpose entertainment and sports complex, on December 15.
■ Schear's Marketplace, a grocery and food court, at Third and Main, in March. For downtown, it was a much-needed retail shot in the arm.

SLICE OF LIFE

One historic structure

The city of Dayton took over the Patterson Homestead, the Federal-style farmhouse and birthplace of NCR magnate John H. Patterson. It's now used as a meeting place, entertainment center and museum depicting the life of Miami Valley pioneers. The Brown Street homestead's original 2,000 acres were bought by Col. Robert Patterson in 1806 when he arrived from Lexington, Kentucky.

Talked about...

■ Landfills (where to build, now that the old one was filling up?).
■ Recycling.
■ Animated TV brat Bart Simpson (whose voice was provided by ex-Kettering resident Nancy Cartwright, starting in 1987).
■ Low-impact exercise aerobics.
■ Earth Day.
■ Low-fat and no-fat meals.

Vital statistics

Miami Valley populations:
■ Beavercreek: 33,626.
■ Centerville: 21,082.
■ Dayton: 182,044.
■ Englewood: 11,432.
■ Fairborn: 31,300.
■ Huber Heights: 38,696.
■ Kettering: 60,569.
■ Miamisburg: 17,834.
■ Moraine: 5,989.
■ Oakwood: 3,392.
■ Trotwood: 8,816.
■ Troy: 19,478.
■ Vandalia: 13,882.
■ Xenia: 24,664.
■ Greene County: 136,731.
■ Miami County: 93,182.
■ Montgomery County: 573,809.

1990

Wet, wetter, wettest

And everybody thought the year before was wet! By December 4, the Dayton area had already recorded precipitation of 51.40 inches — the dampest year on record here.

High-profile loss

Shut down the Arcade? Patrons were outraged, and 25 tenants and shop owners were stunned. Developer Tom Danis, who bought the ailing structure for $100,000, dropped the bomb right before year's end and announced a 1991 closing date. Danis was mum about his plans for the landmark — which was still vacant, five years later.

Travel problems

Dayton airline passengers anxiously watched as USAir continued slashing operations at Dayton International Airport. USAir, like many other airlines, was hurt by skyrocketing fuel costs and recessionary travel cutbacks. Would USAir shut down its Dayton hub?

Sold...

Philips Industries, to London-based Tomplins plc of Great Britain.

Off to war

Men and women in uniform kissed their loved ones goodbye right before the holiday season. Destination: the Persian Gulf. Trouble was brewing with Iraq, which refused to leave oil-rich Kuwait, and the United States was gearing up for war.

'Irongate'

The accusation was horrible — almost unbelievable. Detroit drug suspect David Green claimed it was a Dayton police officer, John Gamble, who burned his chest with a hot clothes iron during an interrogation in a crack house. People were aghast at such tactics. Gamble and two other officers were fired, and a citizen review board was created for complaints against police.

In 1991, Gamble was shot and killed by Bert E. Watts outside Watts' North Gettysburg Avenue bar. A jury ruled that Watts, who saw Gamble with a knife, fired in self-defense.

More than busing now

Busing was no longer the sole means of desegregation in Dayton schools after the district adopted an expanded magnet-school plan. Schools took on specialty programs, such as fine arts or international studies, meant to make them attractive to kids from all over town.

Designated...

The Wright Flyer III, as a National Historic Landmark. The plane and Wright Hall, at Carillon Historical Park, are now part of the Dayton Aviation Heritage National Historical Park.

Closed...

■ Rubenstein's Department Store, 1100 W. Third St.
■ The old Dayton Walther foundry, manufacturer of truck axles and other automotive parts.

Rejected...

School levy after school levy throughout the Miami Valley.

1991

What would John H. have said?

Patterson's old company held out as long as it could. But in May, word finally came that AT&T had indeed won Dayton's own NCR Corporation for $110 a share, or a whopping $7.4 billion in AT&T stock. AT&T immediately began merging its computer business into NCR's. Gilbert P. Williamson took over as NCR's new chairman and chief executive. The multibillion-dollar coup was the nation's 11th-largest takeover.

Closed...

The Arcade, in March, by developer Tom Danis, the new owner.

Above: Dayton's bicycle patrol officers included (L-R) Gregg Gaby, Donald Howard and Greg Kraft from the Second District. The trio was riding on Fillmore Street in East Dayton.

MILESTONE
War declared

Miami Valley soldiers were among the Western and Arab military forces that served in the Persian Gulf War, which began January 17 with a fierce air attack on Baghdad to force Iraq from Kuwait. The bombing lasted five weeks, followed by a ground offensive beginning February 24 that lasted only 100 hours until the Iraqis agreed to withdraw. President George Bush ordered a ceasefire February 27. The war claimed 148 American lives.

Just like a great big video game

Like Americans everywhere, Miami Valley residents were glued to their TV screens watching the war. Much of the technology that made the air bombardment possible — including the Stealth fighter, the F-15E fighter, laser-guided bombs and state-of-the-art electronics — was rooted close to home, at Wright-Patterson Air Force Base. ■

New museum

A $4.8 million addition to the Dayton Museum of Natural History's old 1958 building opened on October 5. New features: a high-tech planetarium, new Ohio wildlife exhibits and a children's room.

Broken...

Ground, in November, on a 1-million-square-foot, $140 million shopping mall in Beavercreek, developed by Glimcher Company. In addition to the Salem Mall in Trotwood and the Dayton Mall in Miami Township, it would be the metro area's third.

Keeping power lines overhead

Get rid of Dayton's famous electric trolleys? Nah. The Miami Valley Regional Transit Authority's trustees abandoned their 1988 phase-out decision in favor of a plan to renovate the trolleys and improve service.

Above: City Commissioner Richard Zimmer (right) and Kendra McCuistion, Ohio's Little Miss America contestant from Dayton View, helped announce Dayton's new status.

Right: Delco Chassis Plant workers (L-R) Rick Donovan, Bob Steiger and Dennis Maxie picketed.

Mail call? Never mind

Emery Worldwide and the city of Dayton waited to hear if the U.S. Postal Service would locate a new mail-sorting hub here. Indianapolis got it instead.

Grocery store wars

Shoppers smiled and saved as grocery stores such as Kroger, Cub Foods, and Meijer slashed prices and caused a shopping ruckus throughout town. Left in the rubble: at least 20 stores that could no longer compete with the big guys.

Goodbye, Mound

The Miami Valley struggled with the news that the EG&G Mound Plant in Miamisburg — a high-technology mecca for the area, and once a cornerstone of the government's nuclear-weapons program — would close by 1995.

Marked...

Woodland Cemetery's sesquicentennial.

On strike...

Kettering teachers, for three days. It was the district's first walkout.

1991

Fair treatment

It was an expensive coat ($100,000 plus) but there was never a more deserving wearer. Before being returned to his original spot at the head of Main Street downtown, the weathered old statue of Pvt. George Washington Fair was refurbished — in bronze, no less. In the meantime, the beautification project on Main Street continued. (Merchants and drivers wondered if it would ever end.)

Added...

The computerized card catalog, to the Dayton & Montgomery County Public Library.

In...

James Williams, as the new superintendent of Dayton schools. First on Williams' agenda: busing and school violence.

Acquired...

Dayton-based Gem Savings, by National City Bank.

Left: The bronze Civil War statue of Pvt. George Washington Fair, after an absence of 43 years, returned to Main Street.

Below: The last few shoppers on the second floor of the downtown Lazarus store found little merchandise to buy before the store closed.

Bottom: The Wright Cycle Shop on Williams Street had been restored.

1992

So long — we'll miss you

The doors closed on another Dayton landmark — the old Rike-Kumler building — after Lazarus rang up its last sale in downtown Dayton on January 31. The question of what to do with the huge building nagged officials for years to come.

Approved...

The Aviation Heritage National Historical Park, by President George Bush on October 16, after Congress gave its final OK. The long-awaited park was to honor the Wrights and Paul Laurence Dunbar, and to restore local aviation-related historic sites.

Inducted...

Dayton Daily News sports editor Ritter Collett, into the Writers Section of the National Baseball Hall of Fame.

Above: Passengers went their separate ways on the last day of USAir's hub operation in Dayton.

Right: Mound employee Cindy Franklin held a T-shirt she bought at a "Save the Mound" rally in Miamisburg.

SLICE OF LIFE

Talked about...

Job security, plant layoffs, potential closings and the economy.

Tornado!

A twister ripped through Preble and Darke counties in November, leaving part of the village of Arcanum in rubble and racking up $16 million in damage. The twister left a path of destruction 18 miles long and a quarter-mile wide. Amazingly, only 13 people were hurt.

Up, up, and away

Closed in January was USAir's hub at Dayton International Airport. That meant a huge drop in the number of flights here, after travelers had grown used to direct-flight service.

'The Christmas killings'

It was a grisly scene during the season of peace and goodwill. Marvallous Matthew Keene and Heather Mathews, leaders of a looseknit group of youths who spent their days drinking and panhandling, went on a shooting rampage in Dayton over the Christmas holidays. Six people were killed. Keene received a death sentence, and Mathews got two life terms.

Finishing touches

Bus shelters, decorative planters, trees, benches, brick crosswalks, and new lighting were the featured attractions of the $7.5 million Main Street beautification project completed this year. City officials hoped Main Street's fresh new look would make it a more pleasant place for downtowners and visitors alike.

A bunch of garbage

Handling trash rose to the top of the government agenda this year as landfill controversies continued. Moraine's Pinnacle Road Landfill was nearly full, so officials went hunting, hoping a site for a new county landfill would become apparent. (It didn't.) In the meantime, Waste Management, Danis Industries and Rumpke Waste Removal Systems vied for pieces of the waste-handling pie.

Foreclosed upon...

One Dayton Centre (the new name for the Arcade Centre tower), which was having financial troubles already as tenants for high-priced office space moved first to the Citizens Federal Centre tower a block away.

Creating 'defensible space'

Iron gates were erected on many streets in Dayton's Five Oaks neighborhood this year, effectively turning through streets into cul-de-sacs. The reason: to stop drug peddlers and other troublemakers from cruising the area. The city said crime decreased, but Five Oaks residents had mixed feelings about the $450,000 program.

Designated...

Third Street, as Martin Luther King Jr. Way.

Rumors mount at Mound

The Energy Department's plans to close the EG&G Mound Plant in Miamisburg prompted Mound supporters to report that closing the place would waste $2 billion over the next 20 years. While discussions continued, more than 500 high-tech jobs were lost, and 1,700 remained up in the air.

Consolidated...

The former logistics and systems commands, by the Department of Defense. The Air Force's new procurement organization was renamed the Air Force Materiel Command, located at Wright-Patterson Air Force Base.

1993

Economic woes

It was one of the worst years in recent memory for bad economic news in the Dayton area. With all the layoffs, closings, downsizings (or "rightsizings," as CEOs liked to call them), people wondered how the area would weather the losses.

January: Closing

Sears announced the closing of its downtown department store, which would be converted to a Sears outlet store.

April: Cuts

■ The last of NCR's manufacturing work force in Dayton — 125 jobs — was eliminated. The company's name was changed to AT&T Global Information Solutions the next year.

■ 5,500 AT&T/GIS employees were offered early retirement while 25,000 of the company's U.S. employees were asked to consider a voluntary separation package. The goal: to cut 8,000 of the company's 51,000 positions worldwide.

May: Goodbye, Mound

It was announced for certain in May that the EG&G Mound nuclear-weapons plant would close in 1995. Miamisburg started looking for new uses for the plant, hoping to save the $1.8 million in income and corporate profit taxes it generated — nearly 17 percent of the city's general revenue fund. By August, the plant's doors were opened to business executives to drum up ideas for reuse. It was Mound's first-ever open house.

June: Losses

Mead Corporation said it would cut 150 Dayton jobs.

August: More losses

In August, Mead Data Central announced 400 layoffs. The electronic information services company, which also said that 200 more vacant positions would go unfilled, claimed the cuts were needed to save $50 million a year and make the Mead division more profitable.

September: Rightsizing?

First the Mound, and now Kettering's Gentile Air Force Station. Defense downsizing hit the Miami Valley hard after Congress announced in September that Gentile would close and the Defense Electronics Supply Center would relocate to Columbus in 1996. The move would affect 2,100 employees — 800 of whom said they'd rather stay here than move. (What to do with the empty complex? Civic and business leaders jumped on the problem, with ideas ranging from warehouses to movie studios.) ■

Top: Brian Graham, senior computer operator (front), and Steve Ullrich, computer operator, worked in the data center at Mead Data Central.

Above: Meadowdale Elementary School teachers Georchia Higgins and Dennis Robinson greeted students arriving for classes during the Dayton teachers' strike.

Top: Richard Clay Dixon

Above: Mike Turner

Right: Police Chief James Newby displayed 15 kilograms of cocaine seized at the Dayton International Airport.

An unplanned spring break

It was the kids who suffered most when 2,200 teachers, librarians and staff went on strike against the Dayton City School District beginning March 25. Security was tight and emotions ran high during the 16-day walkout, which saw substitute teachers brought in from Cleveland and elsewhere.

Named...

Jerre Stead, in March, as chief executive of AT&T/Global Information Solutions, replacing Gil Williamson.

Finally getting recognition

Folks in bars around Dayton had known him for a long time, but Harley "Red" Allen, bluegrass musician extraordinaire, got his national due with a Grammy nomination. Credited with influencing the bluegrass "high lonesome" vocal style, Allen moved to Dayton in 1950. He died of cancer this year.

Fasting for a cause

U.S. Democratic Rep. Tony Hall of Dayton fasted for three weeks beginning April 5 to protest the elimination of the House Hunger Committee, which he chaired. In the end, Hall's efforts to make the world's hunger problem known spawned a hunger conference organized by the World Bank.

Planned...

A community-wide computer network called Dayton Freenet. Plans were announced in June.

Raided!

Expense account abuse? The Dayton Area Chamber of Commerce came under intense fire this year after Montgomery County sheriff's deputies raided chamber offices and carted away boxes of records allegedly containing evidence that top chamber officials had used their expense accounts for non-chamber business. In the end, three chamber officials resigned, and the chamber was reorganized.

A new shopping mecca

Shoppers embraced a brand-new shopping outlet when the Mall at Fairfield Commons — the Dayton area's first new mall in 20 years — opened in Beavercreek on October 27.

Out...

Dayton Democratic Mayor Richard Clay Dixon, who lost by a mere 397 votes to Republican Mike Turner in the November election. Turner became the only Republican on Dayton's City Commission.

1994

Merged...

The village of Riverside, with Mad River Township, on January 1. Population of Montgomery County's newest city: 26,000.

Died...

■ Dayton industrialist and philanthropist Jesse Philips, 80, on November 29.
■ Candy maker Esther Price, 89, on January 9.
■ Montgomery County Commissioner Donna Moon, 62, on September 19.

Caned!

Was it justified? Cruel and unusual punishment? The community was divided over the flogging of Kettering teen-ager Michael Fay in Singapore on May 5. Fay got the decidedly un-American punishment after pleading guilty to vandalism in Singapore, a nation that keeps crime in check by sentencing vandals to one or more strikes on the buttocks with a rattan cane. Fay's case drew worldwide attention, including a plea by President Bill Clinton to spare the youth of such a sentence.

Looking brighter

In May, GM's Moraine Assembly Plant began production on the 1995 Chevy Blazer and GMC Jimmy after a $300 million retooling effort. By year's end, more workers in the Miami Valley — including auto workers — had jobs this year as overall unemployment dropped below 4 percent.

Announced...

Plans, in May, to locate a 750-job military payroll center at the Gentile Air Force Station in Kettering, which was preparing to close.

Seized...

25 kilos of cocaine, by Dayton police on July 19 at Dayton International Airport. It was the city's biggest-ever cocaine bust.

And they shot their videos here, too

Kim and Kelley Deal, twins from Huber Heights, watched as *Last Splash*, the second album by their rock band The Breeders, shot up the charts to platinum status. The band, which was based in Dayton during all the hoopla, included drummer Jim MacPherson, also of Dayton, and British bassist Josephine Wiggins.

Above: Charlie Ward completed the assembly of antilock brakes at GM's Truck and Bus Plant.

Left: Dr. Harley Flack became Wright State's president.

Miamisburg cheers

Hard work to convert the Mound plant began to pay off in October after Miamisburg officials cashed a $10 million check from the Department of Energy for economic redevelopment of the soon-to-be-closed facility. Total DOE funds allocated for the Mound's economic redevelopment: $28 million. By year's end, eight companies had agreed to set up analytical services and manufacturing facilities at the Mound.

Parks OK'd

Voters gave thumbs up to local parks in November by passing a 10-year, 1.2-mill countywide property tax levy for more and better parks. The Park District of Dayton and Montgomery County immediately went forward with plans to add 3,000 acres of waterfront park land along the county's major rivers. In the meantime, residents looked forward to new boat docks, picnic areas, nature centers and paths for walking, jogging, biking and rollerblading.

Above: Eight-year-old Miranda Morgan admired Degas' work at the Dayton Art Institute.

Predicted: A city deficit

The city of Dayton projected it would be swimming in oceans of red ink by the year 2000 — $40 million of it, in fact — unless spending cuts were made right away. Layoffs were rumored. While city officials said they could cut $8 million, a separate task force issued a report outlining a whopping $31 million in proposed annual cutbacks.

Moved...

The area's oldest Jewish congregation, the Reform Temple Israel, to a new synagogue at Riverbend Park, from its home on Emerson Avenue, where it had gathered since 1927.

Inaugurated...

Dr. Harvey Flack, Wright State University's new president.

Broken...

Ground, on a remodeling and expansion program at the 25-year-old Dayton Mall in Miami Township.

Completed...

A $33 million expansion and modernization at Emery Worldwide's Dayton International Airport hub. It was a milestone for the air freight company, which had struggled throughout the late '80s and early '90s with financial losses. Mid-way through the year, Emery, which employed 2,300, reported year-to-date earnings of $34 million.

Approved...

Dayton's income-tax renewal.

Striding forward

Local black women were making political waves:

■ Elected and sworn in to the Ohio Senate was Democratic state Rep. Rhine McLin of Dayton, the first black woman in that position. She was the daughter of longtime state Rep. C.J. McLin.

■ The first black woman judge in the general division of Montgomery County Common Pleas Court: Adele M. Riley of Trotwood, also a Democrat.

Kiln battle ends

Environmentalists cheered in November after the owner of the Southwestern Portland cement kiln in Greene County near Fairborn threw out plans for burning hazardous waste there. The battle between environmentalists and the plant had lasted four years. According to plant owner Southdown Inc., its hazardous-waste fees weren't sufficient to justify burning the stuff.

Sold...

Mead Data Central, for $1.5 billion, to Anglo-Dutch publisher Reed Elsevier plc on December 2. MDC's name was promptly changed to LEXIS-NEXIS, to reflect the common names of the company's electronic information retrieval databases. Affected by the sale were 2,000 Mead Data employees in Miami Township and 1,700 others worldwide.

Art, art — and more art

The Dayton Art Institute couldn't keep out of the news this year with its announcement of multimillion-dollar art donations by local residents, its two-month Edgar Degas extravaganza (the institute's biggest show ever) and its plans for a major building expansion.

Stores, stores, everywhere stores

New names on the Dayton-area retailing scene — Lowe's, Best Buy, Kohl's and SUN Television & Appliances — sprang up this year, raising new warehouse-like stores in what once were suburban fields.

MILESTONE

Gloom and doom at AT&T/GIS

It was no secret that the company was having problems, but the news, when it came, still hurt. Mounting operating losses at AT&T/Global Information Solutions led to the announcement in September that 1,300 local jobs — 20 percent of the company's Dayton work force — would be lost by year's end. The telecommunications giant said it would split into three publicly traded companies, a restructuring to be completed by 1996. It was the largest corporate breakup in U.S. history. ■

A-10 is A-1

The Flyers were flying high in February when the University of Dayton joined the Atlantic 10 athletic conference. UD had belonged to the Great Midwestern Conference, which announced in 1994 that it would fold.

New name

Delco, a name synonymous with Charles F. Kettering and Dayton itself, was tucked into the history books in February when GM announced a new name for its automotive components group: Delphi.

Sought...

Chapter 11 bankruptcy protection, by Cassano Pizza & Subs, the area's first locally owned pizza chain. Cassano's, founded in 1953, said its 43 restaurants would remain open.

Thomas quits

A financial crisis at Central State University led to the resignation of President Arthur E. Thomas in March. CSU's many debts included more than $1.8 million owed to two state retirement funds.

Left: Courthouse Square, illuminated for the holidays.

Below: The Ohio Korean War Memorial was built in Riverbend Park.

Removed...

A kidney, from popular columnist and author Erma Bombeck. The Dayton native has polycystic kidney disease.

He's back!

Ronald Lowe Sr. — police chief of Chatham County, Georgia, and a former Dayton police major — was named Dayton's police chief in March. He took over for James Newby, who retired.

Gone forever

United Theological Seminary was stunned to learn in May that it had lost a $1.75 million investment with a Pennsylvania foundation that filed for bankruptcy and was investigated for fraud. Private donations helped ease a potential budget crisis after the loss.

Released...

His first solo CD, by jazz saxophonist Norris Turney. After years of expert backup for such greats as Duke Ellington, the 73-year-old Kettering resident got a lot of overdue recognition.

Above: Neal Gittleman conducted the Dayton Philharmonic Orchestra in rehearsal at the Fraze Pavilion in Kettering.

Hired...

Seven additional rangers, by the Park District of Dayton and Montgomery County. The doubled ranger staff, responsible for patrolling 10,000 acres, was made possible by voter approval of a property tax levy in November 1994.

The district changed its name to the Five Rivers Metro Parks.

At home with the Hall of Fame

The nine-month tussle over where to put the National Aviation Hall of Fame ended in July when hall officials announced that the U.S. Air Force Museum would be the new host. Plans called for adding a Hall of Fame wing to the museum in 1996.

Commemorated...

The 200th anniversary of the Greene Ville Treaty signing, on August 3. The landmark treaty between the United States and 12 Indian tribes opened the Miami Valley to peaceful settlement by white pioneers.

Canceled...

Donahue, by WNBC/Channel 4, after 17 years, in August. It looked as though Dayton native Phil Donahue, who pioneered the audience participation talk-show format, might not survive the tabloid talk shows.

Truly gifted

Kettering got a new crown jewel after General Motors gave the city Delco Park, a 66-acre property with five softball diamonds, three soccer fields, a BMX track, two picnic shelters and a large pond. The city had leased the park from GM since 1977. The surprise announcement came during the Kettering Holiday at Home celebration on September 3.

Talk of peace

The world's attention focused on Dayton as U.S. Secretary of State Warren Christopher hosted peace talks between Bosnia, Croatia and Serbia at Wright-Patterson Air Force Base. Ancient hatreds and religious intolerance had fueled a three-year war marked with mass killing, rape and homelessness. The United States hoped its peacemaking role would help end the conflict.

Dedicated...

The Ohio Korean War Memorial and the All Veterans Walkway at Riverbend Park, on September 9. The memorial's granite slabs and bricks bear the names of Ohioans who died in the conflict and the 8,100 still missing.

Began...

Neal Gittleman, as the fourth music director of the Dayton Philharmonic Orchestra. He replaced Isaiah Jackson.

A 22nd air show?

Less than two months after Dayton's 21st official air show, the future of the United States Air and Trade Show was threatened by a financial crisis. After show president Henry Ogrodzinski announced that the 1995 air show lost $100,000, staff were laid off and Ogrodzinski and local officials began scrambling to raise the $2.5 million needed to keep the event afloat over the next seven years. Would there be a 1996 trade show for aviation and aerospace professionals? Would the air show last until the centennial of powered flight in 2003? By fall, it was still anybody's guess.

Opened...

The U.S. Bankruptcy Court, on the first two floors of the Old Post Office at 120 W. Third St. From 1915 to 1975, the Old Post Office housed the region's federal courthouse and had been used for private offices ever since.

DAI heyday

Director Alex Nyerges was cheered as a sort of savior for the Dayton Art Institute, which was relishing its renewed popularity. The DAI — with higher-than-ever attendance and membership up nearly 95 percent since 1992 — spent the year gearing up for its 1996 renovation and expansion.

High waters

St. Paris, Piqua and Ft. Recovery flooded in August. Crops were washed out, homes were damaged, and the region was declared a disaster area.

Died...

Ivonette Wright Miller, 99, favorite niece of the Wright brothers, on October 5. She was the last living person who had flown with Orville Wright piloting the airplane. As she was buried at Woodland Cemetery a replica of the Wright B Flyer flew overhead.

Bankruptcy

Elder-Beerman Stores Corporation filed for protection from creditors under Chapter 11 of the U.S. Bankruptcy Code on October 17. The 112-year-old retailer would keep control of its business while figuring out how to repay its debts. One drastic possibility under consideration: closing the downtown Dayton Elder-Beerman store.

1996

'The world hates change; yet it is the only thing that has brought progress.' — Charles F. Kettering

Bibliography

Akers, Kathy, and Janine Montgomery. *Let's Discover Ohio*. Student's Edition. Kettering: Schuerholz Graphics, 1995.

Aullwood Audubon Center and Farm. *Aullwood Audubon Center and Farm*. Dayton: Aullwood Audubon Center and Farm, date unknown (n.d.)

Aviation Trail Inc. *Aviation Trail, Dayton, Ohio*. Dayton: Aviation Trail, Inc., n.d.

Becker, Carl M., and Patrick B. Nolan. *Keeping the Promise — A Pictorial History of the Miami Conservancy District*. Dayton: Landfall Press, Inc., 1988.

Bernstein, Mark. *Miami Valley Hospital: A Centennial History*. Dayton: Miami Valley Hospital, 1990.

Brentlinger, Dora Class. *Beside the Stillwater: A History of Early Settlements in Northern Montgomery County and the Miami Valley*. Dayton: Polk Grove Church and Butler Township, Vandalia, Ohio: 1973.

Brunsman, August. *A Brief Monograph on the Life and Works of William Maxwell*. Dayton: Carillon Historical Park, 1993.

Brunsman, August. *Let Other Crafts Bring to the World Creative Genius Like That of Wilbur and Orville Wright, Printers*. Kettering: The Trailside Press, 1988.

Brunsman, Charlotte K., and August E. Brunsman. *The Other Career of Wilbur and Orville: Wright & Wright Printers*. Kettering: The Trailside Press, 1989.

Burba, Howard L. *Miami Valley Local History and Various Other Subjects*. [Dayton]: Evening News Publishing Co., 1931.

Carillon Historical Park. *Carillon Historical Park, Dayton, Ohio*. Dayton: Carillon Historical Park, n.d.

Carillon Historical Park. *The Wright Brothers at Carillon Historical Park*. Dayton: Carillon Historical Park, June 1993.

Carillon Park. *The Barney & Smith Car Company*. Dayton: Carillon Park, n.d.

Carillon Park. *The Blacksmith Shop*. Dayton: Carillon Park, n.d.

Carillon Park. *The Conestoga Wagon and the Concord Coach: Part of the Cavalcade of America*. Dayton: Carillon Park, n.d.

Carillon Park. *The Electric Railway*. Dayton: Carillon Park, n.d.

Carillon Park. *The Little Red Schoolhouse*. Dayton: Carillon Park, n.d.

Carillon Park. *The Miami and Erie Canal*. Dayton: Carillon Park, n.d.

Carillon Park. *Milestones in the Mighty Age of Steam: The Grasshopper and The Corliss*. Dayton: Carillon Park, n.d.

Carillon Park. *Newcom Tavern*. Dayton: Carillon Park, n.d.

Carillon Park. *Our Antique Autos*. Dayton: Carillon Park, 1982.

Conover, Charlotte Reeve. *Dayton, Ohio: An Intimate History*. New York: Lewis Historical Publishing Company Inc., 1932.

Conover, Charlotte Reeve. *The Story of Dayton*. Dayton: The Greater Dayton Association; Dayton: The Otterbein Press, 1917.

Cornelisse, Diana Good. *The Foulois House: Its Place in the History of the Miami Valley and American Aviation*. Dayton: History Office, Aeronautical Systems Division, Wright-Patterson Air Force Base, 1991.

Cornelisse, Diana Good. *Remarkable Journey: The Wright Field Heritage in Photographs*. Dayton: History Office, Aeronautical Systems Division, Air Force Systems Command, 1990.

Crouch, Tom D. *The Bishop's Boys: A Life of Wilbur and Orville Wright*. 1st ed. New York: W.W. Norton, 1989.

Curwen, Maskell E. *A Sketch of the History of the City of Dayton*. 2nd ed. Dayton: James Od'ell Jr., 1850.

Dayton Canal Scrapbooks. Vol. 1. [Dayton]: publisher unknown (n.p.), n.d.

Dayton Daily News and *The Journal Herald*. Numerous articles.

The Dayton Foundation. *A History of the Dayton Foundation*. Dayton: The Dayton Foundation, n.d.

Dayton, Illustrated: Published in Nine Parts. International Publishing Co., 1889.

Dayton-Montgomery County Bicentennial Commission. *Dayton 1776-1976: A Pictorial Review*. [Dayton]: Dayton-Montgomery County Bicentennial Commission, 1975.

Dayton-Montgomery County Bicentennial Commission. *The Fife & Drum*. Various issues. Dayton: Dayton-Montgomery County Bicentennial Commission, 1976.

Dayton & Montgomery County Public Library. *Baseball Days, Dayton's North Side Field*. An exhibit. Dayton: Dayton & Montgomery County Public Library, September 6, 1995, through October 31, 1995.

Dayton & Montgomery County Public Library. *Spotlight on Your Library: The Dayton and Montgomery County Public Library Newsletter*. Dayton: Dayton & Montgomery County Public Library, August/September 1994.

Dayton Museum of Natural History. *100 Years of Discovery*. Dayton: Dayton Museum of Natural History, 1993.

Dayton (Ohio) Board of Education. *An Outline of the History of Dayton, Ohio, 1796-1896*. Dayton: W.J. Shuey, United Brethren Publishing House, 1896.

Dayton (Ohio) Police Department. *History of the Police Department of Dayton, Ohio: From Earliest Times to October First 1907*. Dayton: United Brethren Publishing House, 1907.

Dayton's Christmas Magazine: Published in the Interest of the Young Women's League of Dayton, Ohio. Dayton: Otterbein Press, 1909.

Deis, Edward P. *The Story of Wayne Avenue in the '80s and '90s*. Dayton: Edward P. Deis, 1950.

De Turk, William, and Maureen McDougal Willits. *The Deeds Carillon*. 1st ed. Dayton: Carillon Historical Park, 1988.

DeWall, Diane P., and Charles R. Berry. *A History of the Dayton Philharmonic Orchestra: 1933-1983*. Dayton: Carlson Marketing Group, Inc./E.F. MacDonald Motivation, Mead Corporation, and Trulson Graphics Inc., 1983.

Eckert, Allan W. *A Time of Terror: The Great Dayton Flood*. Dayton: Landfall Press Inc., 1965.

Fick, Edward. *Souvenir Program, Street Fair and Midway, Dayton, Ohio, June 26 to July 1, 1899*. [Dayton]: n.p., 1899.

Fisk, Fred C., and Marlin W. Todd. *The Wright Brothers from Bicycle to Biplane*. West Milton, Ohio: Miami Graphics Services Inc., 1990.

Fogle, H. Myrtle. *The Old Log Cabin, or, Newcom Tavern*. Dayton: Dayton Historical Society, 1956.

Forster, Jennifer. *A Dayton Enterprise: The Rike-Kumler Company, 1853-1959*. Dayton: The University of Dayton, 1993.

Frame, Robert. *Craig MacIntosh's Dayton Sketchbook*. Dayton: Landfall Press Inc., 1977 and 1985.

Freedman, Russell. *The Wright Brothers: How They Invented the Airplane*. New York: Holiday House, 1991.

Frontiers of Freedom! Dayton Centennial, Miami Valley Celebration, June 15-22, 1941, Dayton, Ohio. Dayton: n.p., 1941.

Gem City Savings Association. *Gem City Saver*. Dayton: Gem City Savings Association, Late Summer 1978.

Gibbs, E.D. ed. National Cash Register Company. *The NCR.* Various issues. Dayton: The National Cash Register Company, 1894.

Gobrecht, J.C. *History of the National Home for Disabled Volunteer Soldiers: With a Complete Guide-Book to the Central Home at Dayton, Ohio.* Dayton: United Brethren Printing Establishment, 1875.

Greene County Convention & Visitors Bureau. *Greene County, Ohio ... The Colour of Dayton!* Beavercreek, Ohio: Greene County Convention & Visitors Bureau, n.d.

The Greater Dayton Association. *GDA Bulletin.* Various issues. Dayton: Greater Dayton Association, 1914-1915.

The Greater Dayton Association. *GDA Bulletin: First Annual Report of The Greater Dayton Association Covering the Year Nineteen Hundred and Fourteen.* Dayton: The Greater Dayton Association, 1915.

Griep, Robert H. *History of the Original Dayton Flag, Designed by Mabel Hyer Griep, Aug. 16, 1917.* Dayton: R.H. Griep, 1990.

Hall, Agnes Anderson. *Letters from John.* [Dayton]: n.p., n.d.

Hancock, Glee R. *Seventy Years of Electricity.* Dayton: The Dayton Power and Light Company, 1953.

Hellwig, Norris D. *Woodland: 150 Years.* [Dayton]: n.p., 1991.

Hine, Darlene Clark, ed. *Black Women in America: An Historical Encyclopedia.* Brooklyn, New York: Carlson Pub., 1993.

History of Dayton. [Dayton]: n.p., n.d.

The History of Montgomery County, Ohio, Illustrated. Chicago: W.H. Beers & Co.; Evansville, Indiana: Unigraphic Inc., 1882, 1971.

Junior League of Dayton, ed. *Dayton, A History in Photographs.* Dayton: The Junior League of Dayton, Ohio Inc., 1976.

Lambert, Kevin. *An Economic History of Dayton, Ohio, 1840-1890.* Prepared for Economics 274, Dr. Wimmer. [Dayton]: Kevin Lambert, April 9, 1990.

Martin, Russell A. *Historical Sketch of the City of Dayton.* [Dayton]: n.p., 1941.

McClelland, H.L. ed. *Daytonians — Their Story.* Bellbrook, Ohio: n.p., 1992.

McClelland, H.L. *The Gem City Treasure Chest: The Legacy & Traditions of Dayton.* Bellbrook, Ohio: n.p., 1990.

McClelland, H.L. *The Souvenir Book of Dayton Cinemas.* Dayton: n.p., 1989.

Metropolitan Company, Dayton, Ohio. *30 years.* Dayton: Metropolitan Company, 1944.

Microsoft Corporation. *Microsoft Encarta.* Redmond, Washington: Microsoft Corporation, 1993.

Military History of Dayton, Beginning with a History of the Miami Valley One Hundred and Fifty Years Ago. [Dayton]: n.p., n.d.

Montgomery County Historical Society. *'The Finest Thing of its Kind in America!' The Story of the Old Court House, Dayton, Ohio.* Dayton: Montgomery County Historical Society, 1970.

Montgomery County Historical Society. *Going to the Source: A Resource Guide to Montgomery County History.* Dayton: Montgomery County Historical Society, 1982.

Montgomery County Historical Society. *Miami Valley History: A Journal of the Montgomery County Historical Society.* Vol. I. Dayton: Montgomery County Historical Society, 1989.

Montgomery County Historical Society. *Miami Valley History: A Journal of the Montgomery County Historical Society.* Vol. II. Dayton: Montgomery County Historical Society, 1990.

Montgomery County Historical Society. *Miami Valley History: A Journal of the Montgomery County Historical Society.* Vol. III. Dayton: Montgomery County Historical Society, 1991.

Montgomery County Historical Society. *A Short History of Dayton.* Dayton: Montgomery County Historical Society, n.d.

Montgomery County Historical Society. *Who We Are: Edgemont Carillon.* Dayton: Montgomery County Historical Society, n.d.

National Home for Disabled Volunteer Soldiers, Central Branch, Guide to the Central National Soldiers' Home for Visitors and Citizens: With Sketches of Dayton. Dayton: Guide Publishing, 1891.

NCR Factory News, various issues. Dayton: National Cash Register Company, 1940.

O'Keefe, T.G. *The Greater Dayton Newcomer's Guide.* 2nd ed. Dayton: T.G. O'Keefe & Associates, 1969-1970.

Pathways to Flight Partnership. *Pathways to Flight: Celebrating 90 Years of Dayton's Aviation.* Dayton: Pathways to Flight Partnership, 1994.

Pumphrey, Edgar Grant. *The Old Log Cabin, or Newcom Tavern.* Dayton: Dayton Historical Society, 1946.

Rankin, Diana (with "Partners in Excellence" and "Commitment to Progress" chapters by John K. Waters and Teresa Zumwald). *Metropolitan Dayton: Flying High.* Canoga Park, California: Dayton Area Chamber of Commerce by CCA Publications Inc., 1993.

Ronald, Bruce W. and Virginia Ronald. *Dayton: The Gem City.* Tulsa: Continental Heritage Press Inc., 1981.

Rosenfeld, Ruth, Mary Mathews, and Fred Bartenstein. *Cash Registers to Computers: NCR ... The First 100 Years, 1884-1984.* Dayton: Carillon Historical Park, 1984.

Sanders, William L. *Dayton, Gem City of Ohio.* Dayton: *Dayton Daily News,* 1963.

Shannon, Marilyn K., and David A. Simmons. *The Bridges of Carillon Park.* Dayton: Carillon Historical Park, 1986.

Souvenir Committee, Dayton, Ohio, Centennial Celebration, 1896. *Souvenir of Daytonia.* Dayton: n.p., 1896.

Third National Bank & Trust Company, Dayton, Ohio. *This, Our Dayton.* Dayton: Third National Bank & Trust Company, 1938.

Vonada, Damaine. *Ohio Matters of Fact.* Wilmington, Ohio: Orange Frazer Press, 1987 and 1990.

Walker, Lois E., and Shelby E. Wickham. *From Huffman Prairie to the Moon: The History of Wright-Patterson Air Force Base.* Dayton: Office of History, 2750th Air Base Wing, Wright-Patterson Air Force Base, Air Force Logistics Command, 1986.

Wilkie's Bookstore. *The Owl's Nest: News and Reviews from Wilkie's Bookstore.* Vol. 2, Issue 4. Dayton: Wilkie's Bookstore, July-August 1994.

Wright, Orville, pub. *West Side News.* Dayton: Orville Wright, March 1, 1889.

Wright-Patterson Air Force Base. *Legacy.* San Diego: Marcoa Publishing Inc., 1983.

Young, Rosamond, and Catharine Booker. *The Interurban: Ohio's Electric Traction Railway.* Dayton: Carillon Historical Park, 1985.

Young, Rosamond McP., and Catharine F. Booker. *Down at the Depot.* Dayton: Carillon Park, n.d.

Young, Rosamond McPherson, and Catharine Fitzgerald Booker. *The Little Red Caboose.* Dayton: Carillon Park, 1980.